The possibility of literary theory has repeatedly been put at risk by the apparently simple question "What sort of object is a literary text?" The question of the mode of being of the literary work has provoked some of the most intense critical inquiry of recent times. In the work of Heidegger, Adorno, and Derrida, the epistemological status of literature, the problem of language's claim to true representation, challenges our received notions of ontology and, ultimately, being itself. Thus the question "What is literature?" frequently sponsors highly philosophical interrogations of our inherited ways of comprehending the external world.

In *Singularities: extremes of theory in the twentieth century* Thomas Pepper addresses this relation between text, commentary, and critical value in some of the century's most influential literary theorists. Through a rich sequence of nuanced close readings of especially demanding philosophical and literary texts, Pepper challenges the conventional critical response to questions of philosophical difficulty. *Singularities* ultimately offers a critique of the very process of thematic reading itself, and the role interpretation can meaningfully play in the search for critical value. *Singularities* is a highly original interrogation and response to the whole question of truth and meaning in the work of Adorno, Blanchot, de Man, Derrida, Heidegger, and Celan.

Singularities

Extremes of theory in the twentieth century

Literature, Culture, Theory 22

General editors

RICHARD MACKSEY, *The Johns Hopkins University*

and MICHAEL SPRINKER, *State University of New York at Stony Brook*

The Cambridge Literature, Culture, Theory series is dedicated to theoretical studies in the human sciences that have literature and culture as their object of enquiry. Acknowledging the contemporary expansion of cultural studies and the redefinitions of literature that this has entailed, the series includes not only original works of literary theory but also monographs and essay collections on topics and seminal figures from the long history of theoretical speculation on the arts and human communication generally. The concept of theory embraced in the series is broad, including not only the classical disciplines of poetics and rhetoric, but also those of aesthetics, linguistics, psychoanalysis, semiotics, and other cognate sciences that have inflected the systematic study of literature during the past half century.

Singularities

Extremes of theory in the
twentieth century

❖❖❖

THOMAS ADAM PEPPER

University of Aarhus

CAMBRIDGE
UNIVERSITY PRESS

Published by the Press Syndicate of the University of Cambridge
The Pitt Building, Trumpington Street, Cambridge CB2 1RP

Cambridge University Press
The Edinburgh Building, Cambridge CB2 2RU, United Kingdom
40 West 20th Street, New York, NY 10011-4211, USA
10 Stamford Road, Oakleigh, Melbourne 3166, Australia

First published 1997

Printed in the United Kingdom at the University Press, Cambridge

Typeset in 10/12½ Palatino

A catalogue record for this book is available from the British Library

Library of Congress cataloguing in publication data

Pepper, Thomas Adam.
Singularities: extremes of theory in the twentieth century /
Thomas Adam Pepper.
p. cm. (Literature, culture, theory : 21)
Includes bibliographical references and index.
ISBN 0 521 57382 3 (hardback) – ISBN 0 521 57478 1 (paperback)
1. Criticism. 2. Critics. I. Title. II. Series.
801'.95–dc20   96-44961 CIP

ISBN 0 521 57382 3 hardback
ISBN 0 521 57478 1 paperback

placed in the hands of Thomas Winkler

ouro de mina
coração
desejo e sina
tudo mais
pura rotina
Jazz
tocarei seu nome
pra' poder
falar de amor

Contents

Preface. Truth or method

This book is not written to help anybody. It has never been my aim, during the course of writing the essays collected here, to provide anyone – least of all myself – with a set of mini-manuals useful for the study of the authors whose works are discussed. Nor have I seen it as my task to provide a statement of a unifying theme, a red thread that might run through all of these essays and lead the one who might follow it to an overwhelming intention. Not a single one of these exercises was ever conceived of as a conspective statement about a writer's work – least of all my own.

The form of much of what is sold in the current eutrophic–entropic bloom of the critical supermarket is, for the most part, based on a main title – which encapsulates, more or less wittily, the thematic concern of the book – followed by a colon, which indicates to the cursor of the potential scanning mechanism that the words that follow are names or subjects to be cataloged for access in storage-and-retrieval systems. It used to be that classification systems were constructed in order to classify books; now books are written, subjects – in all senses – are produced, in order to conform to the standards of those systems.

This time of so-called postmodernity, in which genres are supposed to be mixed, reveals its truly corporate intention in the way it classifies books, in a way analogous to that in which the university system which produces those who write them insists that would-be apprentices specialize themselves into the most standardized fields so that they will be capable of being recognized by the System. This hysteron proteron of the book-production system and the cynicism and hypocrisy of the academic-unit production system together demonstrate the decadence and profound lack of imagination of this time. This leveling of everything into information is the technological correlate of a nihilistic aestheticism, in which everything is interesting and can be scanned by the eye without any potential scotomization or damage. The damage is already done.

Is it so surprising, then, that we find ourselves in the cliché of the Middle Ages? It is wars, plagues, chaos, and identity politics at every level. But the new medievalism has a very contemporary aspect, too: the intellectual garage sale. Not only in the matter of what passes for intellectual life, particularly in the United States, this is not a good time.

It is a time of massive cynicism and universal lying, in which all qualities have been devalued, or rather suspended, in a wave of reactive consumer populism that seems both inescapable and never-ending. It is a time to burrow in and to write for the future, because there are no readers, and perhaps there never will be again. This is a hard burden for any book – let alone my first book, my little Isaac – to bear.

I cannot help feeling somehow preemptied, cheated. It is not only that now we are postlapsarian and post-Pascalian: even the idea of the shock experience, as a characterization of what we are going through, seems remarkably quaint as a kind of description of the modernity to which, so it is claimed, we no longer belong. This is an age in which one must be classifiable, so that everything one says can be dismissed as mere point of view.

How many *voices* are there? Very few. But if one wants to have one's own, it is necessary to have apprenticed oneself to the ones there are. And so it is necessary to have chosen them with the greatest care; to have been their student; to have listened to them; *to have faced them*; to have measured oneself with and against only the strongest and the most productive – but never to have been locked into the boredom and ultimate self-disappointment of discipleship. To have dallied with it – yes, inevitably; to have seen the depression – yes; to have endured the confrontation – and survived.

But survival is a lonely issue. One is one's only witness. And how can I present an account of my singular experiences? Somebody has to write and somebody has to tell the truth.

Under the pretense of objectivity, a vulgar theoretism has taken over, a theoretism that is blind to its history. Even though I am more or less conventionally captioned as a theorist, a literary theorist, whatever – I think of those T-shirts that say "model/waiter/whatever" – I cannot make any pretense to some kind of lie of objective interest in the objects I have chosen here. I prefer to state my nonobjectivity and my partiality here at the outset. If I am going anywhere, I am moving towards the space where I can show that it is obsessions, which are always those of a subject or of subjects, that show something of the true, not the universal lie of interests. Interests are interesting at one moment, no longer interesting the next. Obsessions last. Interest is the defensive screen of obsession.

Explaining how something so apparently subjective as an obsession can and does have a relation to the true, and that this might be of more than passing interest to the reader–scanner, is very difficult indeed. The first step is to say that I do not think that obsessions are simply personal or simply subjective. I live in the world just as everybody else does, and therefore I cannot – falsely – pretend to say that anything I have to say is so radical, revolutionary, and original that it has no relation to the Out There where I too am. To do so would be to price myself out of the market.

If I were to say something so silly, how could anybody possibly have access to what I do say (supposing they cared to try, which is not a given)? As long as one writes about words signed with other people's names – as long as one writes – one is in a public space along with everybody else. So it is not a matter of subjective impressions.

When Freud self-consciously began the century with the attempt to try to situate his own dreams within the realm of science, he began down this road upon which I find myself. In any case, I find this road to be the only logically possible hope – not only for the reasons stated above, but also because it is a questioning, critical road, one upon which I find myself thinking about how stories, particulars, texts, bear some relation to the truth, also about how something that must be called knowledge of this truth is produced, even if it is not itself capable of being reproduced.

This road allows me to ask my questions starting out from the language in which the sediments of the production of such truth are to be found. There isn't anything else, really, to go on. Long ago, I left behind any impulse to state the truth in some perspicuously stable and universal form. In the realm of reading and writing, which is where I am, such attempts – attempts toward a theory of this or that – always fail to satisfy. They renounce being able to account for what is to be found in the reading of any given or chosen particular, and thus they renounce their claim to bring a set of phenomena under the control of a concept or of a set of concepts. Such theories – of something called narrative, for example, a word I have never understood, even if I use it sometimes – are today's version of the vulgarity of a theory of truth by correspondence.

Since the phenomena do not correspond to the theory in any compelling way, they reveal only the theory's own desire for control, and ultimately, its despair over its lack of control. One can either dispense with the theory (unless it is a statement – not a theory – about the limitations of theory) or with the phenomena (Hegel: "so much worse for the facts"). And *a fortiori* for all the -isms that have fallen out of what is now called High Theory – tinged as this expression is with a nostalgia for a time when people were smarter, if more naïve. The -isms, those *misérables* of the academy, are all more vulgar and more cynical and more opportunistic than Theory ever was – even if the existence of Theory itself is only a phobic, defensive aftereffect, the reaction–formation mirage of the institutional marketplace. It is unfortunate that those concerned, the practitioners of this magical art, rushed to this word and took it upon themselves as a name.

When I started putting these things together I felt like the old, tired J. F. Sebastian in Ridley Scott's *Blade Runner*, who takes a cyborg named Pris, whose brain he has designed, into his apartment, itself crammed with the more mechanical toys he has invented to keep him company among the ruins. He introduces her to them and says: "These are my friends, I make them – I *make* them."

Happily I could never say the same. Now I remember the story of one of the world's more famous and enduring rock stars. Once asked why he didn't visit his children, he responded, "Because I don't know who they are."

There are so many names hidden in this book. I prefer not to make any more unfair use of them by chanting them again at the moments where they themselves cry out. Their own music appears in the proper places, along with strains of Shostakovich's Preludes and Fugues and the ballads of Caetano Veloso. I do not wish to make anyone suffer the indictment of more crass repetition. Cathy Caruth, Shoshana Felman, Ortwin de Graef, Werner Hamacher, Geoffrey Hartman, Jan Mieszkowski, Mary Quaintance, Gene Ray, Jan Rosiek, and Andrzej Warminski have my deep thanks for doing what they could for parts of the manuscript; Richard Macksey, Ray Ryan, Michael Sprinker, and Hilary Hammond for their work on and faith in the project. Thoughts, friendship, and wild patience from Andrew Ash, Howard Bloch, Jack Cameron, Jacques Derrida, Susan Edmunds, David Ellison, John Guillory, Ralph Heyndels, Denis Hollier, George Kateb, Debra Keates, Jan Keppler, Jean-Pol Madou, Janet Malcolm, Louis Marin, Claire Nouvet, Hans-Detlef Otto, Ernst Prelinger, Avital Ronell, Michael Shae, James Swenson, Greta West, and Deborah White were the condition of possibility of my own impatience. Special thanks are due to my colleagues at the Søren Kierkegaard Research Centre at the University of Copenhagen, and in particular to Stacey Ake, Vivian Bentsen, Henrik Blicher, Niels Jørgen Cappelørn, Joakim Garff, Dorothea Glöckner, Darío González, Johnny Kondrup, Karsten Kynde, and Kim Ravn, all of whom kept me alive through the final editing. Much of this book was written with the generous support of the Mellon Foundation, the Mrs. Giles Whiting Foundation, the Alexander von Humboldt-Stiftung, the James L. Knight Foundation, and Danmarks Grundforskningsfond.

Acknowledgments

Versions of parts of this work were first published in other places: "Guilt by (un)free association" in *MLN* 109:5, copyright 1994 by Johns Hopkins University Press; "La Lettre de l'esprit," in Jacques Poulain and Wolfgang Schirmacher, eds., *Penser après Heidegger*, copyright 1992 by Editions L'Harmattan; and "Er, or, borrowing from Peter to pay Paul," in Aris Fioretos, ed., *Word Traces*, copyright 1994 by Johns Hopkins University Press. They are reprinted here with the permission of the publishers.

Abbreviations

AI   Paul de Man, *Aesthetic Ideology*, edited and with an introduction by Andrzej Warminski (Minneapolis: University of Minnesota Press, 1996)

AR   Paul de Man, *Allegories of Reading* (New Haven: Yale University Press, 1979)

BI   Paul de Man, *Blindness and Insight*, second edition, revised (Minneapolis: University of Minnesota Press, 1983)

C   Maurice Blanchot, *Celui qui ne m'accompagnait pas* (Paris: Gallimard, 1953)

CTP   Edgar Allan Poe, *Complete Tales and Poems* (New York: Vintage, 1975)

CW   Paul de Man, *Critical Writings 1953–1978* (Minneapolis: University of Minnesota Press, 1989)

DE   Emmanuel Levinas, *En Découvrant l'existence avec Husserl et Heidegger* (Paris: Vrin, 1982)

E   Jacques Lacan, *Ecrits* (Paris: Seuil, 1966)

FR   Søren Kierkegaard, *Fear and Trembling* and *Repetition*, translation by H. Hong and E. Hong (Princeton: Princeton University Press, 1983)

GO   Maurice Blanchot, *The Gaze of Orpheus* (Barrytown, NY: Station Hill Press, 1981)

GW   Paul Celan, *Gesammelte Werke* I–V (Frankfurt-on-Main: Suhrkamp, 1983)

MM   Theodor W. Adorno, *Minima Moralia* (Frankfurt-on-Main: Suhrkamp, 1951), translation by E. F. N. Jephcott, *Minima Moralia* (London: New Left Books, 1974)

MP   Jacques Derrida, *Margins of Philosophy* (Chicago: University of Chicago Press, 1982)

OS   Jacques Derrida, *De L'esprit* (Paris: Galilée, 1987), translation by G. Bennington and R. Bowlby, *Of Spirit* (Chicago: University of Chicago Press, 1989)

P   Jacques Derrida, *Parages* (Paris: Galilée, 1986)

RC   Paul de Man, *Romanticism and Contemporary Criticism* (Baltimore: Johns Hopkins University Press, 1993)

RMR Lindsay Waters and Wlad Godzich, eds., *Reading de Man Reading* (Minneapolis: University of Minnesota Press, 1989)

RR   Paul de Man, *The Rhetoric of Romanticism* (New York: Columbia University Press, 1984)

RT   Paul de Man, *The Resistance to Theory* (Minneapolis: University of Minnesota Press, 1986)

SP   Jacques Derrida, *Signéponge/Signsponge* (New York: Columbia University Press, 1984)

WH   Martin Heidegger, *Was heißt Denken?* (Tübingen: Niemeyer, 1984)

Introduction: Ode to X,[1] or, the essay as monstrosity

And for a long time I could see no other conclusion than this, that short of having sixteen pockets, each with its stone, I could never reach the goal I had set myself, short of an extraordinary hazard. And if at a pitch I could double the number of my pockets, were it only by dividing each pocket in two, with the help of a few safety-pins let us say, to quadruple them seemed to be more than I could manage. And I did not feel inclined to take all that trouble for a half-measure. For I was beginning to lose all sense of measure, after all this wrestling and wrangling, and to say, All or nothing. And if I was tempted for an instant to establish a more equitable proportion between my stones and my pockets, by reducing the former to the number of the latter, it was only for an instant. For it would have been an admission of defeat. And sitting on the shore, before the sea, the sixteen stones spread out before my eyes, I gazed at them in anger and perplexity . . . And while I gazed thus at my stones, revolving interminable martingales all equally defective, and crushing handfuls of sand, so that the sand ran through my fingers and fell back on the strand, yes, while thus I lulled my mind and part of my body, one day suddenly it dawned on the former, dimly, that I might perhaps achieve my purpose without increasing the number of my pockets, or reducing the number of my stones, but simply by sacrificing the principle of trim. The meaning of this illumination, which suddenly began to sing within me, like a verse of

---

[1] "[N]ot just in the vague or general manner in which any poem of address could be given this title . . ." After these words about the word "prosopopoeia" as a fitting title for a poem by Victor Hugo that in fact bears another name, Paul de Man appends the following note: "As they in fact often are, though preferably by the more euphonic and noble term 'ode' or 'Ode to X.'" The next note to his text reads: "Rather than being a heightened version of sense experience, the erotic is a figure that makes such experience possible. We do not see what we love but we love in the hope of confirming the illusion that we are indeed seeing anything at all" (*RT*, 48, 53).

Isaiah, or of Jeremiah, I did not penetrate at once, and notably the word trim, which I had never met with, in this sense, long remained obscure . . .[2]

I could begin at exactly the same place where I began to write the essays collected in this book – in a time that now belongs to the pastness of a past I hope never to remember – and say: I am fascinated by difficulty. This is what I have learned.

Let me try and state where I think I have come from. At the outset, I tried to formulate a set of observations concerning the relations between text and commentary in the authors whose works I was reading. I insist that the goal was, or should have been, to formulate – that is to say, to bring to utterance – and not to formalize. And thus I insist that among these texts there is no single relation but rather there obtains an open and mobile set of links, a set with no fixed boundaries of relations capable, at any moment, of being broken off and modified, but not exchanged.

For someone whose training began, by predilection, more or less, in the realm of so-called philosophical discourse, it was and still is all too easy to move along at the level of the concept. This is not what I hope to have done, although I have, no doubt, done some of it. But I admonish myself and my readers here, at the end and at the outset, against this. These admonitions toward the specific differences of each text, and against the banality of generalization, are themselves generalities, and fall into well-worn tracks.[3] But now it is long after the end of a long apprenticeship, and I trust I will be forgiven for the attempt to restate, in my own terms, these problems that have come to the fore of the mind and as I see them.

Let's begin again.

In the course of a given rhetorical reading, there is a paradoxical relation between the reasons for the choice of a particular text or

---

[2] Samuel Beckett, *Molloy*, rpt. in *Three Novels by Samuel Beckett* (New York: Grove Press, 1965), 70–71.

[3] The problem of enunciating this tendential attitude as a law, and thus falling into the trap that, like the principle of verifiability, it is not itself verifiable, is in fact the crux that generates so much of the power of Paul de Man's work. In the vocabulary of another tradition, we would have to call this kind of injunction toward the singularity of any text or reading a rule of *grammar*, in Wittgenstein's sense, that is to say, a rule of form. It is only, perhaps, in thinking about – and speaking about – the way in which the evidence of such a law's existence must be everywhere shown, but never said, that we will be able to speak of the recognition of event, act, or occurrence that will allow us to assert that we are no longer simply hyperformalists.

passage for reading and the micrological or histological reading that follows upon this initial choice. This initial decision (the rhetoric of intention is particularly dangerous here, as it is not certain that one ever *chooses* a text, purely and simply) may be an ideological matter (in the technical sense, a question about the *logos*, the meaning of a text); for example, in the case where it seems that a given passage is a crux and that a successful interpretation of this text depends upon its resolution. But what follows in the rhetorical analysis has more to do with lexical considerations: *how* is this text (dis)organized, and what does this (have to) do with or to the presupposition of meaning? My question is, then, how does the lexical reading relate to the original choice of reading material by means of logical (read thematic) considerations? What is the *thematic scar* left by the necessity of the initial choice upon the lexical reading that ensues therefrom; and how does this scar structurally limit the scope of the reading, or its extension (in the logical sense of entities covered by the predicate), what we might call the reading's power? I call the thematic scar the mark left by the initial choice of a text to be read on the rhetorical procedure that treats signifiers (and not concepts). How does this scar necessitate the proviso that comes with any reading, namely, that it is a reading of only *this* text, a particular reading, but one which also confers exemplarity upon the choices it makes and forecloses?

I write these words here, in the language of a critical mode now in desuetude, not out of a desire to remain in the past, but to assert that these projects, and my habitus, began under this sign. If I have moved on – who knows where, and who would be the judge? – I still wish to exercise my liturgical practices, not automatically, compulsively, or in the mode of sterile and unanimated repetition, but in order to try to move towards the future without any false sense of security or liberation that would come from ditching the past. Better to wake up every day and make ready for the journey to Mount Moriah than always to be trying to get back to Ithaca, or to New Haven. So it is not that I shall not have moved, but that I have tried, as hard as I could, to perform my exercises starting from this one place. Accidents always happen along the way. This is the correlate, or perhaps only the restatement, of what I have said already of my desire to temper my conceptual temperament, this tempering being the enunciation of the law I have tried – but no doubt failed – because of my very desire to state it – to internalize.

These tensions of the particular and the general, of the pressure of the move to the ontological and of the more pragmatic nominalism that says "I will have had to or have tried to begin *somewhere*," with *some* text, in some always singular, provisional situation, no matter how well prepared the ground may be – these tensions preoccupy this space even before it is opened outright, more purely and more simply. In this realm of contaminations there is not going to be anything more than the more or less purely and/or simply. They are well known, these tensions, but they can stand bearing out and restatement, in something like an apology for having decided to – that is to say, for having recognized that it is necessary to – leave the discourse of the universal behind and to move to something more like what used to be called – may its name forever and hauntingly be praised! – the essay.

Others have occupied these spaces differently, by working on the peculiarities of the relations between examples and what they can( )(not) be read as exemplifying – for example – or by reading the relations between formalist discourses and the remains, what gets left out of the fields surveyed by these systems as the very conditions of possibility of enunciation of the formal laws themselves. (These gestures can, and can also not be read in the register of the proverbial return of the repressed; but the use of such a vocabulary must also be interrogated in respect of the temporal schemes it brings with it. In truth, it is not a bad choice of words at this moment; for, in foregrounding the temporal sequences imposed or implied, it shows that a purportedly more steady-state and neutral-formalist discourse – which itself can be expanded to include a meta-discourse on its own conditions of possibility and what they exclude – speaks this same language in respect of temporal pattern.)[4]

There is no simultaneity of our finite reasoning, and thus we could say there is always narrative, hence allegory – even if it is impossible, in the case of most narratives, to figure out what their law is or if they have one or to find a general law of narrative.[5]

---

[4] See also de Man, "Sign and Symbol in Hegel's *Aesthetics*," in *AI*.

[5] We could substitute the word "allegory" for the word "sophism" in the title of Lacan's "Le Temps logique et l'assertion de la certitude anticipée: un nouveau sophisme," given the definition of sophism therein. And we should also note that the title of the earliest typescript of de Man's essay now entitled "Allegory" (in *AR*), is "Narrative." *Allegory*, therefore, is the name we use for the *Narrative* that tells the story of the undoing of the concept (often by use of example) in a pseudo-temporal sequence that is, philosophically speaking, called *Sophism*.

But – it is not possible to leave the concept behind, or simply to leave it out. And thus we have to ask: What kind of quilting is always taking place between an avowedly *critical* discourse, a discourse that celebrates (or mourns) the fact of its anaclitic relation to something necessarily anterior, that proclaims its status as an act of receiving something else, if not of a reception – what does reception mean anymore? – and the fact that such a discourse, once it overtly manifests its *ex post facto* nature, often seems to lapse into a vocabulary of necessity, of sufficient grounds, of causal explanation from *before*, as opposed to understanding from *after*? Is there a structure to be discerned behind this apparent *post hoc propter hoc*? Is it only apparent, and is it only a lapse, or a prolapse whose syncopations are dictated, perhaps, by the critical act itself?

Here, then, is my apology. Apology here means: the attempt at a statement of how one has become what one is, of how one came to write what one has written. But an apology for the itinerary back to the essay – to make a comparison (and *is* the point here that comparison always belongs to an inferior genre, is structurally thus always vulgar in its belatedness?) – must work from more formal grounds, perhaps, and less from personal ones. It should be the apology of a necessity of thought, by which any I, thinking these thoughts, would be affected. And yet it is also my apology – a fact for which I make none. It must go like this, or something like this:

I came to the field of literary studies – and not to the study of any specific, national(istic) literature – in order to continue my more or less philosophical investigations, and for essentially pragmatic, worldly reasons. It seemed that there I would be able to pursue the thoughts I wanted to pursue without being bothered by any silly person telling me whether what I was interested in or what compelled me was philosophy or not. I came to this open field, then, to comparative literature, to go on holiday from the more brutally normalizing aspects of the discourse of language-being-on-holiday. And for a while I got caught up in the necessity of the carnivalesque, of the upside-down, topsy-turvy displacements there. But this caught-uppitiness was not an accident. I was disoriented. It took me years of doubt as to even the possibility of refinding my bearings, to come up with these humble excuses for excuses. But here I am, and this does not go without these potentially offensive words of defense. And where am I? In a department of rhetoric, in a department of French, in a department of comparative or general literature, in an independent research center sitting on top of a theology faculty? – I am everywhere and nowhere.

What I call the carnivalesque turned out to be, in fact, one part terror and one part – the major part – a wake, a scene of mourning. The hyperbolic form of this mournful terror could be stated in the constant conjunction of two words: necessary and impossible. How do you tell a story about this bizarre hendiadys, "necessary and impossible?" Where can you begin? Where can you go?

The terror was interiorized and self-imposed: You must adopt, adapt yourself to the discourse of the strictly impersonal, dry, didactic, surgical. You must always maintain the strict tension between the universality of the conceptual apparatus you should want to be abandoning and the sheerly focused, one-pointed attitude aimed always and only at the singularity of the text you are reading. Speak only of what is immediately under your gaze, which should become more and more congruent with the gaze of your words. You may only *show* the relation of these tessera to the whole; you may not *speak* of the form or of the frame, otherwise you will be ostracized. Otherwise your tessera will become our ostra.

While I insist that this terror was self-imposed, that it came out of the necessity of my own project and out of my own movements of thought, I would also like to give some figural examples of the kinds of criticism I have received concerning some of the work between these covers.[6] One colleague said to me, for example: "You should not be writing about de Man [or, I presume, by extension, Derrida], you should be writing about, say, lyric poetry [Celan was the example used, since he was on the boards] in a de Manian fashion." I took this as an example of the kind of false piety toward my teachers I wanted to avoid at all costs, while at the same time I knew I would have to interrogate its reasons. For me so much of the enterprise was invested in the necessity of measuring myself against the standards of my forebears, against their

[6] On the distinction between allegorical interpretation as that which mediates between the world of phenomena and the world of ideas, and figural interpretation, which takes place between two worldly sets of phenomena, see Erich Auerbach, "'Figura,'" in his *Scenes from the Drama of European Literature* (Minneapolis: University of Minnesota Press, 1984).

authority, their fecundity, that, having traveled with them for so many years, I did not feel as though I could fake the false humility of discipleship.

Another European colleague, who himself has made among the most significant contributions to the reading of the aforementioned figures, said to me: "You should be writing, say, about Merleau-Ponty [and some other, purportedly less *contemporary* thinkers]." I took this as a kind of condescension, which I couldn't swallow very well. The implication of the condescension, of his list of names as opposed to my list of names, seemed to me to be of this kind: You are an American in a department of comparative literature, and I am a European trained in the science, *Wissenschaft* – with all its attendant paradoxes – of literary interpretation. You cannot, therefore, because of your in-nate provinciality, approach these subjects, because you cannot approach them from the position of in-nate proximity from which I approach them. So don't bother, because you will always end up showing only your own ignorance.[7]

To this, which shocked me at the time and left me speechless with the shame, first of my own, followed by my recognition of his own much greater presumptuousness, I can only begin to respond now and in retrospect: to do anything other than what I will have set out to do, *here* and *now*, would be a cop-out, for reasons that I hope will have asserted themselves (the future perfect is a lie) constantly throughout this book. (This is an introduction, so I am entitled to lean on this assertion-through-structure I attribute, if a little faithlessly, to what follows: read the book, judge for yourselves. I will judge it more harshly than you will, but let's not get involved in one-upmanship.)

Besides, I write against the self-hating, know-nothingist aspect of American academia, the widespread tendency that respects anyone as long as he or she has an accent. In saying this, my (incorrectly) presumed nationalism will be objected to. But in fact the nationalism is on the side of that repressed (and thus more strongly maintained, more destructive) American self-hatred, which mixes ever more today with a disgusting, nativist and populist (one could say brown) tint.

[7] See my "Fleisch und das Vergessen des Blicks," in Hinderk Emrich and Gary Smith, eds., *Vom Nutzen des Vergessens* (Berlin: Akademie Verlag, 1996), for a detailed reading of what takes place between Merleau-Ponty and Lacan.

And if anyone wants to accuse me of self-indulgence in recounting these stories, or of thus wanting to show my scars, I will insist on the fact that these stories are all true and at the same time are truly allegorical as I tell them here. They tell stories that contain within their individual selves (of) the defective universal structure of similar moves that happen over and over again. And my aim in telling them here, thus, is ethical.

But the last and most interesting objection I can remember was that of a friend, who deepened his friendship with me, as well as his colleagueship, by *counting* the sentences in one of my essays that ended in question marks (I remember only that he mentioned a number, although I myself have never counted anything – I begin and then I lose track). "You do not write ethically," he said.

The depth of our friendship was measured by the years of silence between us that followed. And to this objection I respond: Yours is the most important and the most interesting, the most compelling remark – along with the first objection above – because you are forcing me to interrogate the status and value of the question. In counting, there is an attention to the letter upon which are built things far from banal.

This is what I say now. Then I said, this is a grouping, a tableau of thoughts in motion. The investigations have always hardly begun, and therefore I will make no pretense at stating my remarks in a more assertoric – if not apodictic – form, which would be to mistake the form of the essay for that of the treatise. Now, and in what follows, I want to try to live up to the responsibility of addressing the ethics of the question as a mode of emphasis, or of performance that does not necessarily fall within the bounds of the conventional "rhetorical question." To assert a problematic in the language game of questions does not either deny the validity of asking nor simply and straightforwardly ask, but points to a certain provisionality of the discourse thus advanced, if not promulgated.

And yet: I am uneasy with the "return to the ethical" in contemporary literary – or should I say, theoretical, post-theoretical? – studies. Why?

1. Because, at first appearance, any such "return" (as though one were ever doing anything other than ethics) must begin with an explicit gesture that says, I am not renouncing the attempt at

intrinsic criticism, I am not renouncing the study of the text. Otherwise there is the grave risk that in renouncing or in being seen as renouncing the text, one will merely be aping or be seen as aping the social so-called sciences out of the insecurity that one does not have a paradigm of one's own, a body of positive knowledge or a methodology one can show when accused of knowing nothing. Thus this "(re)turn" can be taken as a reactive gesture, and furthermore as a gesture in the mechanics and service of the most terrible kind of self-hatred. If I am interested in ethics, "the ethical," etc., it has *nothing* to do with a desire to legitimate what I do in the face of the totalitarian stupidity of those who would assume that the digressive structure of my constellations is not "theoretical" – and at the same time not "wordly" – enough. (The desire for *theory*, that is, for control, is a symptom of the same kind of defensiveness as the desire to have one's intellectual concerns dictated by "the world," "the outside," etc.)

2.   Because such a discourse, if it wants to lay claim to having anything to say about ethics, had better start asking questions about the status of a discourse that promises everything for and in a certain experience of the future when this future clearly is not a future which will ever be present to any kind of experience. This is a call to the examination of the provisionality of so much of contemporary thinking. The mechanics of the ethical relation, *pace* Levinas,[8] involve a disruption of the temporal order inasmuch as the temporal order is linked to the categories of consciousness itself. This is why Levinas insists that the trace is the insertion of space into time, or that it disturbs the order of the world irrevocably. *This* is the call of the ethical, in the *irrevocable*, which will not allow us to promise anything for some future, utopian holiday. There is, at several levels, a profoundly anti-Kantian set of implications here, not only ethically, but also metaphysically speaking, and these are most certainly deeply linked.

Provisionality, which I have thus far enunciated as what came out of an attempt at a description of *terror*, turned out to be the way out of mourning and of renunciation. That is to say, I had paralyzed myself, submitted to a paralysis, because I had interpreted the problem of "the end of philosophy in the discourse of criticism" as

---

[8] See his "La Trace de l'autre," in *DE*.

so overwhelmingly insurmountable that *I couldn't move*. It took a long time for me to open my eyes again, to see through my tears, in fact, and to realize that the work of all the figures I was interested in constantly was caught up in gestures of foreclosure, of provisionality – what I have called in some places radical provisionality – in a recourse to the pragmatic, to the occasional, to the event, act, occurrence, singularity – what can and does "fly in from the outside." (From "A large hall, many guests, whom we were receiving," to "Suddenly, the window opened, and I saw ...") I had to turn from the paralysis of renunciation to the more or less ethical attitude of adopting this renunciation as itself what there was to be read and analyzed.

(Often I have contemplated writing an opera, which I destine for the beginning of the millenium. It is called *Freud's Dreams*, and it consists of three acts: the first stages the Dream of Irma's Injection, and concludes with the silent scream of Freud looking down Irma's throat; the second stages the Wolf Dream, and requires cutting and pasting for the insertion of various mythological themes and variations; the third recurs to The Dream of the Burning Child. Why is it that no one has seen or heard that all of these key dreams are about singing, shrieking, screaming, about the relation between silence and screaming? The surgence of the real in each dream [the formula of trimethylamin, the scream of the Wolfman, the dead child who speaks to his father, and says, "Father, don't you see I'm burning?"] – all of these occurrences call out of their contexts the way a text calls out to be read. The first parts of these dreams are regressions toward the absolute singularity of these events, in the way that readings do not dismiss contexts, but try to uncover the moment of their irruption into text.)

Hence the gathering of these essays, painstakingly planned and unplanned, and which I put together under the title *Singularities*. (I could have used many titles – *Mourning Becomes Being, or Toward the Non-Thematic* was another that suggested itself to me. Mourning certainly becomes *my* being. I could write an entire essay that would consist of nothing but titles – that would be good, a strong gesture.) The impulses for these essays came on a number of occasions over several years. The tones and scopes differ wildly.

I begin with love. – Romance, that is. I wrote the essay on Adorno in a deep depression, as a kind of self-analysis, while I was trying to figure out why I fall in love. It flew out of my fingertips, this essay on an aphorism buried in and as the heart of *Minima Moralia*. I was trying to figure out the structural situation of the damaged life: no smaller task would satisfy. I think I did it, but I don't think I'm any wiser. A lot of people heard it and read it and liked it. They even said I had acquired a style. I have never been able to take compliments, and I took this one in a blind rage, as a sheer, aestheticizing derogation of anything I might have to say. I enjoyed writing this essay even more than usual. In its acting out of the battle between the particular and the universal, it commingles intimately with the pages on de Man below. I love Adorno for the eloquence of his scorn.

I would also have liked – this "also" is my *Tendenz*, this last a word about which I have much to say in these pages on Adorno – to write about the aphorism that follows it, called "Gaps." "Gaps" is an aphorism concerned with the idiocy of the demand of academic argumentation that no step be left out. Since everybody has been telling me, my whole life long, that I am always leaving out steps, that I am always writing about at least one too many things, *et cetera qui possunt accidere aut rebus externis*, I also had an affinity, a *Neigung*, for "Gaps." But I left it out, because, after having worked the preceding aphorism, "Morals and the Order of Time," to which I ended up consecrating the entire essay, I decided that I could only move forward if I were to will one thing – and, after the essay was written, the only thing I could have done with "Gaps" would have been to repeat it, word for word, with no commentary.

I could have added it as a postscript and said: See what I mean? And this is what I would have said, had I written about "Gaps": The demand that one not leave out any steps, our inheritance from pre-psychoanalytic Brit-twit culture, has merged, in the last fifteen years, with the fundamentally anti-intellectual (not to mention anti-pleasure, anti-love, anti-life . . .) byword of American populism: that everything should be written so as to be capable of being understood by the average, illiterate American, for whom the *New York Times* is something like what Mallarmé used to be.

The tendency of our all but consumed, consumptive society is to say: If I have to do any work to read it, then forget it. There is no joy anymore, there is the massive imperative toward passivity. Those of us who supposedly teach see this in our supposed students: they want us to do all the work for them, and then they fill out those ridiculous multiple-choice evaluation forms at the end of the semester, and say that we were inadequate because we didn't make it simple enough. This is the mark of a decadent culture that has no possible justification. I call it the schlock experience, and I rest my case on this front.

The principal burden of the essay on Heidegger–Derrida is to consider the role that readings of a certain activity or passivity play in their relationship, and to watch the terms that interpose themselves between these, but do not replace them. First, a search for a voice: What kind of archaeology resuscitates – in a move of thought that seems so necessary for so many thinkers on the contemporary scene – the older middle from the fallen, warring, and sclerotic active and passive? And what kind of fabular telling is necessary to this story, with its recourses to the Fall, in all its cases and senses, to spiritual resuscitation, and to the notion of the modern or of the contemporary itself? This essay proceeds more or less programmatically and in a rather dry fashion, without much polemic. For the most part it was written as a pedagogical exercise and makes no claims to any conspective account of Derrida's readings of Heidegger. Besides, these readings often happen in places other than in Derrida's readings of Heidegger. (In Derrida's *Signéponge*, for example, upon which I do not do much more than touch – even if I feel it up constantly – in a disordering gesture of contiguity. *Signéponge* is a book about touching, about names touching things, about name-things, about what it means to touch a text. It is, if you will, about the laws of touching, and it is one of the pieces of Derrida's writing that moves me most. It is one of the truly great commentaries on Heidegger's Thing, although in this sense and in general it has been almost entirely unappreciated.) Therefore, an attempt at such a conspective reading of Derrida's Heidegger readings would itself not be able to proceed along thematic lines, but would have to read Derrida's own encyclopedia with an eye for all the parabases, the asides.

Reading Heidegger is more or less the permanent parabasis of Derrida's speaking. And, proximally and for the most part, I try to relate Derrida's asides to and about Heidegger to the rhetoric of the provisional, and to its necessity, and to a certain appearance of the vocabulary of necessity itself. I want to take seriously the places where Derrida's analyses of Heidegger assert their *interminable* character, and to interrogate the assertions Derrida makes that everything should go more slowly – infinitely slowly, perhaps – and be all-round more patient – and for reasons that have little to do with the empirical incompleteness of Heidegger's *œuvre*. The *fact* that someone can give a five-hour lecture on Heidegger, which then turns into the first "book" he publishes "on" Heidegger, a kind of "introduction to the reading of Heidegger," and, in the scope of that time and of those pages, keep saying, because of the limits of this situation, I cannot do everything I should do, etc. – these are not contingent statements of personal finiteness, but have something to do with the structure of the work within which the problem of finitude is brought to the fore.

A certain logic of contamination necessitates our taking the provisional seriously. For if we never can be sure, in any last instance, that it will be possible to insure that the conditions of possibility of a discourse can be sheltered from whatever accidents or infelicities may befall the discourse itself, then clearly it will be seen that instances of deferral, and our remarking of them, serve not merely as reminders of the redundant vagaries of, say, an overburdened lecturing schedule, but relate to the very urgent matter of the philosophy of the future itself. We will have to ask how Derrida's continuation of Heidegger's analysis of the future as the most radical of the ecstases shakes out into issues he broaches under the names *monstrosity* and *Heideggerian hope* in an effort to think the future without nostalgia, and whether this attempt does not itself lead to – or is not still a symptomatic correlate of – a certain sentimentality.[9]

Once one of the temporal modes is rendered problematic, they all unwind. The deferral of the future dissolves the present; the dissolution of the present leads us, in problematizing perception as that which cannot take place in a present that does not exist, to the impossibility of any past recaptured. Rather than go in search of time lost in the critique of transcendental phenomenology via the remarking of the trace, we should be asking questions such as:

[9] A sentimentality very much like the nostalgia Tom Lehrer discusses in his introduction to "So Long, Mom" when he says: "I believe that if any songs are going to come out of World War Three we had better start writing them now . . . You might call this one a bit of pre-nostalgia" (Tom Lehrer, *1963: That Was The Year That Was* [Reprise Records, 1965]).

Are we bound to the cardinality of the future as the most important of the ecstases? Had Heidegger not announced his critique of vulgar time consciousness in *Being and Time* in the analysis of being-towards-death, would the future still be, in a logical sense, the lynchpin of the system? Can we perform a critique of vulgar time consciousness starting from the point of view of *any* one of the ecstases, and reach the same conclusions, in a kind of anamorphic mode of projection? Is the survival of the future in its status as the radical itself a kind of lingering anthropologism (or an inescapable anthropomorphism?) in Heidegger's later writings? Or are we bound up in questions of the irreversible, of irreversibility here? These are urgent questions, and it's about time we started asking them. About time, indeed.

It is time to start talking about finitude, which is never simply a personal assertion of one's own exhaustion (to feel exhausted is to know that one is alive), but rather is part of the structure of the critical act itself, of the joint constraints of saying, on the one hand, that certain things, passages, cruxes asserted themselves as demanding consideration; and, on the other hand, that one also must be responsible for making choices, for always already having made some choices. (The critical act is suspended between the pastness of the "asserted" and the future orientation of this "responsibility.")

Let us never forget that Derrida is a critic, that he is a textually oriented kind of guy, and that much of the resistance to his work, in purportedly philosophical circles, stems from the nakedness of his assertion of the critical act itself. He is a teacher of the history of philosophy, and this is what makes him into a commentator on the history of the present. Let no one misunderstand the investigation of provisionality in the context of his work as the attempt to read failure, but rather let it be taken as the positive assertion of the necessity of making provisions for a longer (if not the longest) journey.

My discussion of the work of Paul de Man is about choices. His and mine. It is to a certain degree about the violence of choice and the violence of the necessity of choice. It is about the essay as form. How does de Man use it; how does it relate to what he says and how he says it? How does this form, upon which we fling ourselves, constantly longing, allow us and force us to make choices? This exercise in a non-dogmatic, rough and ready, forensic post-formalism treats the way the provisionality dictated by the paleonymic necessities uncovered in my discussion of Derrida–Heidegger shakes out into the perennial and fragile necessity of the relations between text and commentary.[10] While I defend and illustrate some characteristics of de Man's argumentation, concerning questions of necessity, irreversibility, occurrence, and so on, I make no claim to any full catalog of his rhetorical terms, or to any exhaustive catalog of topoi or of sources. My need is rather to examine and elucidate the inevitable character of much of what de Man has to say, and this especially when, while Derrida's work seems to be being all too easily assimilated – hence buried – into the structure of some kind of superficial history of postmodern ideas, de Man's seems to have encountered resistance of another kind.

The mere fact of someone's work being critical, of its going out of its way to point out the way in which it leans on something anterior, seems to devalue it for those who can assimilate only the Concept. Hence, while Derrida gets falsely assimilated to grand narratives of the end of narrative – of history, of god, of man, and so forth – de Man tends to get treated as a theoretical tendency among others, as one version of the tools in the critical toolbox, as one shelf of provisions in the critical supermarket among others. This is defensiveness or stupidity masking itself as pluralism or eclecticism.

It is at least partly the desire to avoid such banal optimism, the Pollyannaish tendency of thought that would allow us to write up de Man into our steadily growing kit of *allgemeine Texttheorie*, which induces some of the terror attendant to this moment. So I must make it clear, at this point, that if my own approach to de Man blatantly and patently refuses to think of itself, in its no doubt somewhat self-interested representation, as a summarizing and conspective pronouncement on his work, and thus admits that it begins in the proximate, by focusing on things there that present themselves as necessarily of compulsive importance *for me*, it is not because, in my terror, I have inauthentically and all too knowingly opted out of the necessity of some kind of universalizing, totalizing,

---

[10] I will also be concerned with emphasizing de Man's differences from Derrida, which are much deeper than is usually thought to be the case, and which tend to surface in moments of great anxiety – theirs and mine.

apodictic almost, conspective, and axiomatico-deductive approach that would start out from the implicit or explicit assertion of having predigested, thus preempted the entire question.

Working with and through my own terror here means: admitting that my own choices are partial, and not for that reason alone any less interesting for a potential reader. I admit that I begin on open and rough ground as the positive assertion of the condition of possibility of doing anything whatsoever – that is *my* provisional, pragmatic mark. It gets me out of the terror that can paralyze all beginnings; it gets me out of the mindless and passive *equis paribus* of the eclectic approach to theory as a well-stocked supermarket (or door store, or Routledge catalog). It recognizes the provisional character of the ways one can deal with necessity, the very ways in which the discourse of necessity opens out onto the most radical contingency, and puts its figural finger there, to touch this knot, scar, or wound of thought.

I must add here that I am thoroughly disheartened at most attempts to "rescue" or "legitimate" thinkers such as Heidegger, de Man, and Derrida by showing that we can make some kind of politically correct agenda extend from their work (likewise to condemn them). The assumptions involved in this move are quite absurd. I do not pretend to present an exhaustive account of these assumptions, but here is an attempt: "For something to be worthy of being thought or thought through, it has to be able to think, think through, or pronounce upon everything." – This is patently ridiculous, the very "root of all evil" of which Hölderlin writes in asking the question, Why always this search for the one? Not even the physicists have explained everything with one force. Why do we have to have *one* theory? Isn't the demand that one thing satisfy every need of thought on all occasions the very kind of reasoning we should want to get away from? It is true that a certain logic of contamination may dictate that thought cannot be kept pure of politics, but this does not entail that every thought has to produce a politics out of itself any more than it has to produce a cookbook. I cannot imagine anything worse than a Heideggerian cookbook. I have long since given up the arrogance of thinking that I do what I do because it is the most radical, revolutionary, and original force with which to destabilize this or that institution, and I have a fearful distrust of those who continue to make this claim. Their desire is totalitarian, not mine.

What is so problematical about the closeness of close reading that always makes it seem too close for comfort? Especially in these times of retrenchment, should we not abandon the rhetoric of close reading and replace it with that of closer reading, in order to stress its necessarily non-static, performative, and in fact hyperbological dimensions? Yes, on the one hand there is something to be said for the analogy to be drawn between close and closer reading on the one hand and safe and safer sex on the other. But on the other hand, if we go for the closer and think that we can forget about the close, do we not forsake the axes of the hyperbola, and in doing so – it is not simply a question of adhering more or less slavishly to a mathematical model – do we not abandon, or sheerly problematize, the discussion of the materiality of the text as the literal ground of possibility of our discussion? I fear and rejoice that in having put the discussion this acutely, I have led us into the ungrounded – or posited – structure of the ground.

If something is seen to inhabit the realm of the conceptual, it crosses borders relatively easily. But borders crossed by Derrida are not often crossed by de Man. Truly it can be said that almost no one in Europe, in the English-speaking countries or elsewhere, has a clue about him. This is true even in Germany, where Derrida's books, which now pass directly from French into German via Vienna, used to have to be translated into English first before German publishers would take them on.[11] And not only Derrida's books. It is no accident that Foucault's *Les Mots et les choses* passed into German as *Die Ordnung der Dinge*. America may not know to what degree it is a German nation, but Germany buys only cheap American things, even if always under protest.

Why is it, though, that the natively American – de Man, for example – cannot be assimilated by an audience willing to buy everything else, and in such quantities?[12] This essay on de Man imposed its necessity on me first.[13]

---

[11] Perhaps the only happy exception to this *je n'en veux rien savoir* is some of Scandinavia – maybe also some of the countries of former Yugoslavia. What an axis for Europe!

[12] To me, Stanley Cavell and Avital Ronell are preeminent, in their different tonalities, in treating the hidden networks that relate European philosophy to American culture.

[13] Perhaps it is from the position of a teacher that one learns best the difficulty and the resistance of the work of Paul de Man. In pushing the question of the theoretical to its most hyperbolic, he is, perhaps, the most literary of the writers under our gaze.

In contrast, say, to Adorno, Blanchot was the most difficult to write about, and the essay which provided me with the occasions of my utmost resistance and despair. Thus I will say the least about it here. This essay is the product of the first time I ever tried to write anything substantial on a supposed work of supposedly narrative supposed fiction. My evasions took various forms, from attempts at explaining my differences with every available purported commentary on this small book, *Celui qui ne m'accompagnait pas*, to outright confession (and the simultaneous – and endless – narrative of self-justification that it breeds and that breeds it). Never did I feel the stakes to be so high as in writing about this book; never did I feel the responsibility for my own choices to be so great. If *this* book has a center, which emerged late but whose necessity asserted itself so early, it is a weak center, and it is here. While everything between these covers could be considered unfinished, this essay is more unfinished than the others. Here I am most exposed, on the ground that is most bare.

In the pages on Shakespeare–Celan, the hyperbola has come full circle: this apparently most mandarin-textual of readings of a lyric poem also turns out to be about identification. Here, it is not only a matter of the question of poetic identification; it is also a question of the double suicide of a poet and of a critic, Paul Celan and Peter Szondi. Szondi's reduplicative gesture is structured around his attempt – and failure – to mourn the loss of his friend in an act of critical writing – his last. Here, the destructive aspects of identification in and as its impossibility come most horribly to the fore. This essay on a poem turns around the question of what becomes of the name when it is curtailed – if not abbreviated – into a pronoun – and into a stammered one at that. Here too I come more closely by a certain desperation of the lyric voice, which explodes only, in a sense, to be emptied out of anything other than its purely positional function. Thus this essay runs ahead of the end of the book.

I have no illusions to the effect that anybody at all will care about all of this. But now, at least, I'm not scared of what anybody thinks anymore, and I don't write for anyone but myself. The worst thing that could befall this book would be for anybody to adopt any piece of it as doctrine – even though I would defend everything I say here as true.

Introduction

"In this life, things r much harder than in the afterworld / in this life you're on your own," as Prince sings.[14] Here are my fragments of the afterword. I cast my lot here with a dying art, that of the essay. I am speaking about tendential, idiosyncratic things, about choices. I resent the word *personal* for its being too tied up in the rampant criminality and ultimate decay, the wreckage of individualistic culture, its selfishness, by which we are all surrounded, its meanness. My things are bound together, in this assemblage, by impulses, peripeties, dead ends, unfulfilled speculations and hypotheses, unsubstantiated claims, moments of lyricism (I try to extend them for as long a possible), in short, writing, such as we love it to be, the fruit of the fascination with objects over which we have not ceased to joy and to rage – even if these last lapse into the infinite leveling of experience and existence we call perpetual mourning. I am a man disgusted with the mechanical, cynical, and dead aspects of my profession. The worship of death that is the current *argot* of the schools is a set of moves, of cheap tricks. I am not interested in keeping up with the units of professional communication in the journals, which have, for the most part, become McNuggetized. The truth of the current ideological obsession with diversity is a reduction of every diverse element to a sameness, to a threadbare cell in the self-administered *carcere*.

[14] "Let's Go Crazy," on his *Purple Rain* album (Warner Brothers Records, 1984).

❖❖❖

1

Guilt by (un)free association: Adorno on romance *et al.*, with some reference to the schlock experience

❖❖❖

It follows from this that anybody who attempts to come out alive – and survival itself has something nonsensical about it, like dreams in which, having experienced the end of the world, one afterwards crawls from a basement – ought also to be prepared at each moment to end his life.[1]

But this is to condemn and to love in an abusive way.[2]

T. W. Adorno's *Minima Moralia* has a kind of cultish status among us *fin de siècle* intellectuals. Everybody has his own favorite passages, whether longer or more aphoristic, and few would deny that the book is one of the masterpieces of twentieth-century prose overall, to use deliberately a monumental vocabulary very much out of pomo fashion but which no doubt would have appealed to crotchety old Teddie, the last great exponent of high culture, epitome of the stylized figure of the German Jew in the ironic cunning of his sentences. Here, the very recondite character of Adornian statement, its stalwart erudition – precisely what made it unintelligible to the American publishing industry and its consumers, thus necessitating Adorno's second exile as a *Nachjude* in the Germany of its Western Federal Republic phase – all combine with its sublime scorn to come forth in a combination both formidable and charming.

---

[1] *MM*, 39/38. Page numbers refer first to the German, then to the English text. In the course of this essay I also advert to de Man, "Sign and Symbol in Hegel's *Aesthetics*" (in *AI*), an essay which is itself a very complex piece of work, to which I do not pretend to do justice here, but to which I also dedicate much discussion in "Absolute Constructions" below.

[2] Blanchot, "Literature and the Right to Death," in *GO*, 33.

Thematic considerations notwithstanding – the continual references to the conditions of exile, and so on – the reasons why this book bears the subtitle "Reflections from the Damaged Life" follow from its being a book of love perhaps in all possible senses: it is written out of love, and it is about love. Alone the constant, albeit hidden reference to Kierkegaard, and in particular to his *Repetition* – a reference to a book about love from an age not as hypertrophically cynical as our own, a reference shown but never said – is enough to justify the apparent baldness of this assertion.

There are, however, paradoxes in the way in which this book is loved. The first: This book is the bible of a certain élite of literati, while the more technical works written or sponsored by Adorno (I put *The Authoritarian Personality* in the latter category) are consumed by the social scientists to the exclusion of this book of love. The second: This book, so full of scorn at the vulgarity of our everyday *post-histoire*, along with Barthes's *Mythologies* and their dialectico-semioclastic twist and the work of Raymond Williams, could be said to be the blueprint for much of contemporary popular cultural studies. One need only think of Adorno on Jazz-as-regression to see how far away he is from his self-elected intellectual progeny writing about Madonna in the age of their emulation of her in the academic star system. Or, in this light, one might also consider, in this time of the heyday of queer theory, the famously disturbing sentence, from the published translation, of "Tough Baby": "Totalitarianism and homosexuality belong together" (*MM*, 52/46) – the only problem here being that Adorno does not write this. What he does write is "Totalität und Homosexualität gehören zusammen," "totality and homosexuality belong together." Here it would seem that the translator, expecting, perhaps, to see the typical attitude of a Jewish grandfather (or father), has read the text through a rather hallucinatory ideological filter. Adorno is making a post-Hegelian commentary on Plato's *Symposium*, a fact which takes the homophobia of the text much further – and much more interestingly so – than the published translation does.

Perhaps, in this jaded age in which we all are supposed to know better and laugh cruelly lest anyone think us stupid, it is too harsh – oh, how Adorno would have hated that word! – to think that someone else's cynicism has already achieved a refinement we latecomers may never attain.[3] The Adorno cult has spread neither as fast nor as wide as the poststructuralist, postmodern, post-cult, but has remained the province of a few in the know, some of whom also work in the realm of a more French subtlety. *Minima Moralia* is a hard book to read all at once, both because it is simply too delicious and at the same time because it is highly repetitious – I, for one, cannot eat chocolate all day – also because it is not quite repetitious enough, but demands a considerable amount of energy to keep alert so as to be able to follow the dialectical pattern of Adorno's sentences to their often startling and unexpected conclusions, thus to admit that his scorn and his despair are not necessarily one's own.

What is most of all *Adorno's* own, his ownmost possibility, is his name, the first part of which hovers ambivalently between a genitive and a dative, subject and object, active and passive (Theodor: Gift of/from God, Gift to God, Gift *of* God); the last which enacts a bilingual pun: in English, to adorn – and was not Adorno's style, from the very beginning (the Kierkegaard *Habilitation*) accused precisely of excess ornamentation, the obscurantism of its baroque sentence structure? – and in German, *ein Dorn*, a thorn, something irritating, pricking, but nonetheless an inextricable part of beauty. Of his famous middle name, I will begin by citing Peter Sloterdijk's now famous gloss, in order to show how he has missed the point: "With Adorno, the denial of the masculine went so far that he retained only one letter from his father's name, W. The path to the meadow (*Wiesengrund*), however, does not exactly have to be the wrong one (*Holzweg*)."[4] Yes, *Wiesengrund* certainly means meadowland, the pastoral opposite of the rootless exile urban cosmopolite Jew Adorno was. And yes, Adorno does not go for Heidegger's version of method as divagation, the woodpath, *Holzweg* (as opposed to Benjamin's method as disgression, *Umweg*), to be upon which means to be headed for a dead end.

It is no accident that Adorno, some pages after the aphorism we shall shortly read, writes the aphorism: "German words of foreign

---

[3] "It is Proust's courtesy to spare the reader the embarrassment of believing himself cleverer than the author." *MM*, I, 29, 55/49.

[4] Peter Sloterdijk, *Critique of Cynical Reason*, trans. Michael Eldred (Minneapolis: University of Minnesota Press, 1987), xxxv. The German interpolations are those of the translator.

extraction are the Jews of language," a sentence in which, among other things, he in a sense glosses all three of his names: the Greek ambiguity of Theodor, the rootless Yiddishkeit of the Meadow-lands, and the elegantly Italianate thorn in the side of the idea of the language's-being-as-organic-totality of Adorno. The thorn draws blood: it, like Jews and homosexuals, drinks the blood of the body as organic totality, leeching it unto a pale death; or, if not killing immediately, at least stimulating an antigenic, autoim-mune response that eventually kills either one or the other – or both parties. Is the rose or the thorn the gift to or from – or, doubly genitive, in (apologies to Adorno) Heidegger's sense *of* God – or both? What Sloterdijk dares not touch upon, in his Second Generation (see Fassbinder) postwar unconscious, is the fantas-matic, anti-Semitic association of Jews, passivity, effeminacy, and, perhaps, homosexuality that lurks, barely latent, in his sentences about Adorno's "sensitivity" and conception of the sensitive.

Reading this book must be an experience that never spares the reader the constant need to examine his or her specific differences. Identification as a readerly strategy belongs to the New Old Right, which is why we don't have to throw out Adorno because he rejects, for example, Jazz: it is only the uncritical desire to seek a Master, thus to be a Slave, that would demand of a great thinker that his taste always be correct. It is silly enough, but the mistake is so often made that an error of such serious proportions could force an absolute reader–text estrangement or divorce. This is to miss the point of the notion of a or of the critical reader which Adorno promulgates, a notion which refuses to allow the reader off the hook. It also refuses to allow the reader simply to indulge in the (naïvely construed) aesthetic pleasure of turning our author into just another example of an irate parent on the other side of the generation gap.

The theoretical justification behind these apparent *obiter dicta*, however much they may find echoes – or not – in the arena of the politically correct, is not to be found in some recent polemic in the debates surrounding cultural studies, but in a place apparently far removed from them. While the point I am making can be found more or less everywhere in Hegel – for Adorno, His Master's Text – a passage from the *Aesthetics* will serve as well as any to make the point. When Hegel defines allegory as representing the separation of subject from predicate, of individual singularity from the universal conceptuality that is being linked to it, he thinks that he can reproach allegorical intention as being inferior to that, say, of the symbolic.[5] But the moment of this separation reveals itself to be structural and incapable of being eliminated, despite whatever derogations or tonal regrets. This form of non-identification of universal and particular, and our understanding in some way of the non-identity they maintain over the copula, is, in fact, the very possibility of our being able to make meaningful sentences, in which singular terms are related to universals, at all.

It is also, of course, the very possibility of criticism itself that is at issue here, that is to say of the ethical necessity of owning up to *not* identifying with what one reads. For a critic merely to identify with what he or she reads is not only silly – the equivalent of the character played by Woody Allen in his *Zelig* – it is, epistemologically speaking, a massive error, a blatant stupidity. A sentence as simple as "the sky is blue" is dependent, for its interpretation, on this ability to recognize, even without being able necessarily to explain, the kind of relation that is meant, even if what is also *said* is the inability of any universal term to link up with or cover any particular. The structural predicament of allegory, which thus infects all discourse, will not be gotten rid of by demoting it as an aesthetically inferior mode.

And where the particular is of the highest importance, the most important is what is tendency, *Tendenz*, and inclination, *Neigung*. At the moment one thinks oneself to be engaged in the spirit of conspiratorial identification between author and reader (precisely the sort of theatrical conspiracy which constitutes the central irony of Kierkegaard's *œuvre*, with which Adorno was passionately involved from his adolescence and which was the subject of his first book) something intervenes, and one is very likely to miss a beat in this nothing but syncopated book if one isn't careful not to adopt Adorno's or anyone else's scorn entirely as one's own.

The tightness of the aphorisms that make up Adorno's Mini-mabilia is Pascalian.[6] The regression toward the particular of the

---

5 G. W. F. Hegel, *Vorlesungen über die Ästhetik* vol. I (Frankfurt-on-Main:Suhrkamp, 1970), 511–16. See also de Man's argument in *AI*, 103–4.

6 See de Man, "Pascal's Allegory of Persuasion," in *AI*, for an analysis of the way in which chiasmatic attribute-crossing impends upon the form of the Pascalian *Pensée*. The same observation can be applied to de Man himself, in order to explain why the essay, and not the treatise, was his form.

essay, itself the denial of system, cannot be tolerated in a work that makes a claim to totality, even though it can only exist in a silent relation to the assertion of that totality, as Adorno remarks in the little preface – actually not a preface, but a dedication to Max Horkheimer on Valentine's Day, Horkheimer's birthday – to *Minima Moralia*. The difference between a preface – to a book such as *The Phenomenology of Spirit* – and a dedication – to a book such as *Minima Moralia* – is the formal symptom of the full-scale critique of Hegel's conception of Science that Adorno is mounting, not merely a literary device to be philosophically dismissed.

We are compelled to remark that reflection on the tension between essay and treatise produced much of the great work of Adorno and Benjamin both. To see this one need only think of the "Epistemo-Critical Preface" to Benjamin's *The Origin of German Tragic Drama*, and its valorization of the treatise as method in and as digression, in relation to what Adorno says about the form of the essay. I would call this development, in Adorno's "The Essay as Form," regression toward the particular. Adorno quite simply predicates of the essay what Benjamin had said of the treatise fifty years earlier. Both with right: the difference is in the "before" and the "after," pre- and post-1945. Adorno might just as well have written "After Auschwitz, no more treatises." The fact that both of these signal and crucial *essays* are written as paratexts should be reflected upon.[7]

Adorno makes a logical argument for *Minima Moralia*, this most abstractly confessional of books, by reproaching Hegel for his neglect of the particular, in what is itself one of the Latecomer's most stunningly ironic coups:

> Thus Hegel, whose method schooled that of *Minima Moralia*, argued against the mere being-for-itself of subjectivity on many levels. Dialectical theory, abhorring anything isolated, cannot admit aphorisms as such. In the most lenient instance they might, to use a term from the Preface to the *Phenomenology of Mind*, be tolerated as "conversation." But the time for that is past. Nevertheless, this book forgets neither the system's claim to totality, which would suffer nothing to remain outside it, nor that it remonstrates against this claim.

Up to this point in the paragraph, Adorno is merely asserting the fact that he knows well enough where *his* present is falling out of

---

[7] It is all a matter of how one chooses to scan one's emphasis; and thus it is a question of what I will call, in the extremely precise but unfashionable language of the New Critics, *tone*.

the System, but has not yet hit bottom. He has no illusions; he is nobody's – least of all Hegel's – fool. But the truly philosophical moment of critique begins when the baldness of a temporal scheme of later-is-less-naïve (the equivalent of *post hoc propter hoc* in the history of ideas) is left behind for an argument based on grounds internal to Hegel's text itself:

> In his relation to the subject Hegel does not respect the demand that he otherwise passionately upholds: to be in the matter and not "always beyond it," to "penetrate into the immanent content of the matter." If today the subject is vanishing, aphorisms take upon themselves the duty "to consider the evanescent itself as essential." They insist, in opposition to Hegel's practice and yet in accordance with his thought, on negativity: "The life of the mind only attains its truth when discovering itself in absolute desolation. The mind is not this power as a positive which turns away from the negative, as when we say of something that it is null, or false, so much for that and now for something else; it is this power only when looking the negative in the face, dwelling upon it."
>
> (*MM*, Dedication, 8–9/16–17)

Minima Moralia is announced, then, as an attack on the soft underbelly of the Hegelian System. But this attack does not come from outside the system, it is simply the result of attending to the details, the matter, *die Sache*, of Hegel's own system. This is a critical argument.

But, on the other hand, it may now be necessary to take Adorno's assertion of his later-therefore-wiser quite seriously. For, given the protasis of the rebuke, with its temporalizing *Setzung*, even if hypothetically stated ("If today the subject is vanishing . . ."), Adorno is marking something else, his being on the other side of a watershed, attempting an *almost* post-phenomenological investigation from the perspective of the moment of the subject's matutinal evanescence.

It is crucial for his argument, for his attack, that the subject has not entirely vanished yet, else one would hardly be able to write in reference to the System at all. The aphorism will be used to rebuke the System, which, *qua* system, had to throw itself in with the matter of the universal element, precisely in order to be able to enunciate itself as the arrival of Science on the world stage. Hegel is reproached for being at odds with his own intention: to attend to the matter itself should always be the claim of the person who announces himself as the phenomenologist.

The dialectics of this paragraph are clear enough, as is fitting for a dedication or an exoteric paratext. But what is disturbing, in its very obviousness, are these very *moments*, these *puncta*: "The time for that is past," "if today the subject is vanishing . . ." The only way for Adorno to avoid being eaten alive and whole by the Pantagruelian – or perhaps better, phagocytotically vacuolizing or macrophagic – dialectic of the Master, even at the very moment when he is admitting where he himself was "schooled," is to inscribe the entirety of the Hegelian lesson into a history as a moment now over.

This, then, is the work of a mature poet, who has swerved successfully from his father and the father of all of us moderns, in addition to being perhaps the first post-Auschwitz classic. It laments modernity's passing and fully evil flowering on the very eve of what some have hailed as its dissolution. Adorno's Dedication cites *The* Preface, the only one, in order to *get past* the moment of Hegel's preface (Hegel as preface to Adorno), that is to say the emergence of Science, that is, Hegel, on the world scene. And what Adorno the son wants to bring as his gift to the Father (Grandfather?) is the message of the first son who got it, Søren Kierkegaard, who wrote, in his *Repetition*:

The exception explains the general and itself. And if one wants to study the general correctly, one only needs to look around for a true exception. It reveals everything more clearly than does the general. Endless talk about the general becomes boring; there are exceptions. If they cannot be explained, then the general also cannot be explained. The difficulty is usually not noticed because the general is not thought about with passion but with a comfortable superficiality. The exception, on the other hand, thinks the general with intense passion.[8]

It is hardly an accident that the person in our century who cites this maxim from Kierkegaard is Carl Schmitt, the man whose critique of parliamentary democracy during the Weimar Republic, whose formulation of the idea of the "State of Emergency" as the moment at which democratic decision making fails, whose attempt to formulate a theory of sovereignty under the maxim "He who is sovereign is the one who decides the exception," and whose revival of the idea of political theology in our time all coexist

[8] Cited from the end of the first chapter, "Definition of Sovereignty," of Carl Schmitt, *Political Theology: Four Lectures on the Concept of Sovereignty*, trans. George Schwab (Cambridge, MA: MIT Press, 1985), 15.

within the same text. A full-scale reading of *Repetition* would have to account, among other things, for the relation there between the devalorization of recollection (*anamnesis*) and the praise of repetition (in the sense Kierkegaard is trying to give to the term) in terms of the relation of the former to the metaphorical maieutics of Platonic pedophilia and of the latter to the (failed) heterosexual relationship Kierkegaard's narrator describes – even as this same narrator acts out an openly Platonic, homoerotic, and voyeuristic relation to that relationship. One might also repeat, with insistence and with Kierkegaard, in order to gloss Adorno's strategy in respect of Hegel, from a different moment in the dialectic of *Fear and Trembling*, published on the same day as *Repetition*: "the one who will work gives birth to his own father."[9]

Adorno continues in his reproaches:

The dismissive gesture which Hegel, in contradiction to his own insight, constantly accords the individual, derives paradoxically enough from his entanglement in liberalistic thinking. The conception of a totality harmonious through all its antagonisms compels him to assign to individuation, however much he may designate it as a driving moment in the process, an inferior status in the construction of the whole. The knowledge that in pre-history the objective tendency asserts itself over the heads of human beings, indeed by virtue of annihilating individual qualities, without the reconciliation of general and particular – constructed in thought – ever yet being accomplished in history, is distorted in Hegel: with serene indifference he opts once again for liquidation of the particular. Nowhere in his work is the primacy of the whole doubted. The more questionable the transition from reflective isolation to glorified totality becomes in history as in Hegelian logic, the more eagerly philosophy, as the justification of what exists, attaches itself to the triumphal car of objective tendencies. The culmination of the social principle of individuation in the triumph of fatality gives philosophy occasion enough to do so. Hegel, in hypostasizing both bourgeois society and its fundamental category, the individual, did not truly carry through the dialectic between the two. Certainly he perceives, with classical

---

[9] *FR*, 27. What is at issue is the occurrence in the same sentence of two uses of the same verb, which can mean both "to bear" and "to nourish": "[d]en, der ikke vil arbeide, ham passer det paa, hvad der staaer skrevet om Israels Jomfruer, han føder Vind, men den, der vil arbeide, han føder sin egen Fader" (Søren Kierkegaard, *Samlede Værker* vol. v [Copenhagen: Gyldendal, 1963], 27). Some contemporary Kierkegaard scholars would prefer to render this sentence as "he who will work hard nourishes [*føder*] his own father." I thank Henrik Blicher, Niels Jørgen Cappelørn, and Kim Ravn for a discussion of this matter, which I shall pursue elsewhere.

economics, that the totality produces and reproduces itself precisely from the interconnection of the antagonistic interests of its members. But the individual as such he for the most part considers, naïvely, as an irreducible datum – just what in his theory of knowledge he decomposes. Nevertheless, in an individualistic society, the general not only realizes itself through the interplay of particulars, but society is essentially the substance of the individual.   (*MM*, Dedication, 9–10/16–17)

There you have it. The Master has now been rather magisterially treated as a moment in the preface of the son. Exit Daddy, Teddie arrives. But the sweetness of revenge is tempered by a terrible melancholy: these "reflections from the damaged life" attach themselves to the triumphal car of the silly optimism of bourgeois liberalism. But in doing so, they are not one, but at least two steps behind the objective tendencies, which perhaps no longer exist. We are all in the cortège at the end of Sirk's *Imitation of Life*. Hegel's dismissive gesture toward the individual becomes here Adorno's chastising gesture toward one very specific individual – Hegel – at the same time that he is addressing this book of aphorisms to another very specific individual, Max Horkheimer, "in thanks and promise."

The final blow of the lesson is contained in the last sentence of the paragraph, where Adorno tells us what the objective tendencies of this time of writing are, in a corrective gesture, a tribute that Hegel *qua* Hegel cannot take. And, in a move of truly Adornian irony, we find the opposite of what we have, thus far, expected him to say: it is not Hegel's romantic yearning for totality or totalization or any other such history-of-ideas claptrap that forced him toward utter contempt for the individual. Rather it is his engagement precisely with the Protestant and bourgeois ideology of individualism that, rather than pushing him toward giving a stronger valence to the individual in his philosophy, robs, on the contrary, the individual of his weight by making it – the individual – into yet another bloodless form of universality – even if, according to Hegel the bourgeois, it is the very form of our being and of our social being.

(Heiner Müller comments the same theme in respect not of Hegel, but of the continuation of the Prussian state in what Müller sees as its avatar, East German socialism reified into a state apparatus. Müller's description of the East German state as being defined by its lack of relation to femininity is a theme familiar from his *Hamlet Machine* and from the sections of *The Civil Wars* he wrote with Robert Wilson. In these works the primal scene of Frederick the Great's absolute monarchy is represented as his being forced to watch the execution of his male lover for desertion from the army, a crime the young Prince committed as well but which punishment he was spared because of his royal station.[10] As in Adorno, we are in the topos of the relationship between the repression of male homosexuality and absolute power.)

It is the very form of our existence that Adorno reproaches Hegel for ignoring. It is Adorno's ultimate condescension to Hegel's naïveté to be able to broach or to inflict such an ironic blow, to be able to strike a blow at a prejudice that emanates from the level of the axiomatic form of the System itself: the form of the thinking subject is I.[11]

But the most striking aspect of this passage is the fact that it is a reading of Hegel on the Terror. The Terror is the moment in which the pure universality of the law-without-law, the nakedness of the symbolic order, reigns and strips every subject of his or her individuality and right to persist in living. "With serene indifference he opts for the liquidation of the particular": how can we hear this, from Santa Monica, Grand Hotel Abyss, in 1944–45, as anything other than what we will be dealing with presently in our chosen singularity, our exemplary aphorism, "Morals and the Order of Time," as yet indicated but untouched, as "the Fascist eradication of the racial minority itself?" *This* is the objective tendency of *our* hearing. It is not a matter of Freedom, Equality, Brotherhood as the truth of the Revolution that produced the Universal Declaration of the Rights of Man. It is a matter of Jew, Gypsy, Homosexual, Asocial, Mentally Ill; it is a matter of the reduction of humanity to types, of the absorption of the absolute singularity of individuals into the global and leveling universality of predicates, concepts, which reveals the truth of Reason in the Terror. In short, we have reached the state of contemporary identity politics viewed from the point of view of nosology.

But in order to deal with the sweating out of these foreign bodies

[10] See Heiner Müller, *Jenseits der Nation* (Berlin: Rotbuch, 1991).

[11] See G. W. F. Hegel, *Enzyklopädie der philosophischen Wissenschaften im Grundrisse. Erster Teil: Die Wissenschaft der Logik* (Frankfurt-on-Main: Suhrkamp, 1970), 71–76, as well as de Man, "Sign and Symbol," *AI*, 96–100.

reduced to types and thus to concepts and thus to ashes at Auschwitz, I want to talk about the structure of the French Terror. Let us turn for a moment to what Adorno's contemporary, Maurice Blanchot, reviewing Kojève, is saying about similar motifs and about some of the same passages in Hegel, shortly after Adorno writes up the damaged life in California:

Let us acknowledge that in a writer there is a movement which proceeds without pause, and almost without transition, from nothing to every-thing. Let us see in him that negation that is not satisfied with the unreality in which it exists, because it wishes to realize itself and can only do so by negating something real, more real than words, more true than the isolated individual in control: it therefore keeps urging him towards a worldly life and a public existence in order to induce him to conceive how, even as he writes, he can become that very existence. It is at this point that he encounters those decisive moments in history when everything seems put in question, when law, faith, the State, the world above, the world of the past – everything sinks effortlessly, without work, into nothingness. The man knows he has not stepped out of history, but history is now the void, the void in the process of realization; it is *absolute* freedom which has become an event. Such periods are given the name Revolution. At this moment, freedom aspires to be realized in the *immediate* form of *everything* is possible, everything can be done. A fabulous moment – and no one who has experienced it can completely recover from it, since he has experienced history as his own history and his own freedom as universal freedom. These moments are, in fact, fabulous moments: in them, fable speaks; in them, the speech of fable becomes action. That the writer should be tempted by them is completely appropriate. Revolutionary action is in every respect analogous to action as embodied in literature: the passage from nothing to everything, the affirmation of the absolute as event and of every event as absolute. Revolutionary action explodes with the same force and the same facility as the writer who has only to set down a few words side by side in order to change the world. Revolutionary action also has the same demand for purity, and the certainty that everything it does has absolute value, that it is not just any action performed to bring about some desirable and respectable goal, but that it is itself the ultimate goal, the Last Act. This last act is freedom, and the only choice left is between freedom and nothing. This is why, at that point, the only tolerable slogan is: *freedom or death*. Thus the Reign of Terror comes into being. People cease to be individuals working at specific tasks, acting here and only now: each person is universal freedom, and universal freedom knows nothing about elsewhere or tomorrow, or work or a work accomplished. At such times there is nothing left for anyone to do, because everything has been done. No one has a right to a private life any longer, everything is public, and the most guilty person is the suspect – the person who has a secret, who keeps a thought, an intimacy to himself. And in the end no one has a right to his life any longer, to his actually separate and physically distinct existence. This is the meaning of the Reign of Terror.[12]

Revolution is the flower absent from all bouquets. It is the moment of purest negation, when there are no compromises. The compromises always come afterwards. It is in this sense that revolution is fabular or allegorical: as soon as it happens – and since it is, by definition, an extralegal situation, it is hard to speak of agency and to say anything other than it happens, *es ereignet sich*, like the true, it occurs – a certain number of names take on the form of blank subjects that are then filled in during the temporal economy thus opened up and which follows: terrors, reactions, decapitations, consulates, Final Solutions, liquidations, Exterminations.

As far as the nationalist moment here is concerned, the distinction between the Revolutions American and French can be registered by comparing the mottoes: if the French have "Freedom or Death," where both words should be capitalized as allegorical, fabular entities, we have something like "your money or your life," in which both substantives as well as the possessives are written in the lower case.[13] French absolutism here is capital and crucial, providing as it does the motive for the very Hegelian text both Adorno and Blanchot-via-Kojève are commenting: the Preface to Hegel's *Phenomenology*, written, proverbially, that is to say fabularly enough, as Napoleon was sidling up to the gates of Jena, home of the German Romantics (who had been busy working on the theory of irony inside).

Now it is time to zero in on the text we have been slouching towards since the beginning, the aphorism from *Minima Moralia* entitled "Morals and the Order of Time":

– While literature has treated all psychological modes of erotic conflicts, the most simple, mechanical matter of conflict has remained unattended by virtue of its self-evidence. It is the phenomenon of being possessed: that a beloved person refuses her- or himself [*sich uns versagt*] to us not because of inner antagonisms or inhibitions, because of too much

12 Blanchot, "Literature and the Right to Death," *GO*, 37–38.
13 I am thinking of the different inflections Lacan gives to these two expressions, the latter in *Les Quatre concepts fondamentaux de la psychanalyse* (Paris: Seuil, 1972), and the former in "La Science et la vérité," in *E*.

coldness or too much repressed warmth, but rather because a relationship already exists that excludes another. In truth abstract temporal sequence plays the role one would like to ascribe to the hierarchy of feelings. In being previously taken there lies – apart from freedom of choice and of decision – also something of the wholly accidental that seems entirely to contradict the claim of freedom. Especially in a society cured of the anarchy of commodity production, rules would hardly [*schwerlich*] keep watch over the sequence [*Reihenfolge*] in which one gets to know people. Were it otherwise, such an arrangement would have to amount to the most unbearable intrusion upon freedom. From this comes the fact that even the priority of the accidental has powerful grounds on its side: if a newcomer is preferred to some person, one does to this person inevitably an evil thing – in that the past of a shared life is annulled [*annulliert*], experience itself likewise crossed out. The irreversibility of time delivers an objective moral criterion. But it, the criterion, is a sibling of myth, like abstract time itself. The exclusionary character posited in time unfolds according to its own concept toward the exclusionary dominance of hermetically sealed groups, in the end those of big business. Nothing is more touching than the anxiety of the loving woman, lest the newcomer be able to draw love and tenderness – her best possessions, precisely because they do not allow themselves to be possessed – toward herself, precisely because of that newness, which itself is produced by the privilege of the older. But from this stirring up, through which all warmth and everything sheltering immediately dissolve, begins an irresistible way upon which the stations are the disinclination of the little brother for the one later born[14] and the contempt of the fraternity student for his pledge to the immigration laws that keep all non-Caucasians out of Social-Democratic Australia, and unto the Fascist extermination of the racial minority, in which in fact warmth and shelter explode into nothing. As Nietzsche knew, not only were all good things once evil; but the most tender, left to their own momentum [*Schwerkraft*], have the tendency [*Tendenz*] to end up in unimaginable brutality.

It would be superfluous to try to indicate a way out of this entanglement. But the disastrous moment that brings the entire dialectic into play most probably allows itself to be named. It lies in the exclusionary character of the first. The originary relation, in its mere immediacy, already requires [*voraussetzt*] abstract temporal order. Historically, the concept of time is itself modeled on the basis [*Grund*] of the order of ownership. But the wish to possess reflects time as fear of losing, of the irretrievable. What is, is experienced in relation to its possible non-being. Only thus does it really get made into a possession and, thus fixed, into a functional thing that allows for its being exchanged for other, equivalent

---

14 Think, with Avital Ronell, of Freud's "Eine Kindheitserinnerung aus *Dichtung und Wahrheit*." See her *Dictations: on Haunted Writing* (Bloomington: Indiana University Press, 1986).

possessions. Once become entirely a possession, the beloved person simply is no longer looked at. Abstractness in love is the complement of exclusionariness, which deceptively makes its appearance as the opposite, as a clinging to this very one being. But exactly this holding on loses its hold on its object, in that it makes it into an object, and thus misses the person whom it denigrates to "my person." Were people no longer possessions, they could no longer be exchanged. True affection [*Neigung*, preference, inclination] would be one that speaks specifically to the other, that attaches itself to beloved traits [*Züge*] and not to the idol of personhood, the reflection of possession. The specific is not exclusionary: it lacks the drive [*Zug*] toward totality. But in another sense it is nonetheless exclusionary, in the sense that it does not forbid, but by means of its pure concept does not even allow substitution of the experience indissolubly bound up with it to occur. The protection of the entirely determined is that it cannot be repeated, and thus it tolerates the other. To the property relation to the person, to the exclusionary law of priority, belongs exactly this wisdom: God, they are all only people, whichever one it is is not so important after all. Affection that would know nothing of such wisdom would not need fear infidelity, because it would be guarded against faithlessness.   (*MM*, 96–99/78–80)[15]

The intertext for this aphorism clearly establishes it as yet another one of the moments of Adorno's major inheritance from his dead friend, Walter Benjamin. It is to be found in the latter's *One-Way Street*:

He who loves is attached not only to the "faults" of the beloved, not only to the whims and weakness of a woman. Wrinkles in the face, moles, shabby clothes, and a lopsided walk bind him more lastingly and relentlessly than any beauty. This has long been known. And why? If the theory is correct that feeling is not located in the head, that we sentiently experience a window, a cloud, a tree not in our brains but, rather, in the place where we see it, then we are, in looking at our beloved, too, outside ourselves. But in a torment of tension and ravishment. Our feeling, dazzled, flutters like a flock of birds in the woman's radiance. And as birds seek refuge in the leafy recesses of a tree, feelings escape into the shaded wrinkles, the awkward movements and inconspicuous blemishes of the body we love, where they can lie low in safety. And no passer-by would guess that it is just here, in what is defective and censurable, that the fleeting darts of adoration nestle.[16]

But the discovery of this "source," interesting at the level of

---

[15] Here I offer my own translation of this aphorism. For his help with this I thank Dr. Jan Keppler.

[16] Walter Benjamin, *Reflections*, trans. E. F. N. Jephcott (New York: Harcourt, Brace, Jovanovitch, 1978), 68.

topological *factum*, highlights the very strong degree of difference between what appears here as the antique innocence of Benjamin's perception-oriented observation, drawn from classical philosophy, and Adorno's own, more modern, dialectical strategy. This difference could be summed up, at first glance, as a difference between the number two and the number three. Adorno's passage performs a dialectical expansion on Benjamin's theme of the beloved trait, a meditation the stakes of which go far indeed down the road to totality with which we have thus far been concerned. Thus, since Adorno's text is far from a simple redaction, it is necessary to perform a closer analysis of it, in order to see how the rewrite is accomplished. For the purposes of this reading, and in order to neutralize the possibility of diversion into the dead end of a phenomenalizing reading, we pause for a moment at Adorno's moral at the end, and then move immediately back to the beginning to follow the text in its own sequence.

One might well ask, after the end of Adorno's statement, rather: But without such "wisdom," how can there be any *true* affection? And this in so many senses: Time, experienced by the subject as anxiety before death and other endings – and this by lovers most of all – or rather, the demand to spend time, to do time, the demand on a beloved that we do time together, etc., cannot be tempered, pragmatically speaking, without the irony, this time of consciousness, necessary to shrugging the shoulders and simply waiting for the other to come, if ever. I take this as both psychologically and phenomenologically true, and therefore, linguistically, almost certainly uninteresting. To demand of the would-be conquering lover that he simply give the love object space out of infinite love for that love object is to ask too much from anyone who has not acquired enough wisdom to know not to be impatient enough to fall in love in the first place. As Kierkegaard knows, every love is the first love, and following from this, in and as its inevitable disappointment (as Bataille knows, for it is the experience he shares with us as the experience motivating his *L'expérience intérieure*), is the realization that, to love and not to do so in an abusive manner, it is counterproductive or even destructive to desire to be everything.

But down to brass tacks. Literature is a collection of particulars, of singularities, and, as such, it is a set that forms the totality that treats all the psychological species of erotic conflict. This is not what Adorno says, but it is worthy of being thought, as a definition of literature. But the simplest has escaped being included in this baroque catalog. What is the simplest? It is what the logicians call material implication, cause and effect, what Kant himself knew to be unanalyzable at the conceptual level.[17]

The fact of the simplest having escaped notice is not insignificant. As atom, the simplest itself has no epistemic valence until it combines, until it is sequenced into a series of moments in which it will receive its value as *first*. The potential love object refuses *itself* to us out of a monogamous prior commitment. The assumption here, at least at this point, is that every monad has a valence of one: monogamy is the presumed atomic fact, *Sachverhalt*, to use Wittgenstein's Tractarian term with rigid precision.

But at this point the dialectic has already come into play, for the monad is only seen to be monadic in relation to its complement. Abstract temporal sequence is abstract here because it applies structurally to all subjects *qua* subjects. It is not as though there might be any way to sidestep this predicament, which is why the references to prehistory and to history, both in the passage from the Dedication cited above as well as here, are so interesting. The reference to prehistory (*Vorgeschichte*) is Adorno's way of denouncing the idyll of a mythic time before time in which such debased relations would not have obtained.

We are limited to analyzing the structure of the events in question, but this proves to be quite a lot. For what we are up against is the very birth of consciousness in the Oedipal triangle, the primal repression of the Father's No. The parental pair is, after all, the first dyad. After all, Teddie will marry into Mommy's name, contracting Daddy's land holdings into that celebrated W. Not might makes right, but time makes right: (The) I got (t)here

---

[17] The use of the word *Reihenfolge* here hints at the Transcendental Aesthetic in the *Critique of Pure Reason*. Sequence, in Kant's Transcendental Aesthetic, is the form of inner perception as time itself, and hence logically precedes that other logical form, space, which can only be treated once the inner form of time has been established. Likewise causality, also a form, is not analyzable in the way that objects given to experience within these forms are. The forms of subjectivity are not part of the experience of the subject. They are the conditions of its possibility. All of which makes Adorno's aphorism out to be playing for the highest stakes indeed, since what is at issue is this miming of the founding text of modern transcendental–critical discourse.

first. Or at least that is the story it tells after getting there. In psychoanalytic terms, this law of priority, of temporal relations, is called the Oedipus Complex, which can be summarized for our purposes here in Lacan's lapidary "if you do that again, I'll cut it off."[18]

In the matter of constraint, or, as Adorno puts it here, of freedom of choice and decision, there is more than a hint of the F. W. Schlegelian language of irony as unrelieved arbitrariness, *unbedingte Willkür*. The accidental fact of time makes right not only seems, but is in flat contradiction to the claims of freedom. Lest we be mistaken for speaking only of things as they are in that fallen state of commodity fetishism (Adorno's supposedly secular equivalent for Pascal's state of Man's Fallenness), Adorno spells it out: even in a society cured of such human relations as object relations, it would not be possible to predict or to plan better, to regulate the order in which one met people. One would have to say, precisely in such a "cured" society, that the arbitrariness of quickies would be even more manifest, because even more purely related to some kind of myth or *clinamen* of spontaneous desire.

But the fact is, Adorno has just explained to us not only why such a society is not possible, but, in fact, unimaginable. In fact, it is the matter of this already announced abstract sequencing operation, itself structurally unavoidable, that is precisely the explanation for why commodity production is inevitable, at least in a society based on the not-yet vanished atom of the subject. What we are dealing with here is a metaphorical catastrophe of the first order. We thought that the false, inauthentic relations among people were going to be at least partially accounted for by the evil contingencies of our production system; and now what we have discovered to be the case is the opposite: namely that the fetishism of the production system is determined by the abstract element that imposes itself in and as sequence in human relationships.

The sentence "historically, the concept of time is itself modeled on the basis of the order of ownership," in the second paragraph of our aphorism, is not to be read as a statement of the historical truth or falsehood of the twinned origin of these concepts. Rather, this generalization at this moment in the narrative of this fable repeats what has already been said: reification, making the person into

[18] See his *Télévision* (Paris: Seuil, 1974), 48.

"my person," thus implying possession, must bring a before and a potential after along with it. Thus we might want to say not that these two concepts are historically linked, but rather that history *is* precisely what we call what is constituted in this linkage. The only time or place within which such relations would not obtain would neither be in history nor in pre-history, but in no history at all. For time to be time, such relations must exist.

Hence pre-history, as well as the post-history toward which more vulgar readings of Kojève yearn, are both delusions. Only myth can name the idyllic non-time when such relations did not obtain. Myth is thus both more and less than pre- or post-history: it is the name here for the negation of history. The tendential inevitability of the obtaining of the situation Adorno is describing (as opposed to the one for which he erases all hope) is evidence enough that neither such pre-history nor its after the fact mirror image has anything to do with actual or potentially existing states of affairs. Rather, these names with unreal referents can only serve as structural moments in the unfolding of the story in their being denounced as the impossible.

This is why the "objective moral criterion" delivered by "the irreversibility of time" – irreversibility and time being, for all intents and purposes, the same here – is a sibling of myth: the myth in question is that of an "abstract time" that would exist without being filled by the kinds of events that occur in and as historical time. The myth here *is* the myth of a pre- or a post-history that would not be historical, that is a time which would not be defined, as our time is defined, by the commodified relations that obtain for us. On the other hand, "if today the subject is vanishing," this would also imply that time, as part of the form of the subject, is vanishing too.

But the question is, isn't the subject always vanishing? Hasn't the subject always been vanishing? If the structural faults to which Adorno points in the constitution of the System in fact are there, then the answer is yes. But vanishing may not imply the perfection of its activity; so that time and the subject in fact never vanish absolutely into the mythic, abstract time-without-the-subject that the subject projects into the past as pre-history or a different future, the possibility of deliverance into which is given the lie by the contrary-to-fact subjunctive verbs in which this time after time is described.

And when time is troubled, so is experience. Why is experience deleted, why are things misused, annulled? Because what is happening here is that relations are being dictated by rhetorical figures. Substitutions are taking place at the level of entities because the chiastic, hypallagous rhetorical structure demands it. The structure always wants a matched, mathed, mathematized crossing. And so the eraser or cursor moves over one term, deletes it, and fills in the blank with another individual, whose substitutability occurs by virtue of that person's being the bearer of a name to which, for the purposes of this very operation, he or she may be reduced, has to be reduced.[19] And a name can also, in this context, be reduced to a number.

There is the name and the thing. But discourse, like and as the Terror, is capable of taking the name of the thing and combining it with other thingly and abstract-thingly (it does not matter if the referent exists materially or not) names, which are then read and used as a template for mixing and matching the phenomenal entities. The annulment, the effacement of previous experience, is the very operation of the verb *tilgen* Hegel assigns to the function of the name when he says, in the *Encyclopedia*, it is in names that we think, and when he proclaims that the sign must be declared to be something great because it allows us to subject the material world to the powers of mind in exchanging qualities in discourse that cannot be exchanged in so-called reality, which has, by now, fully earned its scare quotes, those linguistico-phenomenological brackets.[20] The priority of the fortuitous assigns to chance the power of unrelieved arbitrariness, what Merleau-Ponty will call, shortly before his death, the irony of things. It has powerful arguments on its side because it assigns to fate the ultimate power of the subject, that of defacing-refacing the world according to its wishes.

But now we enter a new dimension, with the bringing into play of the question of irreversibility. For it is the irreversibility of

---

[19] This is the very meaning of ideology as the mistaking of linguistic for phenomenal structures, such as Paul de Man defines it in "The Resistance to Theory" in the book of the same title. The pre-history of this moment in this essay would seem to be the essay "Roland Barthes and the Limits of Structuralism," now in Paul de Man, *RC*.

[20] See G. W. F. Hegel, *Enzyklopädie der philosophischen Wissenschaften im Grundrisse. Dritter Teil: Die Philosophie des Geistes* (Frankfurt-on-Main: Suhrkamp, 1970), 277–88, also de Man, "Sign and Symbol," *AI*, 101–3.

sequence – the revenge, to speak metaleptically, of the young on the old – that dictates the entire schema.[21] Property is irreversibility: this in the sense of property as in "life, liberty and . . .," as well as in the sense of *Merkmale*, that which a subject acquires in taking on predicates. The fact that we can go from A to B but not back again sets things up so that what is done is done. It is related to myth in the sense that it is, *qua* abstract, part of that allegorico-fabular dimension of template structures we use to negotiate our stories about ourselves, one of the stories we tell ourselves in order to live. This is the myth of history.

And now comes that conspiracy-theory-laden moment when we explode into the discourse labeled "Marxist": the exclusivity in time takes us to inherently hermetic groups, big business. This is just to say, the combines, the constellations that come together to keep ahold of what they have by having more are the material instantiations of the steady accretion disks of these figures. Pull back from the totalization: the little woman appears, defenseless Olive Oyl, waiting for Popeye to come rescue her from the evil usurper.

What happens here is that the initial couple of stable, heterosexual nature and origin (they always must needs be the same, in this context, at this moment), the man and woman, who can move "naturally" – but, remember, we are in a post-Pascalian universe, where nature has been effaced – over the copula, have drifted into being the couple of the first partner and her youthful or new replacement.[22] What we are dealing with now is catty bitchery. And it is her or their own – structural – fault, because if she didn't have her arms around him in public, the character ready to rob her of her prize wouldn't know to take her cue.

We are approaching the moral of the end of this paragraph, in which a series of parallel totalizations is presented. And here is where the moral of the story gets complicated and therefore interesting, *qua* fable. Perspective has been collapsed: we have moved back from big business to the innocence of the atom. And now it is a matter of showing how this telescopic maneuver has been accomplished. The motif that gets globalized is not necessar-

---

[21] I have seen a T-shirt that says: "Age and cunning will always win out over youth and beauty." Why is one so fearful if one has so much to hope for?

[22] For all those who blame the contemporary French and their minions for having invented the sex–gender distinction: Go back and read Pascal.

ily simply a heterosexual partner's fear of replacement, but rather the fear before the evident structure of replaceability in general. For the next link in the chain is the little boy's fear of being replaced by his younger brother, or the fraternity student's contempt for his "fag" – as Jephcott translates it, his pledge, "Fuchs" in German, "fox," his younger cadet.[23]

There is an important twist on the Oedipal cliché here: usually what one is referring to when one makes reference to Oedipal anxiety is the anxiety of the infant. But what of the anxiety of the Father, what of *his* anxiety at the arrival of a possible replacement in the child? One might call this the neglected, countertransferential dimension of the Oedipus Complex. But it is also necessary to make the link between the inter-generational aggression implied in the all too familiar idea of Oedipal conflict and the sibling aggression, the intra-generational competition Freud discusses, for example, in "Eine Kindheitserinnerung aus *Dichtung und Wahrheit*."[24] Only now can we move on to the racism of so-called democratic societies, and thence to Fascism, the negative-theological name for ultimate horror in our certainly exhausted, if not yet ended, century and millenium – a millenium that runs from the poems of Guillaume IX d'Aquitaine until now.[25]

It is time to comment the famous line from the aphorism "Tough Baby,"[26] where Adorno tells us that "Homosexuality and Totality belong together." The sublimated homosexual urges to which Freud often pointed as the homosocial glue of society are, Adorno is saying, not very far off from the paranoia (with its foreclosive trait of lack of connection to any other) that Freud also ascribes to the same repressed, homosexual urges. In both cases, however, it is the *repression* of homosexual drives that is at issue. But it is the violence of the latter, of paranoia, that needs to designate an object

---

23 "Fuchs" was Foucault's nickname during his student days. Fox is the name of the character who loses everything (property, properties) over the course of his hazing in Rainer Werner Fassbinder's *Faustrecht der Freiheit* (1975, Federal Republic of Germany; English title: *Fox*). The director himself plays the title role.
24 In Sigmund Freud, *Studienausgabe* vol. x, eds. Mitscherlich, Richards, Strachey, and Grubrich-Simitis (Frankfurt-on-Main: Fischer, 1969).
25 The appearance of Nietzsche's name here has as much to do with his talents as an aphorist as with his being the author of *The Genealogy of Morals*. A corrective for the philosophical forgetting of what Nieztsche meant by the gay science would have to begin with Roger Dragonetti, *Le Gai savoir dans la rhétorique courtoise* (Paris: Seuil, 1982).   26 This title is in English in the original.

as foreign in order to call itself whole, to constitute itself as a totality. So the older brother, who is supposed to identify with Daddy, must neutralize the threat of the newcomer, the younger brother, in passing on the threat of castration, thus of feminization, which is how the feminized–castrated male becomes the object of fear: if it can happen to him, it can happen to me. This is the fear that must be kept at bay in the designation of this figure as foreign, other. In between the first loving couple and the various constitutions of social bodies around a figure to be excluded, then, come the situations in which the persecution of the newcomer presents itself as the strategic excuse by means of which the hyperbological extension toward totality will be made.[27] But Adorno, for whom the distinction between male homosociality and male homosexuality is no distinction at all, himself does not seem to see, in "Tough Baby," that it is the matter of priority he is discussing in "Morals and the Order of Time" that is even more primordial than the gender relations it conditions or engenders.

After this piece of writing, which dates from the end of the War, I think it would be preposterous to blame the French defenders of reading Heidegger for being Fascist thinkers, or at least of being tainted. Their point, rather, is that it is Heidegger who, in producing an integral reading of the tradition – even if this reading leaves much out and does great violence – has given us the tools to think of Fascism as the monstrosity of Western culture, not as something that flew in, on a given day, from the outside. It is clear that this is no excuse for not reading the French, nor for not reading Heidegger either, given that it is now clear that one would have to call Adorno thus tainted as well.

And the fact is, he is, we all are, and should be. For it is this very desire for purity itself, this desire not to be involved, not to be tainted, because the subject *qua* subject knows precisely that if it is involved, it risks losing what it "has," being replaced – it is this

---

27 Lacan is in the same register when he proclaims racism to be on the rise. (See his *Télévision*.) Racism is one name for paranoia, the psychotic–foreclosive maneuver by which one's own object is thrown out into the field of the real in order to return as a hallucination. Television presents or materializes this very fact: the far comes back into the near as a framed, inscribed object presented to the unity of a single – in this case collective – gaze. Reason and race come from the same etymon, which is a figural way of relating the unity of the logos to its exclusion of other *types*.

desire for purity that, pursued to the end, led to Auschwitz, the marginal place in the light of the East where Germany sweated out its hysterical fantasm of the Jews as a foreign body. The literalization of the figure of the atopic Jew through mass carbonization, so that there not be a trace, is, in this sense, the horrible realization of the psychotic–foreclosive fantasy of cleaning up one's territory so that it be absolutely immaculate, pure, *rein*.

Nietzsche told us this fable: How one gets from the bad to the good through dilution and legitimation; also how, moving in the direction in which Adorno is rigorously drifting, how one gets from the good to the ugly. Now that the fatal sequence has been sequenced, and the unquestionable but dreaded truth has been uttered, it is a matter of asking, what now? Since we cannot get out of this trap (what Paul de Man might call a predicament, something predicated, spoken before and after, prejudiced, demanded [*vorausgesetzt*] by sequence) what is left?

The structure of this *pensée* cuts it almost exactly in two.[28] The first part gives us the figure, and itself consists of two parts, that is to say, the delivery of the figure as the mechanism of replaceability, and the explosive movement toward totalization that is generated as soon as one realizes that the chain of substitutability or replaceability can be hyperbolically extended to cover the entire social field[29] conceived of as a text, that is to say, the entire tropological field.[30]

In seeing this, we see as well that the reason why this one of the aphorisms singles itself out as exceptional, as requiring special handling, is because it is a rather pure version of a tropological model, that is to say, of substitution or substitutability as such. "Abstract temporal sequence" is precisely what Paul de Man will

---

[28] If this is not exactly unique within the covers of *Minima Moralia*, it is still interesting, as Adorno's next unit of form above the sentence is the paragraph – or, in the other direction, the one-liner.

[29] Lacan has a similar insight toward the end of his 1948 essay on Logical Time, where he attempts to make the structure of subjectivation triadic, and then to extend his cellular–triadic model toward a field that could always add one more subject, hence be globalized to account for social structures.

[30] The notion of *the* tropological field, like the notion of *the* language game, is in fact generated by this tropological urge towards totalization. The totality of the world does not exist as totality except in language. *This* is the truth of the always-already of the abstract.

call the story of the figure in the course of its undoing, decomposition in and as the text, that is to say, narrative, that is to say, allegory.[31] Temporality, for us, is not, then, as it was for Kant, the form of inner experience, therefore the first form, but the form of textual procedure, of the way in which argument and storytelling inextricably commingle in and as precisely what we call text.

The second part of Adorno's now disfigured maxim, then, plays the part of the moral of this fable, what we might call, in its belated phase, its consolation:

> It would be superfluous to try to indicate a way out of this entanglement. But the disastrous moment that brings the entire dialectic into play most probably allows itself to be named. It lies in the exclusionary character of the first. The originary relation, in its mere immediacy, already requires [*voraussetzt*] abstract temporal order.

I say *consolation* advisedly, for what we are dealing with should be called the consolation of critique in that very Kantian sense of mapping out and knowing the scope and limits of the region one is in. The knowing of the structure has to serve – has to because it is the only thing that can serve – as the consolation for a machine of unstoppable, inevitable, rigorous, impersonal and therefore brutal ubiquity. At least we can *name* it, and, in naming it, we can, among other things, inscribe it as one punctum in the scansion of moments that is this book of mourning, *Minima Moralia*. We can inscribe it as one moment cleverly hidden to look like just one moment among others, even if it perhaps, figurally speaking, brings all the other moments into play, prefigures them – if it doesn't contain them outright, absolutely.

The original relationship, in its mere immediacy – *bloße Unmittelbarkeit* (let not the sense of lack of mediation in the technical sense be lost from this mere immediacy) – already establishes the conditions for (*voraussetzt*) abstract temporal sequence. Triumph of the dialectic as cortège. The *already* of this sentence conditions the abstract temporal sequence. Immediacy is an aftereffect, a *Nachtrag*, in Freudian terms, of the mediations that follow immediately upon this wavering dyad of the first loving duo. Wanting to possess makes for fear of loss, of that which cannot be brought

---

[31] The textual model of the figure in the course of its undoing–decomposition is the paradigm for all texts de Man offers early in that essay. See de Man, *AR*, 205–7, also the critique of Genette in "Reading (Proust)" within the same covers. I return to both moments in chapter 3.

back, *Unwiederbringlichkeit*. This sentence gives the logical explanation for the purported historical explanation of the last. What is,
is experienced in relation to its not only potential but, in fact,
inevitable non-being. This sentence brings (whether Adorno
wishes it or not) an entire Heideggerian register into play, and
with a very interesting twist.

For if Heidegger's Dasein is the being for which Being is an issue
– the being for which Being is an issue precisely because it, Dasein,
is continually exposed, held out over the possibility of its non-
Being – then Adorno's commentary takes Heidegger's topos out of
a certain kind of self-interested, deep-structure narcissism into the
realm of care about others; while at the same time it exposes the
presumed charity of that care for others or the significant other as
self-interest about and for one's own property. Christian charity is
revealed as the theologically sanitized version of private property
– what we knew all along. Only thus is the other truly a possession,
when it is transfixed into some functional form as a commodity –
which form allows it to be exchanged for other, equivalent
possessions.

Time for the subject is time for a transaction. Once become a
property – not *Merkmal* here, but *Besitz*, a possession, but a prop to
be moved around also – the beloved is in fact no longer seen. Its
first figure has been effaced. Abstraction in love, this turning the
beloved into a bloodless placeholder, is the complement, that
which completes exclusionariness, which manifests itself deceptively as the opposite, as this holding fast to this one being, the one
that is *thus, dies eine so Seiende*.[32] The object is lost to the degree to
which it is objectified, and misses, wrongs (*verfehlt*) the person
whom it reduces to mine.

It might appear to be a reduction of this lofty melancholy to say
so, but we are still in the thick of the Hegelian topos of the relation
between universals, concepts, and particulars here. But the crucial
difference between Hegel and Adorno is the melancholy tone of
the latter as opposed to the scientific optimism of the former. It is
much like the morning after the night before. And Adorno is
writing, in 1944, at dawn on the day after. Dawn on the first
postmodern day: the discourse of the concept is *over*. The bringing

---

[32] The reference to the (mistaken) idealization by the young man of his beloved, as
this is described by the narrator, Constantin Constantius, in Kierkegaard's
Repetition, is Adorno's unmistakable signature here.

of the other under a concept led to the extermination, *Vernichtung*, in which all otherly qualities were effaced to zero.

This is the inversion, the logical end of Blanchot's fable of the fable of the French Revolution, of the allegorical dance of Reason, Progress, Enlightenment: *fabula rasa*. This is the sad dance of the realization, not of the impossibility of bringing all particulars under the concept – to say that would be fatuous – but of realizing what happens when this is done. This is mass murder, extermination, holocaust. This is the very moment of our realization that the key to allegory is its failure, its ability, not to teach a stable lesson, but only to tell the story of the disjunction between subject and predicate, universal and particular. Totalitarian Hegelian optimism about the march of the dialectic has to be read against the young Hegel's own warnings, against his "Who Thinks Abstractly?," for example, which dates from the same year as the *Phenomenology*, and to which Adorno's diction points here.

"If people were no longer possessions, they could no longer be exchanged" is this paragraph's complement to the last's "even, and precisely, in a society cured of the anarchy of commodity production, it would hardly be possible for rules to surveil the order in which one met people." But this time, the need for Adorno to struggle against the hopelessness which he himself is in the process of teaching, in this after of the last paragraph's before, forces him to make this instantaneous idyll of a hypothesis out of what he has already shown to be impossible: the shimmering phantasm of post-commodity romance. True affection would be – but *is* not – one that speaks specifically to the other, and becomes attached to beloved features – predicates – and not to the idol of personality, the Idol that is the mirror image of personality.

But in the realm of the imaginary that is the realm in which human relations are constructed, there is only the *méconnaissance* of the idols.[33] To speak, as Hegel did not cease to remind us, is to speak in the realm of the general. The particular is lost as soon as one begins to speak. There is only one option: love and be silent. There are no words for this one love. The specific is not exclusive; it does not close out other things. The beloved in one port is

---

[33] The potential for false idealization inherent in Lacan's essay on "The Mirror Stage," which postdates the essay on "Logical Time," makes the dyadic structure of the "Mirror Stage" essay an anachronic regression from the rigor of the other essay's triadic model.

different, after all, from each one in every other. Or I might say, every beloved not has, but *is*, its own harbor. In this sense, each love *is* exclusive or exclusionary: because, having gone through this allegorical regression to the singular, we realize that our moral vision is precluded from the vulgarity of impossible, hence inappropriate comparisons – even though this is all that our language, which is a language of particular and universal terms, can do.

Adorno's language either helps him or trips him up: he says, the specific lacks the trait, pull, almost the drive – *Zug* – to totality. But the last sentence has told us that true affection attaches itself to the traits, *Züge*, of the other, not to their harmonized image, itself always, as Lacan tells us, a totality *qua* image. Attention to the beloved traits, *Züge*, of the specific love non-object keeps that object from being reduced to being prey to the holocaust of totality or of totalization, the train, *Zug*, on the way to totality, into the all. The singular and plural of this word cannot be reconciled with each other, for the singular, *Zug*, in its sense of "drive," connotes a unity of direction, a single motion in the direction of the all – an idol to be sure – that the plural, *Züge*, in its senses of "traits," thus of plurality and disparity – but not of the idol of totality – would oppose. It is the lower gods, the idols, that are praised with the promise of the All. They listen for praise like children, infants learning to speak by collecting together their traits into a false image, Man, in the mirror.

The specific precludes replacement in this exclusivity of a higher power, radicalized – as they said in the seventies and early eighties – its essence precludes it. But its essence precludes it because, in a manner of speaking, its essence is to have no essence.[34] Thus: "But in another sense nonetheless it *is* exclusionary, in that the substitution [Adorno substitues the Latin *Substitution* for the German *Ersetzung*] of the experience indissolubly bound up with it [*ihm*, the specific] doesn't forbid, but through its pure concept [*reinen Begriff*] doesn't allow it even to come up."

Now, with the entrance of the language of the concept, that is to say, of language, what can be said in the realm of the general, not merely meant, opined, *gemeint*, onto the scene, we see that what

---

[34] This is what the other is, in Levinasian ethics, as it is mapped out in its greatest statement, *Otherwise Than Being or Beyond Essence*, which began with an essay called "Substitution."

Adorno is dreaming is the idyll of the world in which to each object, or subject, there is a concept. Or better yet: for each object, there is one aphorism. But this is, then, the end of the concept, the end of philosophy. The protection of the completely determined, determined through all its properties, is that it cannot be repeated, and therefore that it tolerates the other, allows for, makes room for, is patient for the other. Let there not be only or dead repetition.

Kierkegaard's entrance here, of whose book of this title Adorno is writing the canniest abstract, should confuse and disorient, if not simply terrify. For from Kierkegaard's narrative, it is not really possible to figure out if repetition in his sense, as opposed to melancholy recollection (which is what Adorno paraphrases and condemns here) exists or is possible. The question is not (only?) "Will I go back to Berlin?," but "Can I go back to Berlin?," to love, true love, to Hegel, to the System, to philosophy. And the fact that Adorno says repetition when he is paraphrasing what Kierkegaard, in the book *Repetition*, calls recollection, would tend to indicate that Adorno does not put much faith in the possibility of repeating, let alone understanding, what Kierkegaard meant by repetition.

To the property relation to human beings, to the exclusive right of priority, this kind of *ius primae noctis*, valid for all nights before the morning after, belongs exactly this wisdom: God, it's only people, and it's no big thing which one. Inclination which would know nothing of such wisdom – the published translation misses the contrary-to-fact subjunctive – would not need fear infidelity, for it would be fast protected from faithlessness. But it is precisely the contrary-to-fact mood of every verb in this last sentence that tells us that we have all drunk of this wisdom, and that all we can do, to continue with that old Cole Porter song, is sigh a little. No matter how present, *this* sound bite is always and can only be an *ars amatoria* in the pluperfect tense. This is why, though the time be long, the true will indeed come to pass. But what about love?

True love was always in another.

❖❖

2

Anamorphoses of grammar: Derrida on Heidegger

❖❖

Spaced-out time: of the noun and the verb

I would like to discuss several topoi in Heidegger's writings which are incontestably prominent, incontestably important one could say, given the amount and prominence of attention they have received both from Heidegger himself as well as from some of his readers. These gestures are also somewhat difficult to relate to each other, even if they are often marked or remarked very close together, whether within the same essay, or in the temporal order of Heidegger's works. These topoi, then, or marks, or sites – I deliberately shy away from calling them *themes*, even though topos can also mean this, for reasons that are evident from my introduction – are the middle voice, a grammatical category Heidegger evokes from very early on in his work; the double genitive, which comes to the fore in its most explicit statement in the first paragraph of the *Letter on Humanism*;[1] and the crosswise through- or overstrike, the *kreuzweise Durchstreichung*, which Heidegger places over the word "Sein," "Being," in 1955.[2]

Each of these marks taken separately has already generated a certain amount of commentary, to the point where one sees the

---

[1] Now collected in *Wegmarken* (Frankfurt-on-Main: Klostermann, 1976). Henceforth indicated by *W*, followed by page number in text. English translation by Frank Capuzzi and J. Glenn Gray in Martin Heidegger, *Basic Writings* (New York: Harper and Row, 1977). Henceforth indicated by *BW*, followed by page number in text.

[2] See Martin Heidegger, *The Question of Being*, original text with a translation by William Kluback and Jean T. Wilde (New Haven: Twayne, 1960). Henceforth *ZS*, followed by page number in text.

words "under erasure" quite often in the writing of people who pay no attention to Heidegger whatsoever. But the aim of this discussion is to try to relate these marks in such a way as to help with the understanding of some of the more grand Heideggerian themes, which may turn out to be more dependent on some of the more prosaic aspects of grammatical functions than on the Hölderlinian prosody that commands such critical attention.

The difficulty of articulating the relation between these marks may not, as I hope to show, have to do with the fact that these relations are recondite and only of importance to a certain mandarin scholasticism. Given the influence Heidegger's thinking has already had on so much thinking in our time, and given that he has produced such a monumental reading of the tradition, it should be important to get clear on what his version of our tradition is. And I want to insist on this: it *is* our tradition. And given, too, the importance Heidegger assigns to the role of language in the tradition and in his own thinking, it should not be considered egregious to try to take a look at places where Heidegger tells some very specific stories about certain pieces of language, or makes some formally innovative gestures.

On the contrary, what I hope to make at least a little bit more clear is that the difficulty of stating these relations has to do with their rhetorical over- or hyper-proximity to each other. The links between them are hard to get at because nothing is hidden here; because these recurrent elements of Heidegger's text seem almost to slide together at the edges. Often one finds oneself thinking of one of these marks, and then only later realizes that another has somehow insinuated itself into consideration. In retrospect, it becomes difficult to tell the story of how one got from A to B, or of how one might possibly get back again. Are these relations reversible? That is to say, is there a logical hierarchy at issue in the emergence and progression of these marks? Is it necessary to construe some temporal or transitive relation between them, from A to B to C, or are the relations symmetrical, in the strictly logical sense, where A is to B as B is to A?

In the latter case, these three figures, if one will, might appear to be anamorphoses or projections of some common and unique source, which itself might lie hidden, *ein Ungedachtes*, more deeply within Heidegger's encyclopedia. And given the strength of the motif of gathering in Heidegger's later work, this would be a comforting possibility. The challenging thing would be to see if these figures or functions did not, ultimately, blend to the one color, but were somehow related without a single, binding trait. Very little is sure here, except perhaps that nothing will be gained in this project if one dismisses Heidegger's use of these grammatical categories as incorrect or improper, in the way in which the oneiric quality of certain of his purportedly philological pronouncements has been used to suggest the unwholesomeness of his entire project. Such a dismissal is also comforting, because it dispenses with the need to figure out what that project, if it is one, might be.

Dealing with these more grammatical and less semantically organized categories should allow us to bypass these reservations about spuriousness in order to ask questions that might be more pertinent, such as: What do the *moves* Heidegger makes allow him – and his readers – to accomplish in other places? Or, what has Heidegger *invented* by trotting out his version of a kind of grammar of thinking, to use an expression he himself would no doubt abominate because of its technicist overtones? These are some of the questions and kinds of questions I address here. And this being an exercise in practical rhetoric, I would like to start out rather pedantically with what is on the surface, and see how much I can try to tie together, rather than to start with the certainty of an overwhelming thematic, hidden or not, of which these marks would be emanations.

The middle voice is the first of these categories to emerge in the sequence of Heidegger's writings, and the least original or fanciful, given that the middle is indeed a codified grammatical category. It makes its appearance very early on indeed, in the second introduction to *Being and Time*, more specifically in paragraph 7, section A, where Heidegger writes:

The Greek expression *phainomenon*, to which the term "phenomenon" goes back, is derived from the verb *phainesthai*, which signifies "to show itself." Thus *phainomenon* means that which shows itself, the manifest [*das, was sich zeigt, das Sichzeigende, das Offenbare*]. *Phainesthai* itself is a *middle-voiced* form which comes from *phaino* – to bring to the light of day, to put in the light. *Phaino* comes from the stem *pha* –, like *phos*, the light, that which is bright – in other words, that wherein something can become manifest, visible in itself. Thus we must *keep in mind* that the expression *"phenomenon"* signifies *that which shows itself in itself*, the manifest. Accordingly the *phainomena* or "phenomena" are the totality of what lies in the light of day or can be brought to the light – what the Greeks sometimes identified with *ta onta* (entities). Now an entity can show itself *from* itself [*von ihm selbst her*] in many ways, depending in each case on the kind of access we have to it. Indeed it is even possible for an entity to show itself as something which in itself it is *not* . . .[3]

The title of this paragraph is "The Phenomenological Method of Investigation." And, after Heidegger has himself rather pedantically opted to split the meaning of phenomenology into its components, *phenomenon* and *logos*, the passage with which we are concerned is the beginning of this bifurcated propaedeutic. This deployment of the middle voice could be called more of a mention than a use; but its location is key, and the author himself has chosen to emphasize it.

After having gone through the structure of Dasein – the chief allegorical personage of Heidegger's early drama – as a questioning entity, "the being for whom Being is an issue," in the first introduction, it is already clear by the time we reach this particular lesson in etymology that Dasein is the particular entity whose phenomenality is being especially described in this passage, where Heidegger names the middle voice. He does so in order to supplement the verbs of manifestation, which are written reflexively in German, such as *sich zeigen*, and which the English translators feel compelled to add to their text in editorial brackets.[4] What Heidegger gets out of the invocation of the middle here is a certain porousness of reflexion for the self-interrogating phenomenon of Dasein.

Whereas a certain French structuralist line of thought on the

3 Martin Heidegger, *Being and Time*, trans. John Macquarrie and Edward Robinson (New York: Harper, 1962), 51. German interpolations from Martin Heidegger, *Sein und Zeit*, 15th edn (Tübingen: Niemeyer, 1979), 28–29. Emphasis in original.
4 The twentieth century is the century of the middle voice. See in this regard the discussion of obsessional neurosis in Sigmund Freud, "Instincts and Their Vicissitudes," in *The Complete Psychological Works of Sigmund Freud*, vol. XIV ed. James Strachey (London: Hogarth Press, 1966–74); Emile Benveniste, "Actif et moyen dans le verbe," in his *Problèmes de linguistique générale* (Paris: Gallimard, 1966); Jacques Lacan, "Voix moyenne/voie moyenne," in his *Le Séminaire* vol. III, *Les Psychoses* (Paris: Gallimard, 1981); and Roland Barthes, "To Write: an Intransitive Verb?," in Richard Macksey and Eugenio Donato, eds., *The Structuralist Controversy: the Languages of Criticism and the Sciences of Man* (Baltimore: Johns Hopkins University Press, 1970).

same topic concentrates, following upon Benveniste, on the subjective aspects of the middle-voice register, summoning up the usual lists of Greek verbs of mental action, birth and death – if not copulation – and so on, what Heidegger concentrates on here is nothing so subjective, nothing so anthropological, to use his own word. The last sentence of the citation opens up the space of the rest of the book, which treats the modes of opacity of Dasein's phenomenal character, the intimate evasions of the perspicuous that belong to the structures (for the Heidegger of *Being and Time*, they are the structures of everydayness, averageness, the structures grouped around the word *Nivellierung*, the leveling-down of the commitment to the ontological in the everyday) of a being that finds itself in the world, *in medias res*, and must *ask back* about more fundamental matters.

The assertion of the middleness of the phenomenon in question is tantamount to the self-assertion and the self-reassurance of its ability to carry out its project. (In this case, the project is the writing of *Being and Time* itself, a project that Heidegger breaks off after the first part.) This project might thus be said to depend upon the ability to stay in the middle position without allowing itself to be stuck or struck into the positions of the simple activity of the mastery of the technicist world view Heidegger will decry until his death – or, for that matter, into the abject passivity which would be its mirror image. It could even be said that the nonsubjective character of Heidegger's employment – as opposed to the more subjective expositions of the category in the French line – of the middle opens up the space in which he can claim, years later, that the understanding of the analytic of Dasein as an anthropology is an error, an error notoriously perpetrated by the French.

So I would like to risk asserting that the possibility of Heidegger's insistence that the analysis of Dasein is not an anthropology – a reading he will insist is a misreading with ever more clipped strenuousness – may depend on this initial point-of-departure-as-refusal to subjectivize this middle category. And this will prove to be crucial to the story he will have to go on to tell, to the future of his own project, in which the discussion of Dasein is increasingly given up precisely because it is necessarily being (mis)read into these subjective terms.

But, more specifically, what else does this attempt to stay in the middle imply for Heidegger himself later on down the line? Having given a call-note from the introduction to *Being and Time*, I move now to an essay that dates from immediately after the Second World War, when Jean Beaufret, from that moment on the anointed prince of the French Heideggerian orthodoxy, addresses to Heidegger the question "How can we give meaning back to the word humanism today?," in what is basically an invitation to the master to respond to Sartre's "Existentialism is a Humanism." Heidegger's letter of 1946–47 is known as the *Letter on Humanism*, which it is more than safe to say is the first major text of Heidegger's new life. In the sense that it is addressed to disciples of the true faith, it is indeed a pastoral letter; but it is also a letter written in the late pastoral mode that is to characterize the later Heideggerian wordpath with ever greater sentimentality and mournful loss, as though such mourning became Being, or vice versa. Heidegger inaugurates the elegy of his long postwar career with the following passage, the first of his long letter:

We are still far from pondering the essence of action decisively enough. We view action only as causing an effect. The actuality of the effect is valued according to its utility. But the essence of action is accomplishment. To accomplish means to unfold something into the fullness of its essence . . . *producere*. Therefore only what already is can really be accomplished. But what "is" above all is Being. Thinking accomplishes the relation of Being to the essence of man. It does not make or cause the relation. Thinking brings this relation to Being solely as something handed over to it from Being. Such offering consists in the fact that in thinking Being comes to language. Language is the house of Being. In its home man dwells. Those who think and those who create with words are the guardians of this home. Their guardianship accomplishes the manifestation of Being insofar as they bring the manifestation to language and maintain it in language through their speech. Thinking does not become action only because some effect issues from it or because it is applied. Thinking acts insofar as it thinks. Such action is presumably the simplest and at the same time the highest, because it concerns the relation of Being to man. But all working or effecting lies in Being and is directed toward beings. Thinking, in contrast, lets itself be claimed by Being so that it can say the truth of Being. Thinking accomplishes this letting. Thinking is *l'engagement par l'Etre pour l'Etre* [engagement by Being for Being]. I do not know whether it is linguistically possible to say both of these ('*par*' and "*pour*") at once, in this way: *penser, c'est l'engagement de l'Etre* [thinking is the engagement of Being]. Here the possessive form "*de l'*..." is supposed to express both subjective and objective genitive. In this regard "subject" and "object" are inappropriate terms of metaphysics, which very early on in the form of Occidental "grammar" and "logic" seized control of the interpretation of language. We today can only begin to descry what is concealed in that occurrence. The liberation of language from grammar into a more original essential framework is reserved for thought and poetic creation. Thinking is not merely *l'engagement dans l'action* for and by beings, in the sense of the actuality of the present situation. Thinking is *l'engagement* by and for the truth of Being. The history of Being is never past but stands ever before; it sustains and defines every *condition et situation humaine*. In order to learn how to experience the aforementioned essence of thinking *purely*, [emphasis TAP] and that means at the same time to carry it through, we must free ourselves from the technical interpretation of thinking. The beginnings of that interpretation reach back to Plato and Aristotle.   (*BW*, 193–94)

In what kind of language is it best to enunciate the relation of the essence of man to Being? It is the language in which the engagement by Being for Being (itself) is expressed through man as a sort of *porte-parole*. Before dealing with the French sentence – Heidegger's own – that stands at the center of this paragraph, and before commenting the irony of its Latinity, I would like to underscore the way in which the reflection that belongs to the phenomenon, guaranteed to it by its middle-voice status at the beginning of *Being and Time*, has been transposed much more explicitly here into a relation between Being and itself, with man as the place-holder occupying the function of the "reflexive" relation. Man's activity, thinking, accomplishes this letting.

We will see more of this letting soon. But for the moment, let us note that whereas the *voice* of the phenomenon is a category that pertains to its nature as verb, we have moved here, very subtly, into the nominal register. The phenomenon, which, in its middle participial nature, has been elucidated in its relation to the verbal form, shows itself to itself. But in the case of thinking, as a semisubstantialized verb (the infinitive being the verbal form, which permits, in abstraction, in its de-limitation, the transition to the noun), the phenomenon is characterized in terms of whatever "action" it produces by an obliqueness of agent and of object.

This is a double obliqueness that, Heidegger wants to assert – but why then does he say, "I do not know if it is possible to say these at once . . . ?" – is capable of being condensed into a single genitive construction, in a move that emphasizes case, *casus*, that which befalls the noun. So man, as the "agent" of this "activity," is the site or the placeholder for the accomplishment of Being's relation to Being. I opt deliberately for the longer, apparently redundant locution, because it is precisely at this moment that a phrase such as "Being's relation to itself" or "Being's self-relation" sounds strange, anthropomorphic, and thus inadequate. Thus we have moved, in the figural space of the passage from *Being and Time* to the *Letter on Humanism*, from the register of the verb to the register of the noun.

And, whereas the middleness of the phenomenon, of Dasein-as-phenomenon at the beginning of *Being and Time*, turns out, following upon the last sentence we cited above ("[i]ndeed it is even possible for an entity to show itself as that which it is *not*") to open up the analysis of the homeyness of Dasein's inauthentic, everyday structures (in the proximally and for the most part, etc.); and whereas the story that is told in *Being and Time* is told in terms of fallenness – Heidegger's own word – as an essential structure of Dasein's being in the world; the story that is told here in *this* paragraph from 1947 is more parabolic, and yet, at the same time, written in a more historically determined register, as a fabulized account or version of history.

Dasein's fallenness is every Dasein's fallenness, that which befalls every Dasein at all times; but " 'grammar' " and " 'logic' " here are as though enemy agents, which won an early battle of the giants over the essence of language, supervening upon language as though from its outside in some kind of hostile – no doubt technicist and corporate – takeover, the takeover of and by the Organization Man. We are still far, and Heidegger himself is still far, from discerning what takes place in this occurrence, between the telling of the overt and timeless allegory of Dasein, which, being a story told of every Dasein, happens in a kind of time outside of time, and the telling of the story of a *coup d'état*, or a *coup de langue*, or *de logique*, or *de l'occident*.

How can we imagine language or a language before "grammar" and "logic" seized control of its interpretation? Even if an argument could be made that this was a specific, punctual, historical reference, that Heidegger was referring to a kind of grammatico-logical scholasticism – an epoch in the history of philosophy he knew better than just about anyone, after his dissertation on Scotus – we are presented with no such concrete reference here, but rather with the by now recognizable beginning of the parable of the forgetting of Being in Greek metaphysical speculation. Is it not this speculation, the specularity of this speculation, that gives birth to theory, to the possibility of the *theoria* as the collective agency that legitimates the passage from seeing to telling?[5]

Now that we have seen the way in which this shift from the verb to the noun has been accompanied by the shift from the recounting of the structures of the everyday existence of phenomena to the telling of a pseudo-historical fable of the seizure of power in and as an act of grammatical interpretation, what could be the next step in *this* account, in which I am trying to relate a kind of set of stations of the cross of Heidegger's grammatical recourses?

My next step is indeed the invention of the true, literal cross, the *kreuzweise Durchstreichung*, the crossing-out which Heidegger places over the word "Being," apparently for the first time, in his next major published letter of 1955, written to Ernst Jünger.[6] Consideration of this next epistle begins with the title or the series of titles given it. First, there is the title of Jünger's own treatise, "Über die Linie," which I leave untranslated for a brief moment, followed by Heidegger's own title, "Über die Linie." Between the two titles we have the difference of a case inflection, the accusative of the *trans lineam* meant in the first title, and the ablative of the *de linea* Heidegger prefers to awaken from the indeterminateness of the German homophone.

Yet again we are faced with a moment where Heidegger himself, in his introduction to the published version of this letter, has recourse to the Latinate powers of grammatical codification in order to make his difference with Jünger understood – and this despite his ever more strident insistence on the etiolated relation of the Romans to the Greeks. We see full well that when Heidegger

---

[5] See Wlad Godzich, "The Tiger on the Paper Mat," his foreword to de Man, *RT*. And for an even more potent discussion of the problem, see Jacques Lacan, "Le temps logique et l'assertion de la certitude anticipée: un nouveau sophisme," in *E.* It is not without interest that the publication of Lacan's essay follows Sartre's *L'Existentialisme* very quickly.

[6] Has anyone commented Heidegger's *tendency* to communicate major utterances after the Second World War in letters? Not everything is a letter, but the *Letter on Humanism* and *Über die Linie / Zur Seinsfrage* (not to mention the much later *Zu Denken als Weg / Der Fehl heiliger Namen*) are not simply texts among others. Their postal status insures a certain power or investment of and in their transmission. And the addressees are not arbitrary, either.

wants to be precise he is capable of dropping his derision for exactitude and giving a magisterial lecture in the language not only of the schools, but of the schoolmasters. Heidegger sees his own title, *on or about the line,* as containing the discussion of the more aggressive, frontal motion of Jünger's title, *across the line.*

But when Heidegger publishes this letter, he changes the title rather radically. The line has been replaced with a question: *Concerning the Line* has been transformed into *Zur Seinsfrage, On the Question of Being.* And now we have to move for a moment in between the covers of this work to consider a place where the question and the matter or question of the meridian, the line, come together in a new typographical disposition, the discussion of which piece of typography may help us figure out what this rather dense piece of writing is about.

The homo–paleonymic relation of Jünger's title to Heidegger's own first title is an apt tableau with which to illustrate what happens in this newer letter, obsessed as it is with the matter of the fact that one still speaks the same language whether one remains this side (and what is it to be on *this* side, for us, here, today?) of the line of the risk of utter nihilism, or on the other side. For Jünger, it is only on the other side that one would have passed through the extremity of the focal point of this risk and into the free region of a kind of *dépassement* of this most extreme and negative possibility. Such are the stakes: for Jünger it is a question of *passing through* the possibility of such an experience to another place, a kind of dream of another locality; but for Heidegger it is a question of dwelling on the line, within (the tension of) the space of this line itself. In other words: Is there a zone outside the system, or is the zone the myth of the system, the myth the system fosters in order further to enslave its inhabitants by leading them to think that there is another place – the zone – to which they might escape?[7] It is the task of our time to elaborate a critique of the structure of this *detachment,* of the way in which we have to find our "clearing" in the bombed-out centers of our cities, and of the existence of this other locality as it is revealed in the disintegration not only of our specular image of ourselves into that of a purely meaningless signifier, a sign without signification, a *deutungsloses Zeichen.*

[7] Pynchon's leitmotiv, in *Gravity's Rainbow,* is the cynical inversion of the way in which, for Lévi-Strauss, the *ingénieur* is the myth constructed by the *bricoleur,* the jack-of-all-trades, the only kind of person who actually exists.

Given the whole critique Heidegger has made (in the rest of the *Letter on Humanism,* of which we discussed the beginning a few moments ago) of nihilism as the most extreme and therefore the ownmost form of humanism, and thus of metaphysics, it is hardly surprising that when he is confronted with the task of imagining the topography of sociologico–technological world domination – the where it's at of beings – he gives us a sketch, or a fascicle of sketches, of an examination of the nature of the place itself, of an atopic place which is but a line, and soon enough a cross and a point. He decides that it cannot ever be a question of bypassing the only language we have, which is either permeated through and through with metaphysics or coextensive with it, consubstantial with it – depending on how strong a reading we want to grant. Rather, we must come to grips with the fact that *there is nowhere else to dwell except in the language we already have,* in which the broad avenue toward nihilism is always and necessarily the road that risks being taken.

The great failure of Heidegger's later work, the failure of his reinforcing the structural necessity of the step back with a thematics of laughable sentimentality, is directly related to the fact that the step back, which is always taken so admirably and rigorously when it is a question of thinking through the tradition, of thinking the unthought of the tradition, is not taken at the level of questioning the *serious.* Heidegger is so funny – because so lacking in irony – at the thematic level of the clearing, the woodpath, the shepherd of Being, the church bells ringing far off in the distance, etc. *And yet* it should not be assumed that this kind of provincial nostalgia is an accident, something that flew in the face of Heidegger's achievement from the outside. Far from it: we should have to interrogate Heidegger's lack of thematic irony, his lapse into the peasant half of what Adorno referred to as his peasant cunning.[8] We would have to do this in the same kind of way that Heidegger himself interrogates Jünger's fantasy of moving across the meridian of the extreme threat of nihilism into some other new world. It remains to be worked out how the Heideggerian step back – from the ontic to the ontological, from technics to the essence of technology – is deeply related to the

---

[8] See Theodor W. Adorno, *The Jargon of Authenticity,* trans. Knut Tarnowski (Evanston: Northwestern University Press, 1973).

derogation of and dislike for modernity and all that comes with it, from Jackson Pollock and all manner of cheap American things cataloged over forty years in weary Rilkean tone, to the Bomb. To ignore the way in which Heidegger's (formal–structural) grammatical cunning shakes out into his reactive country discourse is not a mistake, it is an error his text predicts and enacts. We would be foolish if we were simply to think that we could bypass the same danger, or even traverse it, to some new and idyllic land of demystification or of demythification. Heidegger has given us bad, late pastoral, the poetry of nowhere-to-hide conjoined with the reverie of a hiding place.

In order to continue with the Heideggerian operation, I have chosen henceforth deliberately to scatter, pluralize, and hence sacralizingly to desecrate Heidegger's text by destroying the typographical unity of the *kreuzweise Durchstreichung*, which I render henceforth using the following possibilities, somewhat deliberately and somewhat randomly: be~~i~~ng be~~ing~~ be~~ing~~ be~~i~~ing b~~ei~~ng ~~being~~ ~~Sein~~ ~~being~~

This is the strongest possible philosophical strategy. Such a strategy goes even further than that of the text of Derrida I discuss below. It follows Heidegger's own suggestions, at the very end of *Was heißt Denken?*, when he begins to discuss, in the resumé of the transition between the last two lectures of this, his last university course, "*Verschiedenheit* der Ortung," "differentiation of the placing," his own translation of the Platonic *khorismos* of the *khora*.[9] Furthermore, in continuing with this *entartete Frommheit*, this sacralizing desacralization, I am also paying tribute to Levinas's refusal to capitalize the word "being," as well as to Paul Celan's most crucial discussion of Heidegger's text, "Der Meridian," where Celan writes: "Ich finde etwas – wie die Sprache – Immaterielles, aber Irdisches, Terrestrisches, etwas Kreisförmiges, über die beiden Pole in sich selbst Zurückkehrendes und dabei – heitererweise – sogar die Tropen Durchkreuzendes – ich finde . . . einen *Meridian*" ("I find something – like language – nonmaterial, but earthly, terrestrial, something circle-formed, turning back upon itself over both poles and thus – more warmly, happily – thus leveling, disturbing, crossing (out) the tropes,

---

[9] Heidegger, *WH*, 174–75, emphasis in original.

tropics – I find ... a *Meridian*"). "Durchkreuzen" means not only "to cross," but also "to destroy," "to level." It is thus close to "nivellieren"; likewise, "die Tropen" means both "tropics" and "tropes."[10] All of these different types of crosses *do* different things, and all of these things are relevant to the discussion. The now-classical ~~Sein~~ is Heidegger's own, and relates the chi over the word to the fourfold, *das Geviert*, which Heidegger unfolds in his "Das Ding." My other marks do other things with and to Heidegger's: "be×ng," for example, where the cross occurs in translation over the central character, abbreviates Heidegger's cross and emphasizes centrality of position; "~~being~~" puts the crosshairs of a Cartesian gun sight over the matter; "~~being~~" weakens the cross and emphasizes disunity and the materiality of the typographical characters; "b×ing" de-centers the point of gathering in one direction, "b×ng" does so with more or less acuteness; "~~being~~" is standard except for the fact that it is in lower case; "~~being~~" enacts the absolute *Nivellierung* of nihilism, the compulsive scratchings of a madman. I do not make any claim to this list's being exhaustive; rather it is simply an encounter with some possibilities of the computer-real.

Shortly before the first appearance of the actual crossout, Heidegger is thus able to write the following passage:

In which language does the basic outline of thinking speak which indicates a crossing of the line? Is the language of the metaphysics of the will to power, of *Gestalt*, and of values to be rescued across the critical line? What if even the language of metaphysics and metaphysics itself, whether it be that of the living or of the dead God, *as* metaphysics, formed that barrier which forbids a crossing over of the line, that is, the overcoming of nihilism? If that were the case, would not then the crossing of the line necessarily become a transformation of language and demand a transformed relationship to the essence of language? And is not your own relation to language of a kind that it demands from you a different characterization of the concept-language of the sciences? If this language is often represented as nominalism, then we are still entangled in the logico-grammatical conception of language.   (ZS, 71)

Crossing the line into the promised land, the transformation of the relation to language, is part of what the language we speak rules out. If we reject the universalizing aspects of conceptualization as part of the metaphysical baggage we would want to get rid of, in

---

[10] Celan, *GW*, III, 202.

what Heidegger is calling a naïve gesture, the nominalistic cataloging of entities which would remain, after our attempts to banish the universal, would still be part of the same system, a mirror image of what we would have hoped to dispense with. We would be left with a monadological catalog, that is to say a melancholic enumeration, the evidence of our failure – a catalog of objects, and of the relations between them, which would resemble a banalized version of Wittgenstein's *Tractatus*-world. The "logico-grammatical" conception of language would be characteristic of this naïve renunciation of the universal. And we can well see that what Heidegger might have in mind here is the kind of "grammar of all sorts of objects" which has been done in the wake of Wittgenstein's *Philosophical Investigations*, a work which Heidegger would no doubt – even if incorrectly, in our view – have considered to be a key moment in this kind of anthropological account of language – an account that disregards all ontological considerations simply as products of the language games people play. (This is not my view of Wittgenstein's late work at all and is, I believe, an egregious misunderstanding; but it is at the same time a misunderstanding which many self-proclaimed inheritors of Wittgenstein, in the English-speaking, as well as in the French and German, worlds have perpetrated with glee. The attempt at formalizing the structures of the *Philosophical Investigations* into an exhaustive catalog of what we do with words utterly fails to take into account Wittgenstein's mode of presentation, of which it makes a mockery. Wittgenstein's book refuses to be a book in the classical sense, and teaches nothing if not the futility of all such exhaustive attempts at formalization, while having a good deal to say about their inevitability as well. Inasmuch as the project of extracting doctrine from the purportedly confused and distracted works of the later Wittgenstein is the work of contemporary professional philosophers, Wittgenstein's work must be rescued from them.)

After asserting the failure of both the scientific worldview *and* of any purportedly post-metaphysical crossing over (and this crossing over does begin to sound – does it not? – like the crossing over which Kafka mentions as the word of the prophets in his parable on parables), after asserting the failure of both of these to give us a path through to the essence of nihilism, Heidegger gives us a meditation on what a "good definition," an adequate description, in the register of adequation and of mimesis, might be:

Where does this essence [of nihilism] come from? . . . We do not thoughtlessly ask too much when we look for the place and discuss the essence of the line. But is this any different from the attempt to achieve what you ask for, namely "a good definition of nihilism?" It looks as if thinking were continually being led, or driven like a fool, as though in a magic circle around the Same . . . But perhaps the circle is a hidden spiral. Perhaps it has narrowed in the interim. This means that the ways in which we are approaching the essence of nihilism are changing. The "goodness" of the rightfully demanded "good definition" finds its confirmation in our giving up the wish to define insofar as this must be established on assertions in which thinking dies out. However, it is a gain, which is slight because it is only negative, if we learn to notice that no *information* [emphasis TAP] can be given about nothingness and Being and nihilism, about their essence and about the essence (verbal) of the essence (nominal) which can be presented tangibly in the form of *assertions* [emphasis TAP].

It is a gain insofar as we learn that that to which the "good definition" is to apply, the essence of nihilism, leads us into a realm which requires a different language. If turning-towards belongs to "Being" and in such a way that the latter is based on the former, then "Being" is dissolved in this turning. It now becomes questionable what Being which has reverted into and been absorbed by its essence is henceforth to be thought of. Accordingly, a thoughtful glance ahead into this realm of "Being" can only write it as ~~Being~~. The drawing of these crossed lines at first only repels, especially the almost ineradicable habit of conceiving "Being" as something standing by itself and only coming at times face to face with man. According to this conception it looks as if man were excluded from "Being." However, he is not only not excluded, that is, he is not only encompassed into "Being," but "Being," using the essence of man, is obliged to abandon the appearance of the for-itself, for which reason, it is also of a different nature than the conception of totality would like to have it, which encompasses the subject–object relationship.

The sign of the crossed lines can, to be sure, according to what has been said, not be a merely negative sign of crossing out . . . The being present as such turns towards the essence of man in which the turning-towards is first completed, insofar as the human being remembers it. Man in his essence is the memory of Being, but of ~~Being~~. This means that the essence of man is a part of that which in the crossed intersected lines of Being puts thinking under the claim of an earlier demand. Being present is grounded in the turning-towards which as such turns the essence of man into it so that the latter may dissipate itself for it.

Nothingness would have to be written, and that means thought of, just like ~~Being~~. (ZS, 81–83)

The collusion of several different registers in this paragraph (including the vectoral–tropological notion of the sign and its relation to man's relation to the thinking of Being) is utterly Pascalian. But there is also, yet again, a pervasive reference to Hölderlin's *deutungsloses Zeichen* of "Mnemosyne,"[11] itself a key text for *Was heißt Denken?*, Heidegger's last university lecture course (1951–52). Unfortunately, the published translators occult these relations with the unwarranted translation of *Zeichen* as "symbol," a translation which represents a thorough misunderstanding of Heidegger's text inasmuch as what is at issue here is the very possibility of a sign's loss of signification, i.e., precisely that which can befall a sign, but not a symbol. If, for Pascal, the zero is the lynchpin for the joining of the orders of number on the one hand and nature on the other, then the figure of Christ, in the *Pensées*, occupies the same structural function as the zero, that of the point of intersection of the chi of the human and the divine.[12]

The *kreuzweise Durchstreichung* becomes only more Pascalian in Heidegger's glosses on what is gathered at the juncture of the lines. The reading of Being as b̶e̶i̶n̶g̶ takes place as a consequence of the gesture of believing that somehow one can move *through* nihilism. The "good description" of the state of nihilism is not adequate, because what is being challenged or what is at issue is the whole regime in which description, the very discourse of adequation in and as description, as the predominant mode of utterance, fails.

Why? The description fails because another language would be required. And it is nowhere, really, to be found. Inasmuch as description speaks in the standard form of a subject-object relation, thus in subject-predicate utterances, it resumes and takes for granted the stigmatization of something like a middle voice into activity and passivity, into a verb with subjects and objects. And it is this stigmatization itself which Heidegger wants to interrogate, not in order to say that it is invalid, but to show what the stakes are and where it leads us – or, and this may be the same thing, where it comes from. While, at first appearance, it moves against the grain of Heidegger's ranting to invoke inventions of the analytic philosophical tradition in order to explain what he could mean when he writes of wanting to interrogate the form of the standard sentence, it is not at all inappropriate here to bring in the Austinian notion of performance as an example of a kind of speaking – or perhaps of

[11] See Friedrich Hölderlin, *Werke und Briefe*, ed. Beißner and Schmidt (Frankfurt-on-Main: Insel, 1969), vol. i, 199–200.

[12] See "Absolute Constructions" below for more on the zero.

writing – which might contain elements that exceed the bounds of descriptive utterance. Heidegger's dwelling on the expression "es gibt Sein," "it gives – Being" – "rather than "there is Being," or "Being is," which begins around this time – that is, after the War – works in this very direction.[13] The "es gibt Sein" eliminates the copulative verb from the utterance; and one is hard-pressed to speak about subject and object in the case of this locution, given what is called the impersonality of such a construction.

Similarly, while the explicit glosses of the middle voice do not appear very often in Heidegger's later writings, we get a proliferation of constructions/locutions that attempt, by means of the use of third-person impersonal constructions like "es gibt Sein," and reflexive verbs combined with the infinitive *lassen* ("to let," of which we spoke a few moments ago), to do what cannot be done. Heidegger *enacts* his failure to find an *other* language, one that would be uncontaminated by the need, for example, to use a two-part reflexive verb in German in order to approximate a one-word Greek middle. The very need to approximate betrays the impossibility of the project. And what we get, in addition to these contortions, is a fabulous story about a prelapsarian time when things stood out in their phenomenality and the advent of modern consciousness, humanism, and nihilism had not yet reduced everything to the uniformity of an industrial grey.

What, then, can be said about these three marks: the middle, the double genitive, and the crosswise overstrike? What are the similarities and what are the differences; and what, if anything, relates them? They are all involved with what we might call the constellation activity–passivity, which in turn is also related to subject–objecthood. The procession between these two vocabularies is the procession from the register of verbal inflections to that of nominal inflections. These two are both related to an attempt to situate standard sentential form within the scheme of the reduction of language to its use value as description. This reduction is itself the ultimate symptom – this reduction of the essence of language to constative, representational value – of the technological age, in which all entities, whether human, linguistic, animal, mineral, or vegetable, are reduced to the status of resources, what

[13] See Martin Heidegger, *On Time and Being*, trans. Joan Stambaugh (New York: Harper and Row, 1972).

Heidegger calls standing reserve. The total reduction of the world horizon to this status is in fact one of Heidegger's major characterizations of the advent of nihilism. Thinking, in the strong sense which Heidegger wants to give to this verbal centaur of a substantialized infinitive, *Denken*, is what he wants to be able to attempt in order to try to understand the force behind this technological injunction – which, as we have seen, is an injunction to the mimesis of adequate description in the linguistic realm.

And therefore Heidegger's strong notion of thinking must not be sheerly mimetic. The task of thinking is to think the crosswise overstrike of Being as a necessity, as the necessary correlate of (the advent of) nihilistic picture-thinking. Thus the difficulty Heidegger has in telling us what his version of thinking is is the latest version of the abyss opened up in the *Sophist*, where the attempt to define mimesis gets caught up in a logical abyss that results from the sharpest dialectical rigor – not from its opposite. Just so for Heidegger, for whom the constant call to and for and from thinking is an absolutely necessary structural recourse to the other scene, a scene which cannot be a *scene*, inasmuch as it is not capable of being *described*. This constant "reference" to some unheard-of language is a necessary tropological anchor for Heidegger, a recourse he cannot do without, given his characterization of descriptive language as inadequate – in fact of his description of the very inadequacy of the language of adequacy and of description.

It is perhaps not irrelevant that the *Sophist* is also the place where the discussion of whether Being *is* takes place. It is a kind of companion piece to the *Parmenides* in this sense. And it is therefore no mere coincidence that the epigraph to *Being and Time*, which, as epigraph, could be said to stand as a kind of motto, an inscribed stele erected at the head of Heidegger's entire corpus, is taken from that dialogue: "For manifestly you have long been aware of what you mean when you use the expression "*being*." We, however, who used to think we understood it, have now become perplexed."[14]

After 1955, we can now give – again flying in the face of Heidegger – a kind of operational definition, and say: Being is that which must be read with the reader's mark of a crosswise

---

[14] Heidegger, *Being and Time*, 19.

overstrike in the age in which representation governs.[15] And what he is trying to imagine, conceive of – our vocabulary fails us here – what he is trying to come up with is what a nonrepresentative regime or government looks like. The notorious Rectoral Address of 1933 is indeed organized around this notion of the mimetic function of the university in its relation to society, itself rather classical. Thus the ascetic turn of Heidegger's postwar work, which insists that the "activity" of thinking cannot fit into or be legislated by institutional constraints, boundaries or fiats, is consonant with a recognition of the need either to leave the university or to give up the university's mimetic function, in an auto-critical and sustained gesture the importance of which should not be underestimated. Heidegger may not give up the university's mimetic function, but his writing functions ever more forcefully in and as an ascesis from the university.

In addition to reading the cross in all of its religiosity, then, and in addition to reading it as a chi, I also insist on this notion of a reader's mark, a scratch over an enigma, which paradoxically makes that enigma legible, even if no longer usable or voiceable. The crossout is the mark of the (il)legibility of the mythical pre-subject–object world, the fabular world to which Heidegger returns over and over again. The existence of this fable of the prelapsarian is clearly not a frill, something with which Heidegger can do away. For its positing, or better, Heidegger's assertion of its once having been posited, is crucial to the very possibility of thinking as the speaking of Being, in fact the speaking after Being, of b̶e̶i̶n̶g. This is how mourning becomes Being; for the thinking of Being can be nothing other than the work of mourning. And Heidegger is caught between the overtly regressive character of his fable and his perennial assertion, as in the passage from the *Letter on Humanism* above, of thinking as a future-oriented activity, the possibility of a future so radically future that it could never be.

But the structure of his text demands it. "Most important in this

---

[15] What does a nonrepresentative government look like for Heidegger? This is a real question after the rectorate, where he tries to give us a sketch, or better a performance of an answer, and where his critique of the university is organized precisely around a critique of mimesis. After the war, we see that the mimetic is all that we have, or what we will always lapse back into, and then we get all the sentimental stories. On these questions, see Philippe Lacoue-Labarthe, "La transcendance finie/t dans la politique," in his *L'Imitation des modernes* (Paris: Galilée, 1987).

thought-provoking time is that we are still not yet thinking," Heidegger writes over and over again in his last lecture course, *Was heißt Denken?*, what we call *What is Called Thinking?* But thinking can only be underway toward the thinking we do not yet have, which itself could only have a place in the realm of the monstrous, the unheard of, that which – to speak etymo-pedantically again – can only be shown, but not said, in any kind of representational utterance.

Again: the use of both the middle register and of the double genitive is related to Heidegger's attempt to tunnel through the obstacles related to trying to think in the language of metaphysics. Metaphysics seems to be inadequate to the task of what *Denken*, half-noun, half-verb, should be concerned with. In the case of the crossout – the most innovative of the marks we have considered – the other two are almost anticipations, in the sense that the temporality implied in such a mark, as a reader's mark, moves backwards toward the time when this mark was not there. Thus the fable of the past that we get in the case of the genitive may indeed persist, but almost need not be told. Thinking Being under a cross is what relates the pastness of the past expressed by the other marks to the way things stand now; and the story told of thinking Being *before* the advent of the cross is a story, again, about a time before the non-limited, in-finite verb *Sein* became substantialized as a noun, or before the distinction between noun and verb.

It is this mark that places the grammatical parables associated with the two previous marks in relation to the story about the global situation. And it is curious that, while the mark of the cross is so pregnant with associations, Heidegger gives us no "etymology," true or false, for this overloaded sign. It can bring to mind the blood of the lamb in order to indicate to the angel of death that it should pass over – a gloss, if you will, which is faithful to Heidegger in its kind of saving or sheltering power – or the cross of the Passion, upon which Being, abandoned in its being forgotten or forsaken, dies; or, as a chi, it is the place where everything comes together in its coming apart, in the traversing of a single point; or perhaps it is the crosshairs of the gun sight of a weapon which is both always ready to be fired and at the same time has been fired in a past so long ago that its present, while bringing our present into being, was itself never really present.

Now, has there been any reception, or perhaps better, any reading of Heidegger's grammar? I do not mean piecemeal, positivistic attempts to flesh out any of his particular claims regarding the historical functioning of a particular category in a given text, attempts that would, according to the preceding, be co-implicated in the pseudo-historical schemata Heidegger himself enunciates. What I have in mind is something else.

Has there been any attempt to interrogate the scheme of these grammatical marks taken together as a scheme, not individually? To try to get at what the stakes are in the very idea of this grammatical scheme or scene, the lengthy scene of instruction of this grammar lesson that is Heidegger's corpus? Already, we can hear him protest: to do a reading of the categories I use as categories is to fall prey to the technicist interpretation of language I disallow, etc. But we have seen already how such a disavowal coexists, at the same time, with a necessary leaning on these texts in order for Heidegger to say what he wants to say – about action, or about nihilism, or about the meaning of the word *phenomenon*. And I recall what we have just gone through to remind that all these are not simply words or marks or examples among others in the Heideggerian corpus. We have already highlighted the duplicity of Heidegger's text on this score and shown the impossibility of maintaining absolute fidelity, whatever that would mean, to his singular intention in order to read him. And this is so even if we read him in the most classical, hermeneutical sense, that is to say, in order to make sense of *more* of what is there in order to have less of a nonsensical remainder. We have thus already earned the right to read everything in Heidegger, to take it all seriously; to read the relations, for example, that obtain between marks and tones – also to read recourses.

Heidegger places himself in the position of reader in respect of the tradition, and that of the reader who maintains that the singularity of the greatness of each of the thinkers whom he reads, the greatness of their singularity, has to do with the fact that each of them thinks *one* great thought, and consequently, one un-thought. What is the status of Heidegger's own thinking? In terms of its unthought? In terms of the singularity of its unthought? What is at stake is not only the fact of whether Heidegger could be said to have an unthought at all – since, inasmuch as the series of metaphysical unthoughts amounts to a series of names for Being, that which Heidegger himself is trying to think – but also its unicity in originary gathering. Heidegger's "unthought" is, if anything, the melancholy tone in which the entire fable is told. It looks as though it is a fable about beginnings. But fables about beginnings have their moral in some kind of pronouncement on an interpretation of the situation of where we are now, and here Heidegger is no exception. The problem attendant to Heidegger's attempt to exempt himself from the predicament of having the same kind of unthought – a name for Being – as all the others is his recognition of the fact of what we can call paleonymy, whose law we have already enunciated above: there is no new language, and yet there is a desire for a new language which can be stated in the old language.

Recently, a name has appeared, and it has appeared glossed by a set of definite descriptions (even if these are always, and in particular in this case, inadequate) that relate it to some of the marks we have been discussing. It is not exactly Heidegger's name, although it attempts to explain itself in relation, perhaps, to some of his attributes:

Now the word *différence* (with an *e*) can never refer either to *différer* as temporization or to *différends* as *polemos*. Thus the word *différance* (with an *a*) is to compensate – economically – this loss of meaning, for *différance* can refer simultaneously to the entire configuration of its meanings. It is immediately and irreducibly polysemic, which will not be indifferent to the economy of my discourse here. In its polysemia this word, of course, like any meaning, must defer to the discourse in which it occurs, its interpretive context; but in a way it defers itself, or at least does so more readily than any other word, the *a* immediately deriving from the present participle (*différant*), thereby bringing us close to the very action of the verb *différer*, before it has even produced an effect constituted as something different or as *différence* (with an *e*). In a conceptuality adhering to classical strictures *"différance"* would be said to designate a constitutive, productive, and originary causality, the process of scission and division which would produce or constitute different things or differences. But, because it brings us close to the infinitive and active kernel of *différer*, *différance* (with an *a*) neutralizes what the infinitive denotes as simply active, just as *mouvance* in our language does not simply mean the fact of moving, of moving oneself or of being moved. No more is resonance the act of resonating. We must consider that in the usage of our language the ending *-ance* remains undecided *between* the active and the passive. And we will see why that which lets itself be designated *différance* is neither simply active nor simply passive, announcing or rather recalling something like the middle voice, saying an operation that is not an operation, an operation that cannot be conceived either as passion or as the action of a subject on an object, or on the basis of the categories of agent or patient, neither on the basis of nor moving toward any of these *terms*. For the middle voice, a certain nontransitivity, may be what philosophy, at its outset, distributed into an active and a passive voice, thereby constituting itself by means of this repression.[16]

What Derrida says is concentrated, if not contained, within the word "différance," his verbal *trouvaille*, is a set of literal, verbal, grammatical markers he wants to emphasize as being able, in a sense, to carry the weight he puts on the word – or, perhaps, to disperse it, to disseminate it, so that it may be absolved and weightless. But the overdetermination of this verbal fact – its roots, in the verbal sense, in Hegel, in Saussure, in Heidegger, in others – does not simply allow us to call this word Derrida's invention. Certainly his intervention in the history of the word is strategic. But this lesson in grammar – admittedly a lesson that points out something new in grammar, if one can imagine such an unheard-of thing – rather comments a word which somehow shows itself to itself in itself, and to us at the same time, but emptied of the connotations of interiority that would seem to attend such *phenomenal* language. The word teaches itself too, in a certain fashion, through Derrida's text, by falling into its pieces, by highlighting its very existence as a mark in its tendency to fall into pieces. Derrida is thus an admirer of his own invention, of his own very transitional object.

– Precisely in the sense that a transitional object is not quite an object, in the sense that a stable object would appear as such to a prior-constituted subject. Rather, the transitional object serves as the kind of nexus of opacity around which the subject–object relationship is constructed. Being itself thus prior to any kind of *perception* (of an object by a subject), it is like grammar, like the material, inasmuch as grammar, the name we give to an aspect of the materiality of language, is capable of being made available to a subject by having an interpretation or meaning imposed upon it. But then it is neither material nor grammar. The mark "différance" thus resists being called a word inasmuch as for it thus to be called would risk allowing its misrepresentation as something that

---

[16] Derrida, "Différance," *MP*, 8–9.

existed, its permanence guaranteed by the stability of a set of meanings. It can always fall into such a description. But such a description, in being semantic rather than grammatical (as here, in Derrida's passage), would not be a commentary on the mark as mark, but as word. And "différance" is the mark for which it could be said that there is more (or less) of a hyperbolic difference between it taken as mark and it taken as word than for any other mark or word.[17]

And yet – all the grammatical categories evoked in Derrida's paragraph are not equal. This paragraph is a passage that moves from a set of determinations – all of which it incorporates, phagocytes, vacuolizes, and simultaneously of which it absolves itself – toward a name for a kind of structurally hovering indetermination:[18] the middle voice. But this version of the middle voice, unlike the one bequeathed to us by the grammarians, has nothing to do with interiority.[19] It even has nothing to do with the interiority of Heidegger's gloss on "phenomenon" above. *Différance* operates here as typography, without any register that could be interpreted as any kind of auto-affection whatsoever. This is where the importance of Derrida's *grammatical* treatment lies, and why he has to say "something like the middle voice," rather than to presume to name the middle voice itself.

But this does not mean that Derrida is simply out of the realm of the fictions of the history of grammar, and that he too does not tell his own fables. For at the ending of this passage, the story that is

---

[17] This is a reading of the moment in Levinas at which he insists that the only way to escape the solipsism of idealism is to consider the trace-character of the sign, even if every trace, in its entry into the world, tends to be mistaken *for* a sign.

[18] If not attention. We would have to interrogate what the implications of naming the middle voice are for what is classically conceived of as the analytic attitude itself, "hovering attention." Such an interrogation would have much to say that would problematize any kind of hierarchization of importance between transferential and countertransferential phenomena. It would have to take account of the fact that Freud himself names the middle voice in the register of the obsessional neurotic, and, even more particularly, in the context of the simultaneous activity–passivity of the scopic drive. We would have to try to work out in what way the shift from eye to ear in and as the very bracketing constitutive of the analytic situation itself would be implicated in this activity. It is in this sense that all psychoanalysis takes place, ideally, in its most pure form, over the telephone.

[19] Even if, in the end, it *accounts for* interiority. For this we would have to move to the end of Derrida's essay, and on into the next essay in his *Margins*, "Ousia and Grammē: Note on a Note in *Being and Time*."

being told, in the context of an analysis of a word that would seem to absolve itself of any kind of relation to an originary, productive causality, is a story about what perhaps happened at and as the beginning, at and as the outset. The irruption of philosophy – and we are closer than ever here to the notion of the arrival on the scene of some entity called philosophy in and as the forgetting of Being – may be said to have taken place when the middle was somehow struck[20] into the active and passive.

But the difference between the register of the middle and the combined register of the active–passive system has always been construed as the difference between the interiority of middle verbs – the fact that, as Benveniste says, their action takes place interior to the verbal subject – and active or passive verbs, whose action takes place exterior to the subject of enunciation.[21] And this paradigmatic distinction must, according to the logic of paleonymy and contamination so dear to Derrida, be transferred onto the way we try to think, or better, to write. This is an account of what is up (or down) with the mark "différance."

For the way in which this word falls apart, from the outset, seems somehow to depend, fantastically and unimaginably, in a sheerly fabular (which is not to say untrue) fashion, on the image of an interiority that opened up, whose contents fell out – at and as the outset of philosophy, for example. This is kenosis of the Word, but no apocatastasis.

Derrida's entire argument is that the image should be resisted. But his argument about contamination also demands that the temporal aspect of the story in*terve*ne in a story about grammar, about *langue*, that is to say about the mechanics of a linguistic function that, as such, has to be taken, methodologically speaking,

---

[20] Heidegger uses the word "geprägt" in *Zur Seinsfrage*. But both earlier, in his lecture course of 1936 on *Schelling's Treatise on the Essence of Human Freedom*, and later, in his essay on Trakl (in *Unterwegs zur Sprache* [Pfullingen: Neske, 1959]), he begins to speak of the register of *Geschlecht* in its relationship to *schlagen* and *Schlag*. For the most important commentary on these words, see the series of essays entitled "Geschlecht" by Jacques Derrida, which begins in his *Psyché* (Paris: Galilée, 1987).

[21] According to Benveniste, the original diathetical distinction is between active and middle, between verbs the action of which takes place outside the locutor (a register that thus includes what we today think of as both active and passive verbs), and verbs the action of which takes place within the locutor. The traces of this linguistic *factum* can be seen in Greek middle-voice verbs and in Latin deponent verbs.

as having no history inasmuch as it would be structurally related to other linguistic functions. This account thus leans – simultaneously – on the cardinal precept of synchronic linguistics (language is a system of pure differences with no positive terms – this puts it in terms of the sign – language is a system of functions which taken together make up a grammar – this puts it in terms of function, of grammar) as well as on the nostalgia for the story of the origin that is denounced in the very absolution of the mark under consideration from a notion of origin.

To this extent I readily admit that I have said nothing new. What is said here is already in Derrida's text and will be remarked by any careful reader. But rather than leaving the trajectory of this exercise as a kind of setting-in-place of Derrida within a series whose other terms are (as I have set them up) Heidegger, Heidegger, and Heidegger, we should see which aspects of Heidegger are being combined with which, and by virtue of what kind of intervention. For how can we fail to remark the fact that, whereas the question of the middle voice emerged first in Heidegger very early on, in the first introduction to *Being and Time*, the fabular element of what we would have to do in order to think Being – by tunneling through the history of its forgetting to its provenance before the advent of subjectivity and objectivity, of activity and passivity – takes place later, in a place where middleness as such is not mentioned, but where we can recognize it as (barely even) latent?

Derrida's account combines the naming of the middle category with the fabulous account of pre-history; but it does so by emptying out the middle category of the consciousness-laden significance of interior action. "That which lets itself be designated *différance*" can be mistaken for a term, but is not a term, because it *is* not anything. Likewise that which lets itself thus be called or designated – in other words shown, like a monstrosity – *différance*, can only "announce or recall *something like* the middle voice" [my emphasis], because if it were assimilable to any grammatico-categorial order it would lose its relation to appearing or disappearing, to its auto-performative, if not auto-affective character (and we have to restrict the *auto* immediately as being inadequate to our purposes here, because it would still presume the stability of some previously existing entity).

It is awkward, but in a sense I have to begin again. Up to this point, my argument has been very *neat*. I have shown that there is a set of relations among members of a kind of set of grammatical categories trotted out at several moments in Heidegger's corpus. And, having shown three examples of the kinds of marks I am talking about, I will assume that henceforth I have proposed a series, rather than a set, that anyone can now extend with his own examples. It is not a question of cataloging or of enumerating *all* the places where Heidegger uses or mentions the middle voice, the double genitive, the crosswise overstrike. I have shown that the emphasis given to these kinds of uses and mentions is pervasive and repetitive enough to demand (constantly hovering) attention, and that it should henceforth be impossible to read Heidegger except by taking these things we have called grammatical recourses seriously, especially in the project of reading a text that has so many not very nice things to say about grammar.

Why have we done this?

1. Because it seems to us that there is a certain nexus of relations entwining the use of such categories and what we have already announced as the mark (once again I hesitate to use the word "theme") of the *provisional* such as it pervades Heidegger's text. Everything in Heidegger is a prolegomenon to something else: the First Part of *Being and Time* is a propaedeutic to the non-existent second part; the *Letter on Humanism* announces a history of Being that is never complete but stands ever before; what we know as Heidegger's last text, the prose poem *Der Fehl heiliger Namen*, announces, at and as its end, that only a *séjour à la campagne* in the form of remaining in the clearing would allow us a look into that which *is* today, inasmuch as it is defaulting, etc. We are all so and too familiar with these ever-preparatory statements, which hold out such tantalizing possibilities.

We are also to that degree uncomfortable with them. When those of us who remain fascinated – perhaps the word *interested* is too active and deliberate – by the ever-proclaimed interminable character of reading Heidegger are assailed by a more conventionally historicist reading of the history of philosophy as the history of ideas, we tend to reproduce these same faltering gestures, even in the midst and at the height of our very discomfort with them. Therefore it is time for some honesty about these gestures of stalling and about the gesture of returning to the ground, always to the ground of unthought presuppositions which, I insist, are also the presuppositions of the activity that reduces the history of thinking to the history of ideas and their representations.

Perhaps it is time, therefore, to move on to some attempt to thematize this *recourse*, the recourse to the question of the horizon, lest Heidegger's mourning poem be allowed to repeat itself in our own bedtime rituals. Let us try, therefore, to refuse to be taken in – to put the whole thing in language that is all too polemical – by this series of stammers on the question of the future, and to read these gestures as a stammer, as what Freud would call compulsive, repeated behavior, as when he says, speaking of his grandson in *Beyond the Pleasure Principle*: "and it was truly a long time before this riddling and compulsive repetitious act betrayed its meaning to me."[22] We all know by now that the mere statement of the fact of a repetition does not break the repetitive pattern.

And we all know that the analysis of repetition tends to take us into the realm of the unanalyzable, of the real as that which always returns to the same place. We do not, therefore, pretend that we are involved in any kind of exorcism. We do know, however, that we have nothing to say, and have said nothing, unless we try to treat – if only perhaps to repeat – what appears to us as a repetition.

We have the sense that this attempt to relate the kinds of marks we have been addressing thus far, and the kinds of things we have called fables in which they are embedded – we know that to relate these kinds of fables about the past to the tasks that are held in store for some monstrous future, and thus to the rhetoric of the provisional, is going to be extremely difficult.

2. It seems that someone has tried to produce a persistent meditation on these characteristics of the Heideggerian text, and to relate them to all the themes we have announced, even in his very deployment of the rhetoric of the provisional itself as a

---

[22] My translation of the sentence: "[U]nd es dauerte ziemlich lange, bis das rätselhafte und andauernd wiederholte Tun mir seinen Sinn verriet." Let us remember that all this is being foisted onto a two-year-old child. But why should any adult be granted the privilege of being exempted from the harshness of a reading we would inflict upon a two-year old? Let us read Heidegger as a very inventive child. But let no one think that we are psychoanalyzing him. See Sigmund Freud, *Das Ich und das Es und andere metapsychologische Schriften* (Frankfurt-on-Main: Fischer, 1960), 127.

gesture that cannot be avoided, and that person is Jacques Derrida. Already we have examined the degree to which a crucial passage in Derrida's itinerary can be seen to be a kind of differential redoubling of a certain number of terms in Heidegger's series; how his own activity is a kind of parody of a certain kind of Heideggerian thinking. Let us take for granted, in our own liturgical act of repetition, that a certain experience will come in watching this kind of repetition take place, even if that means entering into it ourselves.[23] This kind of parody admits its own instability, and thus subscribes to no stable notion of the mimetic, which would allow something called a parody to be dismissed as *mere* parody.

Derrida's dream: the gist of geist[24]

Toward the end of Jacques Derrida's 1987 essay on Heidegger, *Of Spirit*,[25] there is a footnote, itself several pages long, within which is to be found the following paragraph, itself placed within square brackets and thus twice removed from the body of the text:

Pause for a moment: to dream of what the Heideggerian corpus would look like the day when, with all the application and consistency required, the operations prescribed by him at one moment or another would indeed have been carried out: "avoid" the word "spirit," at the very least place it in quotation marks, then cross through all the names referring to the world whenever one is speaking of something which, like the animal, has no *Dasein*, and therefore no or only a little world, then place the word "Being" everywhere under a cross, and finally cross through without a cross all the question marks when it's a question of language, i.e., indirectly, of everything, etc. One can imagine the surface of a text given over to the gnawing, ruminant, and silent voracity of such an animal-machine and its

---

23. I use the word "liturgical" here in the etymological sense exposed by Emmanuel Levinas in "La trace de l'autre." Liturgical here thus means a putting out of funds at a loss, which does not quite mean the same thing as kneeling and praying so that you will believe.

24. *Oxford English Dictionary*: "*Gist* ... Also ... *giste* ... *geist* ... 1. A stopping place or lodging ... a list of stopping places or stages in a monarch's progress ... *Gist* ... 1. *Law*. The real ground or point (of an action, indictment, etc.) ... 2. The substance or pith of a matter, the essence or main part."

25. Jacques Derrida, *De l'esprit: Heidegger et la question* (Paris: Galilée, 1987), translated by Geoff Bennington and Rachel Bowlby as *Of Spirit: Heidegger and the Question* (Chicago: University of Chicago Press, 1989). Henceforth OS, followed by page numbers in the English and French editions.

implacable "logic." This would not only be simply "without spirit," but a figure of evil. The perverse reading of Heidegger. End of pause.

(*OS*, 134/152–53)

One of the most evident features of this extraordinarily pregnant pause is that it speaks to each of the four principal themes Derrida has announced from the beginning of his book, namely those of the question, of technology, of animality, and, in a rather eschatological way, of epochality. Thus this paragraph is, in its own way, a kind of response to the questioning demand that follows upon Derrida's announcement of these preoccupations: how to knot these themes together, or is such a knotting a desirable aim or even possible?

Given the comprehensive scope of this short parabasis – comprehensive in regard to Derrida's announcement of his own major concerns – the actual diction and structure of these few sentences is curiously impersonal, evasive, and nonpropositional. At this moment at which Derrida risks knotting together the topoi he has at the outset and expressly chosen as his own, the reader finds him- or herself removed from the main discourse, first by the structural periphrasis of a footnote, then by the *non sequitur* signaled by the square brackets, and finally by a string of infinitives and verbs the grammatical subject of which is the third-person impersonal. Each of these forms of distance makes it difficult to decide whether what is coming down is a directive to do what is necessary, a desire for future gratification expressed in a momentary reverie, or some combination of both. The author's propositional attitude is itself curiously suspended. Suspended, that is, until almost the end, where the necessity of this dream is denounced in the harsh expressions "figure of evil" and "perverse reading of Heidegger."

Why should this reverie-reading be, not only perverse, but indeed an evil reading of Heidegger's corpus, his textual body? We can try to imagine for ourselves a set of responses from the voice of Heidegger's corpse thus affected:

First, it would be evil because it would pretend to do away with the thus morcellated body of Heidegger, whose features would, after such a reading, be visible – or better, legible – only through the wounds, scars, and punctures of this impersonally disfiguring reader's stylus. Thus, the reading performed under the directives of this pause would put an end to the meditative pause of reading

– Heidegger – having thus actively aided in the process of corporeal decomposition.

Second, even if Heidegger wants us, after a certain moment in his own itinerary – a moment which for Derrida is marked by the publication of the essay on Trakl in 1954 – to avoid "spirit," that may not mean that he wants us actively to engage in such anti-spiritual and impious mutilation. Such disfiguration would only testify to a desire for a revenge. It would be of *Geist*, all right, but the *Geist* would be the *Geist der Rache*.

Third, such a disfiguration, by carrying out Heidegger's pre-scriptions, his own kind of spiritual-anti-spiritual *Führung* with regard to his own text, would be mechanical, that is to say, it would be unthinking (according to Heidegger). It would not be able to hold itself back from crossing out all question marks, all occurrences of the word "Being." Thus it would welcome this reading's entry into the zone of utter nihilism. It would be to go badly *trans lineam* and not to tarry, thoughtfully and compellingly, in the tightrope-walking act of the one who walks the line and thinks *de linea*.

Fourth, humanity, thus placed in the position of being unable to read Being except as ~~Being~~, is not far from being world-poor in the way in which the animal is world-poor. And thus such a reading would deport man from his essence – in contradistinction to that of the animal – that is, it would remove him from his rightful dwelling place within the ontological difference. (And what is this, if not Heidegger's surreptitious reintroduction of a humanism beyond humanism in his own purportedly anti-humanist cause?) We would have to meditate here on the difference between the animal, which cannot think the Being of beings, and thus does not have the opening of the world in the ontological difference, and a humanity which, being able to read Being only as crossed out, would itself have *lost* access to the world in its nihilistic forgetting of the ontological difference.[26]

These might be some of the reasons that the spirit of Derrida's letter here speaks of perversion and of evil. I might add that, like many desires expressed in dreams, these reasons have a kind of mutually contradictory kettle logic about them: how else would it

---

[26] See Heidegger's remarks on animality in his *Die Grundbegriffe der Metaphysik, Martin Heidegger Gesamtausgabe*, 29–30 (Frankfurt-on-Main: Klostermann, 1983).

be possible for there to be a revengeful animal-machine? Only, perhaps, in a dream.

But let us try to wake up, if only for a moment, from this nightmare of evil and of mutilating perversion and ask: Is there a possible outside of this dream? Whose is this dream which is denounced as being so awful? And can we avoid being implicated in this dream? Should we even want to?

What the stakes of these questions amount to is whether the evil under discussion is something which can be avoided or is something inevitable, whether it is intrinsic to a reading of Heidegger or extrinsic. If we were to find that such a reading of Heidegger had already begun as a move within his own text, then it would be difficult to dismiss this evil and perverse pause as merely a dream, or simply as *Derrida's* dream. Or, if we thought more of dreams, so that calling something a dream was not tantamount to a dismissal but was itself a positive notation of a phenomenon whose manifestation was worthy of our attention and investigation, then we would not necessarily be able to see our way out of this dream. Perhaps what is in fact gratified in Derrida's – although, as we will see in a moment, it may not be uniquely his or his at all – dream is the wish to see the inexorability of this reading *as* a dream in the first place. It would in fact turn out to be not the presentation of a thought too outrageous to be presented in any way other than in that of a dream, but the manifestation of a certain dis-ease in the rigorous proximity of Derrida's text to Heidegger's own in these pages.

While what I am suggesting about a possible wish in Derrida's text to shelter itself from contamination certainly goes against what is often taken to be Derrida's stated intention, namely to insist upon contamination of the ontological difference wherever it might occur in Heidegger, or of Heidegger's text by his own, it is worth saying that such moments of contiguity are anxious moments and are not to be felt without ambivalence. In respect of this it is worth noting that *Of Spirit* marks what is for Derrida an unprecedented change of tone, exemplified, for example, in his distancing of his reading of Heidegger from his reading of Freud, a distancing that leaves its mark in the extremely rare, highly qualified, and always very general references to something called "psychoanalysis" in these pages. These references tend to be explicit about the inability of psychoanalysis to contribute to a discussion of the matter of Being, or to mark the use of words like "foreclosion" as being unable to qualify certain moments of the Heideggerian trajectory inasmuch as they are too embedded in the discourse of psychoanalysis. This distancing would have been inconceivable as recently as in the major essays of *The Post Card*,[27] and the presence of these contra-restrictions in the absence of any complementary pro-choices indicates yet again the degree of proximity of Derrida's voice to Heidegger's own here.

Often would-be dismissals of Derrida take place around the site of the purported perversity of his readings or of his supposedly cavalier treatment of texts. The ignorance of these pseudo-attacks is wearying and boring. The more interesting matter is that of the places within Derrida's own text, such as in the passage under consideration, where there is a commingling of voices, of the voices of Derrida and of the text about which he writes, to the point that it becomes impossible to distinguish them. This is a fact worthy of interrogation, particularly, as is the case here, when the other voice is that of Heidegger, with the summoning of whose text a certain register of inevitability and of necessity always comes powerfully into play.

What is often mistaken as perversity in Derrida is perhaps best summed up under the heading of *tone*. Professional philosophers are not, in general, trained to treat tone as a matter worthy of consideration in philosophical discourse. Even among students of literature a more rigorous and sustained reflection on the language game of tone is an important project which has not received enough recent consideration. This is no doubt due to moves on the part of many theoreticians of literature to try to distance themselves from the ideological baggage of some of the New Critics. But the New Critics are still models of what reading can do, and the matter of tone is an instance of the way in which institutional philosophy (how much of any other kind is there today?) could benefit from the intervention of so-called literary discourse. The widely proclaimed need for a corrective to the literary excesses of the American literary reception of Derrida misses the point in this respect: there will be *no* real reception of Derrida as long as such "literary" dimensions as tone are avoided in a call for textually oriented critics simply to give up their calling and speak a purely

---

[27] Jacques Derrida, *La Carte postale de Socrate à Freud et au–delà* (Paris: Aubier-Flammarion, 1981).

conceptually oriented discourse. Philosophers will get it wrong as long as their reading proceeds at a purely conceptual level; likewise critics who ignore aspects of transcendental–critical discourse and insist that there is only the random play of the signifier miss the point.

Whose "evil" is this anyway? Who is denouncing the desire to follow Heidegger's own prescriptions *vis à vis* his own text as evil? Is Derrida passing this judgment on his own momentary reverie, as though censoring it in order to allow it into consciousness and into print? Did it go through his consciousness at all? There is no clear narrative break in Derrida's pause that would indicate the passage from something we could call Derrida's voice to that of Heidegger. *This* contamination is what is indeed so startling about this paragraph; and it may mark with even greater insistence than heretofore the radical *continuity* between what are conventionally thought of as Heidegger's and Derrida's texts.

Let us retreat from the large and weighty generality of these questions and attempt to reformulate them, perhaps in a more pragmatic manner. Are there places in his corpus where Heidegger has gone back, in a kind of recursive scanning, and made the kinds of (thus self-inflicted) reader's marks which are the matter of Derrida's dream?

The opening paragraphs of the *Letter on Humanism* are a case in point, at least in the version Friedrich Wilhelm von Herrmann has given us in the 1976 *Gesamtausgabe* edition of *Wegmarken*, which contains what, in the context of this *Ausgabe letzter Hand*, we might take to be Heidegger's last version of this historically decisive text. At the end of the first paragraph, as a note to the word "Sein" in the sentence "Das Sein als das Element des Denkens ist in der technischen Auslegung des Denkens preisgegeben" ("Being, as the element of thinking, is abandoned by the technical interpretation of thinking"), occurs the following marginal note: "Sein als Ereignis: die Sage; Denken; Entsagen die Sage des Ereignisses" ("Being as Ereignis: the Legend; Thinking: To renounce the legend of the Ereignis"). And then, more noticeable for our purposes, the following sentence, "Die Strenge des Denkens besteht im Unterschied zu den Wissenschaften nicht bloß in der künstlichen, das heißt technischen-theoretischen Exaktheit der Begriffe" ("The rigor of thinking, in contrast to that of the sciences, does not consist merely in the artificial, that is, technico-theoretical exactness of concepts"), has been marked with the following marginalium: "das Denken hier schon angesetzt als Denken der Wahrheit des ~~Seins~~" ("thinking here already put forth as thinking of the truth of ~~Being~~") (*W*, 315).

These two marginalia were found by von Herrmann in Heidegger's copy of the 1949 Klostermann edition of the *Letter*.[28] It is not possible to say exactly when they were made. But while the 1955 text of *Zur Seinsfrage*, the text in which Heidegger first *published* the *kreuzweise Durchstreichung*, is itself fairly untouched by Heidegger's later hand (at least according to von Herrmann's indications), the *Letter* (as well as the following essay in the *Gesamtausgabe Wegmarken* volume, the introduction to *What is Metaphysics?*) contains several similar notes, in which Heidegger has crossed out the word "Sein" in marginalia the editor also takes from Heidegger's copy of the fifth (1949) edition of that text.

Regardless as to whether Heidegger began to write the word ~~being~~ in 1949, the point is that the cross operates as a reader's mark, moving back from its first – printed – occurrence in the 1955 text of *The Question of Being*. Regardless of the exact date of Heidegger's marginalia, and of their vulgar-temporal relation to the first publication of the crossout of Being in *Zur Seinsfrage* – prospective or retrospective – the point is that Heidegger *did* make the gesture of moving backwards – or forwards – through his own corpus and of leaving there the marks of the prescriptions he makes in other, earlier or later, texts.

Thus it cannot be asserted that Derrida's dream is simply *his* dream, for it is Heidegger himself who began the process of the conversion of his own text into his – Heidegger's or Derrida's – dream text. My question above, namely, "What is evil in respect of all this?," might now be given yet another formulation: Having shown what I have shown of Heidegger's scanning of his own text, the question concerning evil might now be posed as the question of knowing where to start or to stop – or better yet, of *not* knowing where to start or to stop – crossing out. And this, of course, only pushes the question one step further back. For with the master himself having secured for us perhaps an exemplary reading of his own texts, how are we other, presumably later readers to know

[28] Martin Heidegger, *Über den Humanismus* (Frankfurt-on-Main: Klostermann, 1949).

when we would be writing "good" crosses and when we would be writing "evil" ones?[29]

It may be possible to give our question – which is not a rhetorical question in the superficial sense – a different inflection than we have done so far, one which seems to belong to another thematic which also runs through Heidegger's work. The opening of the *Letter on Humanism* is concerned with a discussion of the relationship of the essence of human action to thinking. Let us recall it.

"Thinking," says Heidegger, "accomplishes the relation of Being to the essence of Man," and is not simply to be thought of as that which leads to action, but as the "action" of the accomplishment of this relation itself. Following upon this opening statement is the introduction of the famous double genitive: "penser," (says Heidegger in the language in which Jean Beaufret addresses him, and speaking presumably of Sartre) "c'est l'engagement pour l'Etre par l'Etre," upon which utterance Heidegger then asks the question as to whether it is possible to state this more economically and say: "penser, c'est l'engagement de l'Etre" (*BW*, 193–94, *W*, 313–14).

The grammatical vehicle of the double genitive permits the expression of a simultaneously double subject-object relation, in which the nouns on both sides of the particle are both subject and object to and of each other. Yet, at the same time, there is the familiar parable – the legend, *die Sage* – Heidegger immediately goes on to tell about how this is an attempt to say in our language what we can only say approximately, after its fall in its having been taken over by the villains of "Western 'grammar' and 'logic.'" Can we even imagine this? In the light of this story, we realize that we must add that in this genitive, not only are both terms *both* subjective and objective, but they are both also neither. They are something else, related in some other way than can be said with these terms, which are *our* terms, the only ones we have. Thus what is expressed in the double genitive is the paradoxical tension of this flickering simultaneity.

This is related to another of our already discussed grammatical

---

[29] The ceremony at which the four questions are asked, always by the youngest present, is the Passover *Seder*, which commemorates the passing of the Angel of Death, and the sparing of the firstborn of the Israelites by marking in the blood of the lamb on their doorways. This mark thus selects and saves, by condemning that which is *not* crossed out. And Derrida's little *Geist*-Haggadah is also a book about a deportation and a destruction. Conversations preparatory to the writing of *Of Spirit* took place in New Haven during Passover in 1986.

themes, that of the middle voice. The double genitive, used for the attempt to tunnel back to a pre-grammatical, pre-metaphysical *Ursprache*, is another version of what we have been exposed to as early as *Being and Time* in a thematic manner, and as late as in the discussion of the "es gibt Sein" of *On Time and Being*. And beyond those well-known texts, I want to argue, we must also read it in a crucial utterance, in the 1974 prose poem *Der Fehl heiliger Namen*.[30]

In this very late text, which Lacoue-Labarthe and Munier have referred to as a kind of testament, there occurs the following, definitional sentence: "Dichten – meint hier: sich sagen lassen den reinen Anruf des Anwesens als solchen, und sei dieses auch nur und gerade ein Anwesen des Entzuges und des Vorenthaltes," "Poetizing – means here: to let say to oneself the pure call of coming to presence as such, even if this be only and precisely the coming to presence of a withdrawal and of a holding back." – This would be the conventional translation of the "sich sagen lassen." But, I want to argue, it should not be "to let *one* say to *oneself* the pure call of coming to presence as such," etc., but rather "to let (*it*) say to *itself* the pure call of coming to presence as such." This is a sentence in which the infinitive–accusative construction "sich sagen lassen *den* reinen Anruf" should be read not in the sense that the pure call is the object of what we would conventionally call a reflexive verb, but as the subject–object, as it were, of that verb, in the manner in which the Latin poets wrote accusative–infinitive constructions as devices for the purpose of transliterating, if not translating, Greek middle-voice verbs. How ironic that when Heidegger wants to write Greek in German – given his famous remarks to the *Spiegel* about how the French have to speak German when they want to think, otherwise they don't make it – he, Heidegger, has to speak a postlapsarian Latin.

In fact, after the parenthesis in Derrida's note which I have discussed above, the note proper continues outside the brackets:

To the extent that, in this singular situation which relates it to a pledge of this kind, thought is a "listening" (*Hören*) and a letting-oneself-say (*Sichsagenlassen*), and not a questioning (*kein Fragen*), then, says Heidegger, "we must still cross through the question marks." Which, he adds, does not mean a return to the habitual form of the title. That is no longer

---

[30] First published, with a translation by Philippe Lacoue-Labarthe and Roger Munier, in *Contre toute attente* 3/4, now reprinted in Martin Heidegger, *Denkerfahrungen* (Frankfurt-on-Main: Klostermann, 1983).

possible. The "letting itself be said" which urges the crossing through of the question mark is not a passive docility, much less an uncritical compliance. But no more is it a negative activity busy submitting everything to a denial that crosses through [*une dénégation raturante*]. It subscribes. Before us, before everything, below or above everything, it inscribes the question, negation or denial, it en-gages them without limits in the correspondence with *langue* or *parole* (*Sprache*). *Parole* must *first* pray, address itself to us: put in us its trust, its confidence, depend on us, and even have *already* done it (*muß sich die Sprache zuvor uns zusagen oder gar schon zugesagt haben*). The *already* is essential here, saying something of the essence of this *parole* and of what en-gages in it. At the moment when, in the present, it entrusts or addresses itself to us, it has *already* done so, and this past never returns, never again becomes present, it always goes back to an older event which will have already engaged us in this subscribing to the en-gage.   (*OS*, 134–35/153)

Ignoring Bennington and Bowlby's incorrect translation of "Sich-sagenlassen" as "letting-oneself-say," what Derrida himself is saying here is that to the extent that thought participates in or is (de)constituted by this kind of middle-voiced verb, the question, as such, is still a form that contains within it too much of the propositional (the matter which is asked after in the question). The performance of the middle verb, which posits the subject which can then, later, *ask* the question, is itself the prayer of a spoken word, a word given (*parole*), of a speech act without an agent or speaker. Speech, in its address to an as yet non-existent *we* or *us*, addresses us, conjures us into the response of our own speech, which only then *asks after* it.

Evil here, then, would assume another form of and in a translation, in the fall, as Heidegger ubiquitously puts it in this theologically loaded setup, from the unspeakable language of thinking into the subject–object-relations language of metaphysics. But the fact is that this *Ursprache* is a kind of dream, a fantastic dream of something which never existed and which could never exist, except as the fabular product of Heidegger's own story, a story in which thinking, lost with the violent overthrow of pre-Socratic language by Socratic and ontological–metaphysical questioning, is to be regained with Heidegger himself, in *his* instauration of thinking. Too late for the gods, have we not read, and too early for Being. Being's *Dichten*, just begun again, is Heidegger. And poetry is of course that which tells this story, the telling of this very story, in the interregnum between thinking of early and thinking of late: After all, is not what is most thought-provoking, in this thought-provoking time, the fact that we still are not yet thinking? Thinking may never have existed and may never exist, but poetry is every true word which can be spoken in this middle age between the original gift of the subject to thinking and our own, belated thinking.

Evil, then, is the name of a fabular structure, in the rhetorical–descriptive sense of the word fable. It is a story that can be told in terms of animal-machines macerating the corpses of texts such as those of Heidegger, or in terms of the arrival of the latest forms of subjectivity and of nihilism. It is always told as the story of the regression away from a primary event, in other words, as the story of a Fall. But it is a name for this circular structure of a Fall from that which never existed – except, that is, in this (pastoral) narrative – into that which *is* today – and always, or into that which itself may never exist. Here evil is the structure of time.

I would like to suggest that Heidegger thinks this structure everywhere, and to discuss the sentence which the editors excerpted to serve as the title from the *Spiegel* interview of 1966–76 (the editors in this case may be assumed to include Heidegger, who, as we know, himself closely reviewed the protocols of the discussion), "Nur noch ein Gott kann uns retten."[31] This sentence has most often been translated into English as the apocalyptic or even post-apocalyptic cry or reactionary moan of Heidegger, practicing his "peasant cunning." "Only a god can save us," as we are told in one translation into English, or "only a god can save us now," as we read in another.[32] But what if we read what Heidegger said not as "nur noch ein *Gott* kann uns retten," but as "nur *noch ein* Gott kann uns retten", only *another* god can save us now? This would be a more gnostically truthful statement in which god, the other god, or more modestly, an other god, would be the god not of the pure presence-absence of our standard theologies, but a god which had within it this movement of the Fall into its creation and into time. This true story of god tells another story about the fabular necessity of evil.

---

[31] See "Nur noch ein Gott kann uns retten": Spiegel-Gespräch mit Martin Heidegger am 23 September 1966 in *Der Spiegel*, 31 May 1976.

[32] For the one and the other – but not for another – see " 'Only a God Can Save Us' ": *Der Spiegel*'s Interview with Martin Heidegger, in *Philosophy Today*, 20:4, 4; and " 'Only a God Can Save Us Now' ": an Interview with Martin Heidegger, in the *Graduate Faculty Philosophy Journal*, 6:1.

3

Absolute constructions: an essay at Paul de Man

[N]ot less blatant . . . for being different . . .[1]

To crack a nut is truly no feat, so no one would ever dare to collect an audience in order to entertain it with nut-cracking. But if all the same one does do that and succeeds in entertaining the public, then it cannot be a matter of simple nut-cracking. Or it is a matter of nut-cracking, but it turns out that we have overlooked the art of cracking nuts because we were too skilled in it and that this newcomer to it first shows us its real nature, even finding it useful in making his effects to be rather less expert in nut-cracking than most of us.[2]

Getting started

It is all a matter of arrangement, that is to say, of constellation. Hence the melancholy that comes of putting things in order, things that have been collected, like quotations and questions, minor obsessions, over a very long period of time.

I have tried to construct a kind of rebus. A rebus of gestures, I am almost tempted to say motifs, out of the work of Paul de Man. Into this have flowed all the things I have been thinking about for many years, a certain number of micrologies, not so much about reading

---

[1] See de Man, *BI*, 127: "With perfect right, within the logic of his own argument, which would consider these passages as redundant or dealt with elsewhere in the commentary. The validity of my emphasis has to stand on its own merits and be responsible for its own omissions, not less blatant than Derrida's for being different." This is the only unnumbered note in *BI*.

[2] Franz Kafka, "Josephine the Singer, or the Mouse Folk," in his *The Complete Stories*, ed. Nahum Glatzer (New York: Schocken, 1971), 361–62.

de Man reading as about reading de Man writing. I have tracked certain words and phrases, involuntarily, and the cross-references and crisscross references have waited, patiently, and proliferated. Now the moment of arrangement has come. I have to construct a certain set of internal relations within a text. The languages that have offered themselves for the task are the only words I have. These words are sometimes tied to a theological sphere, sometimes tied to the sphere of poetics, to themes and gestures from the history of philosophy, always to the hovering attention of psychoanalysis. There is also a certain language of tone and of the humors that has asserted itself over the years.

Several years ago, filled only with theoretical zeal, I would have disdained the language of tone, for example, as being merely impressionistic or imprecise, in any case as belonging to another era of criticism. Now I ask myself, what is or should be the reading of philosophical texts that goes on in departments of literature, if it is not to be reduced to a vulgar kind of theoretism that seeks only to emulate a macho, hard-core discourse of concepts?

I have been terrified of this essay. The prospect of amassing all of my scattered notes and observations fills me with an anxiety more severe than that I feel on leaving the house every morning. The possibility haunts me that, having cracked, I think, pretty much every one of de Man's codes at one time or another, I might lose the sequence, or never find the thread of my own narrative in which I would subject the rest of the world to the exhilaration of my own anxieties.

This essay has had almost as many titles as it has had failed beginnings, all of them defective and mournful corpses which I yet want to subsume within this newer one. "Absolute Constructions," the title of the present version, an attempt at an attempt, presents itself in the current circumstances as perfect.

In its grammatical usage, an absolute construction is so called because it is independent of its grammatical surroundings. Ablative in Latin, genitive in Greek, the kind of clause to which I refer has something of the unconditioned condition about it. I take as an example a sentence fragment I heard awhile ago in a café, when someone at the neighboring table uttered the expression: "Assuming that Jupiter is not necessarily a right-wing planet . . ." – That is an example of an absolute construction. Or it can be, depending on whether what follows is or is not modified by it. If what follows modifies "Jupiter," then the phrase is not absolute; but if the sentence into which I splice my string continues "I will go on to write about Paul de Man," or "I will go on to draw connections between aspects of Paul de Man's texts that have not yet been drawn, and between his texts and others whose echoes I hear and read there," then I have performed a kind of absolute construction, one whose very logic of (in)dependence depends, for its structure, on what I do with it.

The figurology of this kind of grammar is even richer, though. For already it is enmeshed in the later work of Paul de Man, at all the moments, starting with "The Rhetoric of Temporality," when the emphasis begins to fall on so-called grammatical figures, most particularly on the non-tropes associated with what de Man, in a discussion of irony, calls anacoluthon or parabasis, or, citing F. W. Schlegel, permanent parabasis. These moments are associated with attempts de Man is in the course of examining to define or de-define irony. They are figures of the break, of the break between sign and meaning, between consciousness and speaking, between consciousness and itself.

When I insert the absolute construction into this series, I coordinate it with lists of things that don't or won't coordinate, that won't cooperate in our attempts to ordinate them.[3] Absolute constructions can therefore serve as another name for the kind of disjunction or *enchevêtrement* that de Man, in his later work as in his earlier work, is often at pains to assert. Between the statement of literature and that of criticism, between "literary experience and literary theory," (*AI*, 91), between the author's – or reader's – self and work, between the center of a work and the origin of that work, between the holy or sacred and the word that ruins it. It is not simply a question of adding another name to the series, however; or it should not be, unless we can demonstrate the heuristic value of this name over the alternatives.

Therefore I want to point out a tension in the structure of the absolute construction of the kind I mentioned more or less humorously above. The absoluteness of "assuming that Jupiter is

---

[3] Recall the moment in de Man's discussion of Benjamin's "The Task of the Translator" where translation is likened and unlikened to several different discourses, those of epistemology, criticism or literary theory, and history, things that are alike only in that they are not like that from which they spring. (*RT*, 82–83.)

not necessarily a right-wing planet" is, to use the kind of language de Man would use, positional. Its absoluteness, its independence is dependent on what follows or precedes.

And yet this positional character does not depend on any matter of ideation, or even of figuration, but sheerly on grammar, sheerly on the mechanical. We are not far away from moments in the *Philosophical Investigations* where Wittgenstein discusses the possibilities of language games constructed entirely of questions or of jokes, but does not want to say that this would make the form of the question or the joke irrelevant. For what would not be *said*, the specificity of a question as a verbal form among others, would be *shown* as the form of the standard utterance in those hypothetical languages.[4] We are also, however, not far from the end of the first paragraph of de Man's essay, "The Resistance to Theory," where we learn that "[t]he difficult and inconclusive history of literary theory indicates that this is indeed the case [the critical status of the object of inquiry in question] for literature in an even more manifest manner than for other verbal occurrences such as jokes, for example, or even dreams." (*RT*, 4). "Critical" should be taken here in its relation to "crisis."[5] Even if de Man always denounces the cry of a crisis as the attempt to recuperate patterns of language into historicizing discourse that would purport but would always fail to explain these patterns, I insist that we are always in at least one crisis in de Man. It can be a manic kind of crisis, as I will discuss at length below, or, perhaps, a nuclear crisis: "As we say of bombs that they overkill, we can say of literature that it over-means" (*RC*, 171).

But the subtle put-down of psychoanalysis is even more the most direct kind of praise: it says that the ontological status of an entity that may not even turn out to exist (namely literature) has to be thought along the lines, analogous if not identical, developed to discuss the kinds of verbal phenomena taken seriously perhaps for the first time by psychoanalysis. Literature is an even more

---

[4] That's a little bit violent to the Wittgenstein of the *Investigations*, inasmuch as it is there that the saying/showing distinction originally put forth in the *Tractatus* breaks down, but we still need to lean on it in order to describe how and where it breaks down. We cannot get rid of it absolutely. This logic of paleonymic survival is what we shall have learned from Derrida and Heidegger as a tool in the reading of the history of philosophy: deconstruction is not simply an infantile–leftist overturning. We're always going to be climbing the ladder.

[5] De Man explores this relation in "Criticism and Crisis," the first chapter of *BI*.

complex code. Hence the preliminary characterization of the difficulties of the craggy field of literary theory, the ontological status of whose object is so difficult that one always, in the characteristic de Manian move, thus has to begin by a retreat away from the general question – "What is literature?" – to a discussion of the example, in the same way that Freud's most pedagogical texts, the *Introductory Lectures*, work – on jokes, slips, and dreams – by example.

The term *absolute constructions* also refers to all my scraps, drafts, and notes: in order to write this I must be free of them; for they oppress me maddeningly. Thus this attempt, if it is to succeed, must break out of the paralysis imposed upon it from the outset by the accretion disk of this circle of thoughts. Obviously, however, and at the same time, the expression "absolute constructions" refers to the whole register of what we have come to call fictions, made objects that preoccupy us as pieces of language. In order to consider these made objects, I may have to treat them somewhat as found objects, what Kurt Schwitters called Merz. Merz is the art of the *bricoleur*, the jack-of-all-trades. It is also a name for shit.

This must be a thinking that is differently enabled from the more surgical aspects of the cryogenic eye surgery everybody thinks Paul de Man performs. But "[t]he validity of my emphasis has to stand on its own merits, not less blatant . . . for being different," as de Man says at the center of the very essay where he is about to make his critical swerve from Derrida, and where it is a question thus of his proto-Oedipal individuation from this younger, blinding source, a light from which de Man, to use another of his favorite figures, frequently must shelter himself.[6] If Derrida thinks that he is the son, a sentiment he expresses in "Psyche,"[7] his mourning poem to de Man, written within a couple of weeks of de Man's death, the situation presented to us in the agrammatical little starred note from which I take my epigraph is at least a little more complex. Who is to say whether de Man and Derrida actually had heterotextual or even incestuous encounters in writing about each other, or whether the strength of the paradoxes of primary narcissism has had them have encounters only with themselves? The truth, as always, is somewhere in between, in the middle.

---

[6] Neil Hertz has written a commentary on shelter – among other things – in de Man. See his "Lurid Figures" in *RMR*.

[7] In Jacques Derrida, *Psyché* (Paris: Galilée, 1987). English in *WG*.

Absolute constructions: how are these constructed? And how to comment them? Well, I have had to leave surgery behind and adopt the Yiddishkeit of a little bit of tinkering. I will proceed in a manner I call locating strings. I weave my absolute constructions, my delusional musings on de Man's text, out of strings I find therein. But who knows if these strings are there, if there is a necessary link between the things I string together, or if I should be in doubt as to my own sanity, as Saussure was when he discovered the anagrams? Some of these strings, needless to say, split into more than one and even more than two fibers, no two fibers running all the way through the gross constituent units of the string, *à la* Wittgenstein's commentary on the red threads of the British Navy. I weave my constructions out of strings, the kinds of strings Winnicott's child-patients play with – perhaps in imitation of the telephone – and which thus serve, in that analysis, as transitional objects.

Pre-emptying the question: the father's nos

It is necessary to own up to the violence of making an incision into any text in order to say something about it. In any choice of a point of entry, there are only the Borgesian alternatives – an infinite number – that have been left out. It is easy to write in a systematic and resumptive manner, to assume that by creating a system out of anything one has absolved oneself of the anxiety of having made one's own mark, touched something. Thus the system will always bear the scar of this denial. It is more difficult to try, at the terrible risk of failing, to make one's own choices in regard to a text which is really only a set of texts purportedly about other texts, whose author refused to write systematically – and yet there are always those very carefully couched and coy moments. Such is always the case with the text of Paul de Man, into whose text I have already delved here, having made my fitful beginning.

Some will already say: You have already lost, because you have subjectivized everything. I say: Yes, I have made my beginning, but nothing is foreclosed – yet. Whoever tries to read this text, the text of Paul de Man, will lie if they do not make such a statement about the beginning. De Man's text has such a beguiling, fascinating power over those who have already been seduced. This is the trap: if I take everything he seems to say *to the letter*, what I will never do is comment his text. For his text says: Do not read me, read what I read, or, like the lesson of the Good Samaritan – or of the Dead Father, or Grandfather, or of the Evil Grandmother – go and do thou likewise. But this is not to have dealt with the seduction, or to have accounted for the fact that we have come to be reading him and taking him seriously at all, as though this were the most self-evident thing. So to the ones who make these objections, I say, in continuing with my beginning, that I take my own risks; that this is what I think everyone should be doing; and that whatever the stronger move is will prove itself in the long run (perhaps to be the wrong one). Otherwise one is condemned to sheerly mechanical repetition, paralysis, or gross systematization. And none of these alternatives is acceptable.

Make it hard.

Let us not think that we have put all the traps to rest, however. The injunction to read what I, Paul de Man, read, not what I write, this *noli me legere* itself has further complications. For its reason is not ungrounded, but would seem to appear to allow itself to be paraphrased thus: Every text will have its singular (un)raveling, and any attempt to put one and one and one together to get a master text will result in a falsification of the occurrences of each of the texts, which can thus only be lined up in the violence of an infinite or open enumerative series, a hypotactic non-pattern which already does violence enough, even if one has already developed a sophisticated reading of the series of commas separating the terms of the series, which is in fact possible.

Every text will have its singular (un)raveling, the navel of its own dream. That means: if a system could only take its tools from a given text, and if every text refuses to be a system in its own way, then what we are left with is an injunction to the most sheer nominalism. We can only say: this, this, this. Even putting an "and" before the last member of the series has a certain violence of the summary about it. To put all these failed deictics *in a line* is even more violent; for before we think about the commas, we should think about the absolute falsification involved in pretending that such absolutely heterogeneous occurrences as texts *occur* in series at all, rather than admitting what is true, namely that we make these series.

The *no* of this nominalism explains itself thus: Do not write about me, do not take me as text,[8] because if you do, you will get lost in an

---

[8] "... einen Text als Text ablesen zu können, ohne eine Interpretation dazwischen zu mengen, ist die späteste Form der 'inneren Erfahrung,' – vielleicht eine kaum mögliche . . ." (Nietzsche, cited in the epigraph to "The Rhetoric of Blindness"

endless series of qualifications, self-recriminations, Chinese boxes, vicious regressions, reservations – as you in fact already have begun to do. You will always be writing and unwriting at the same time; you will not have the olympian stature of mind which would be necessary to write about me; you will leave out missing steps, your argument will be flawed; you will always have started in the wrong place; everything will devolve into a kind of obsessional neurotic behavior – and I have seen it happen. Even in deciding to write about me – or in feeling compelled to write about me, whatever – you still will have had to submit to my law, that is to say to the law of the text I have laid down before you; for that is the lesson I have taught you.

Make it harder.

I myself have enough piety still left in me to worry about this. (Sorting out what true piety is will have to come out at the other end – and this is not the last of the promises I will have to make, in my impatience and in my need to get on with it – promises which will have to be fulfilled and no doubt also defaulted upon later.) – To be saying to myself, already: Nobody you will want to take this seriously will do so, because you have already violated too many codes, of honor, of an unspoken kind of textual ethics, perhaps of *omertà*. I want to get to the root of this ethics, and see what's going on there. I want to take my own risks. I want to do my own cutting and pasting. I want to write my own essay. I want many things – some of them I'm sure I don't even know and probably never will, and no doubt can't have. At least the appearance of extreme violence is necessary. I'm not sure it could be carried out in an utterly tranquil tone, as others have tried to do.

Read my lips (*noli me legere*)

Let's try to get down to some brass tacks. Make it hardest.

In reading de Man, what I want most to avoid is piety. Piety is not the same as high fidelity. Paul de Man's text seems to say: Do not read me, read the things I read as I read them and go out and multiply readings of everything in the universe as I would have done them, read my lips; read me. Only don't read me.

[*BI*, 102]). This epigraph serves as a warning to anyone who might be foolish enough to believe that Paul de Man even dreams of taking a text as text, without any element of selection, arbitrariness, or compulsion on the part of the reader.

Don't come too close. Or the game will be up. Don't read my lips.[9]

This silent injunction must be thought and fought. De Man must be read in the same way in which he reads – with both care and a certain amount of perversity. (I hesitate to say arbitrariness, lest anyone think the worst, but I will have more to say about arbitrariness anon.) Paul de Man must be taken apart and put back together again so that all the cracks are visible. I think of his comments on Benjamin:

All you have to do, to see that, is translate correctly, instead of translating like Zohn – who made this difficult passage very clear – but who in the process of making it clear made it say something completely different. Zohn said, "fragments of a vessel which are to be glued together must match one another in the smallest detail." Benjamin said, translated by Carol Jacobs, word by word, "fragments of a vessel, in order to be *articulated* together" – which is much better than *glued* together, which has a totally irrelevant concreteness – "must *follow* one another in the smallest detail" – which is not at all the same as *match* one another. What is already present in this difference is that we have *folgen*, not *gleichen*, not to match. We have a metonymic, a successive pattern, in which things follow, rather than a metaphorical unifying pattern in which things become one by resemblance. They do not match each other, they follow each other; they are already metonyms and not metaphors; as such they are certainly less working towards a convincing tropological totalization than if we use the term "match." (*RT*, 90–91)

This is the way I hope to work with the text of Paul de Man. In order to do this it is necessary for me *not* to do certain things. One of the things it is necessary for me not to do is to think that one should take apart only one of his essays and consider it along with the text it hopes and purports to read, its intertext.[10] I cannot do this, and it is necessary for my project not to do this. It is a work of

---

[9] The superb pages on de Man in John Guillory's *Cultural Capital* (Chicago: University of Chicago Press, 1993) discuss the matter of the discipleship following upon de Man as a matter of transference transferred. It is astonishing for me to see many of the insights it took me years to glean from closer readings of de Man's text presented by Guillory in the thick description of an institutional context. Unfortunately, his work has remained unread by those whose predicament is best described in it.

[10] This would be to perform the same kind of analysis as that of positivists working on Foucault, who would take *Les Mots et les choses* apart, chapter by chapter, and say how Foucault got x or y discourse wrong. The point is rather that there is something important to be learned from the pattern – if it exists – of deflection that shines forth from the whole.

patience and of a kind of piety to which I am constitutionally unsuited. I have been marking up Paul de Man's texts for fifteen years with little notes in my own steadily evolving – and sometimes dissolving, I cannot truly say that I still know what all my old marks mean, I am a memory, among other things – code. If I were to sit down with fresh copies of all the books and essays still scattered, or manuscripts not yet printed, I would get ahold of a box of pens of different colors and use them according to some legend I would construct – now, at this closeness or distance. (I'm sure I would forget everything and it would all fall to pieces the very same day.) But I do not have these clean copies and will not: already I have enough stories to tell about Paul de Man's stories, scattered in all my little notes, in the margins and on the flyleaves of all his books, in computer files, and now here.

If I were to undertake this kind of patient, systematic *Toposforschung*, automatically it would preclude dealing with the material in the fashion I think will be most fruitful for me, that is in reading across the corpus and commenting the things that stick out to me by virtue of their (in)consistency, urgency, compulsion to repeat, general weirdness, recurring hypogrammata and their deformations, and so on. I can only hope that the necessity of the account will turn out to be not merely personal, even if it is a little bit idiosyncratic; and that in the end my assertion of the necessity at least of beginning with these gestures will spare me having to confront the accusation of having written merely an impressionistic account, or a case study in obsessional appreciation.

The other thing I must not, will not do is to attempt any kind of conspective approach. It would be folly to try this or to pretend to say anything about Paul de Man's *œuvre*, as a rule and as a whole. I say this too here at the outset, and in addition I assert that such attempts on the part of others have struck me thus far as notoriously wrong-headed, boring, and sloppy. So I will not and must not be conspective; and I must not merely be singular in terms of my textual object choices. There are intellectual grounds for what might at first glance appear to be these apparently violently and apodictically stated versions of my own arbitrariness, capriciousness, willfulness, sloppiness, orneriness, or laziness – I have adventured a couple of these already.

Treatment of a single text, while it can be very strong indeed, risks losing the strength of being able to observe repetitions, even wearying repetitions. It also risks canonizing a certain vestige of organic form in respect of de Man's essays, which is the very organicity-as-monumentalization they predict, and the necessity of the interrogation of which they also ceaselessly demand. To attack seems to mean, first off, to make something fall to pieces. But to make something fall to pieces ruins nothing, but monumentalizes contrariwise.

On the other hand, trying to do everything risks banalizing generalization and massive superficiality, and, even more, risks falsifying all of the detotalizing and anti-systematic power (which is not in itself simple, but strongly ambivalent), which is such a strong and deep current in de Man's work. I would maintain that this work is elastic enough – even in its very non-compromising tone and continually deployed rhetoric of necessity – to have generated both these kinds of approach. The move toward the singular, what we might call regression toward the particular, is itself generated by the kind of *noli me legere* adumbrated above.[11]

The desire to will oneself to speak about only one thing is to a certain degree generated by the kind of silent injunction emanating from de Man's texts and which says: Read only one thing at a time, do only one thing at a time. To do only one thing is hard enough – the hardest thing, in fact – and to try to do any more with me (maybe even to try to do anything with me) is suicidal, because I will have spun such a web (a web some of you are still spinning for me, after I'm dead) or so many webs, that you will lose your own thread, or never find one for yourself, if you try to do anything more than follow the constructions I have secreted (away) one by one. Do as I tell you.

The opposite path, the urge towards systematization, is generated by the kinds of universalizing and totalizing statements that occur all over de Man's texts, no matter how carefully couched, and which go hand in hand with these more severely nominalistic injunctions. Still, the relation between these two strategies – let us call them particularizing and universalizing for the moment – is not symmetrical in the light of what can be gained. The particular approach will always win out. It will always *show more*. The universalizing approach will always lose out; it will always show less, contenting itself, even as it self-destructs, in a

---

[11] This is *not* Blanchot's *noli me legere*. For his version of that kind of solitude of the work, see his *L'Espace littéraire* (Paris: Gallimard, 1955).

kind of repetition of the Neoplatonic dictum of the one differing in itself.

I am opting, then, for a middle approach (not the same as eclecticism), out of the necessity of dealing with repeated tics across the corpus. But my sympathy is with the singular approach. I hope that my own attempt will not be judged to be merely eclectic and random. Eclecticism is a weakness to be avoided. In trying out several approaches (historical, biographical, stylistic, psycho-analytic, rhetorical, philosophical, chronological), I can only hope that the essential will always slip through.

It's not about tropes

I want to stress the never-ending battle between word and image. This new attack having been made, I want to talk, for a brief moment, about the image of the word.[12]

The Saussurean image of the sign as twofold, as signifier and signified, has held us captive. This captivity was necessary for a long time and for many historical reasons, which mostly have to do with Derrida's project, and not with the project of Paul de Man, with which we are concerned here. Saussure's image of the sign is an *image* of the sign. Mostly, *that* is the problem. I am not trying to contest the value of a methodological working hypothesis, or to condemn a supposed truth that has become a shibboleth of *literary* theory. I make these remarks in the spirit in which Adorno's title *Aesthetic Theory* has, first and foremost, to be read not only as a theory of the aesthetic, but also and simultaneously, by the necessity of thought, as a statement on the aesthetics of *theory*, of the theoretical gaze as it is related to the *aisthesis* of vision and sight. Theory taken as an aesthetic object, an aspect of theoretical process internal to theory itself – taken uncritically, as it is so often in the contemporary marketplace – now serves the same role that organic form served in post-romantic criticism. It is the aesthetic-cism and the aestheticization of theory that have made it possible for the market to move from what is now called High Theory, itself already old and useless, to cultural studies, conceived of here

---

[12] I have a floating debt to the pages of Jerome Christensen, "From Rhetoric to Corporate Populism: a Romantic Critique of the Academy in an Age of High Gossip," in *Critical Inquiry* 16:2 (Winter 1990). The years since the publication of this little-noticed essay have only borne out its truth.

under all the ruses it takes in order to avoid the accusation of political aestheticism.

So I am simply calling attention to an axiomatic fact, or, if that expression offend as pleonastically redundant, I should rather say that I would like to point out a rule of thoughtful grammar. If we want to take seriously the gap, say, between reading and seeing – in other words, if we want to talk about what, in Paul de Man's terms, might have to do with what a "non-phenomenal reading" might look like – we may have to begin by dealing with the idea that language, or any element of it, *looks like* anything.[13]

It is by beginning thus that we can begin to think about reading Paul de Man's work *backwards*. If we read his work backwards, a certain physiognomy will be seen to emerge. It will not be the physiognomy of an interiorizing consciousness that has reading experiences; nor will it be, necessarily, that of the rhetorician, who sees the navel of each text to be a catachrestic *figure*, whether it be catachresis, thus nakedly named, or prosopopoeia, or any of those others. It is the face of the grammarian.

This face recognizes *metonymies, parabases, anacoluthons, allegories,* and all the *-taxes* (hypotaxis, parataxis, and, most of all, syntax). These are not the names of tropes, strictly speaking. They are para-figural, in that they involve no substitutions. They are grammatical inasmuch as they have to do with *sequence*. They do not depend on a twofold image of the sign. Here is the moment at which we can say truthfully that de Man is not only farthest from himself when he uses the word *deconstruction* (or farthest from Derrida), but when he speaks of binary oppositions, which always turn out to be a kind of ruse or diversion. But this is precisely the kind of talk many of de Man's readers, including some of the most astute, seem to take from him. I want to avoid all talk of binaries *per se*. I hope I will not *use* them, even if I may have to *mention* them. The binary opposition is the first outward displacement of the twofold image of the sign which, as I have already said, I want to avoid. In all its anamorphs it remains an unread metaphor, a sleeping figure, and should not simply be repeated *ad nauseam*.

The sign has no *intimité* for Paul de Man. It is *entamé*, or pre-emptied, as he translates this word (although it is not only in

[13] The moments where the word "deconstruction" becomes an image for de Man must be analyzed along these lines. In particular I have in mind the preface to *AR* and the "Interview with Stefano Rosso" in *RT*.

his reading of Derrida reading Rousseau that he uses this neologism, it also occurs in his reading of Jauss).[14] The sign is to be thought of as having no interiority, as "having" only absolute exteriority, although the verb *to have* here should be replaced by the more honest word *to be characterized by*. The sign has no interiority which would allow it to be a well-wrought urn of aesthetic experience, which, after de Man's reading of Hegel, certainly becomes inconceivable, if not unthinkable, according to a certain logic of the rote, grammatical exteriority of the signifier "I" not as a sign, but as a syncategorematic function.

Paul de Man does not want to be held captive by the image of the sign. As this is the case, he – and I – will speak less of the sign and more of syntax or position. And I will try to show that this will make it easier to discuss certain problems, such as the problem of materiality, in the work of Paul de Man.

Thus I insist that there is a change of emphasis, and a sense of discovery, that takes place within his *œuvre*. I view with suspicion attempts to neutralize this change of emphasis, this discovery of the grammatical as a major focus, as integral to our sense of the work. The attempt to see all of the later de Man as somehow necessarily and entirely prefigured in his early work verges on the attribution to his text of a kind of theological power: that it always will have been right and never wrong.

This tendency mistakes a search for *understanding* – let us be brutally hermeneutical for a moment – for a desire causally, scientifically, thus also theologically, to *explain* his text. And whatever one may think about the rigidity of the distinction between explanation and understanding, between the natural sciences and the human sciences, it must be agreed that if one tampers with one member of the pair – for the moment what it means to understand – one is tampering not only with the other, but with the whole. The analysis of texts with the tools of descriptive poetics may look as though it elides the attempt to understand as such in favor of the decision for the attempt to explain how understanding is produced. But such a would-be placing of poetics in the field of the sciences ultimately would be rendered impossible (1) by virtue of the fact that poetics, like the

---

[14] See Paul de Man, "Introduction," in Hans Robert Jauss, *Toward an Aesthetic of Reception* (Minneapolis: University of Minnesota Press, 1982), now reprinted under the title "Reading and History" in *RT*.

linguistics upon which it is based, would still be without any principle of causality which would give it predictive power, and (2) because the hallucination of a pure poetic analysis, devoid of all hermeneutic decision, will always have to evanesce before one simple question: Why *this* text?

That is to say, any dream of a purely poetic analysis can only come into existence by foreclosing its relation to the choice of text to be read, an initial choice which leaves what I call a pragmatic or thematic scar on the critical act. This is the moment at which criticism stops the text it reads in cutting it, in cutting the passage to be read out and inserting it into the critical narrative – which can then proceed to work along the lines of descriptive poetics or to talk about food, sex, or the housing crisis – whatever. De Man understood this incisive aspect of the critical act very well and elaborates it in a discussion of Friedrich Schlegel's theory of irony. Crisis, too, is about *choice*, about deciding. There is a crisis at the beginning and a crisis at the end. Beginning, the first cut, text production, is one performative:

But [the tropological system] is not just that, because it is also a performative system, to the extent that it is based on an original act of positing that exists in a linguistic mode in the form of the catachresis, of the power of *setzen*, which is the beginning of the system and which itself is a performative rather than a cognitive. There is first a performative, the act of positing, the original catachresis, which then moves to a system of tropes; a kind of anamorphosis of tropes takes place, in which all the tropological systems are engendered, as a result of this original act of positing. (*AI*, 176)

But a similar disruption is required in order to bring things to a halt:

Benjamin . . . sees the impact of the parabasis much better [than Szondi]. He sees the destructive power, the negative power, of the parabasis, fully. He sees that "the ironization of form consists in a deliberate destruction of the form" – not at all an aesthetic recuperation but, to the contrary, a radical, complete destruction of the form, which he calls "the critical act," which undoes the form by analysis, which by demystification destroys the form. (*AI*, 182)

The moment of cutting, of saying, arbitrarily, "es gibt aber ein Halten," stops the form and is the moment of perihelion, when the form begins to disintegrate under the critical gaze.[15] This is the

---

[15] See his comments on Benjamin's "The Task of the Translator" in *RT*.

moment of the beginning of critical narrative, that second- or third-level narrative that tells the story of the text, that is to say, of the posited figure in the course of its decomposition, that is to say, criticism, that is to say, allegory. Allegory is very much like translation in the sense in which de Man reads Benjamin. It stops the original; it kills the original by making you aware that it was already dead; which, in the language of this current passage, means it undoes the form, shows how the text works, which is a kind of demystification that ruins the totalizing illusion that may have been produced by the text. The moments of cutting are *not* symmetrical though: the first moment is an act of production, the second, the one that stops and says, "assuming that Jupiter is not necessarily a right-wing planet, *I will go on to write about Paul de Man*," is an act of the reader or critic, who also, however, in beginning to spin his own narrative, is making the first kind of performative – but one that can only be read as such by *another* act of reading, criticism, cutting.

Structurally speaking, any act of criticism is ironic in the sense that it speaks aside from, takes its point of departure from another text. And this situation is not capable of being neutralized by any self-proclaimed and prosaic desire to be *true* or *faithful* to the mother text. Even the most prosaic criticism is ironic in this sense. And the beginning of criticism as the twisting out of poetic form into critical narrative, this becoming prose of poetry or of literature, is the very height of this irony.

Of course, there is a certain reflux action, for prose and criticism also become poetic. The line that could be said to begin with Longinus extends to Baudelaire and Flaubert and to Stein. And the dream of a pure prose, a prose consisting only of automatism, is a dream, just as the dream of pure poetry was the dream of the age that invented the modern prose poem. But for all those who blame Paul de Man for the blurring of these distinctions, I remind them that this notion of the becoming prose of poetry and the becoming poetry of prose was the staple of the poetics of Roman Jakobson. It is precisely what Jakobson was referring to in his celebrated formulation, "the poetry of grammar, the grammar of poetry."[16] One of the silliest – because most

---

[16] See his "Linguistics and Poetics," now in Roman Jakobson, *Language in Literature*, ed. S. Rudy and K. Pomorska (Cambridge, MA: Harvard University Press, 1987).

ignorant – of the charges currently floating around about so-called post-structuralism (I myself don't know what this is, or if it exists, and yet at the same time I feel compelled to defend it, even though I know that this is an impossible task, given that it may have its existence only as a trumped-up object of fear and hysteria, a paper tiger) is the idea that this current menace is responsible for the breakdown of the purportedly clear distinctions between poetry and prose, between literature and criticism. These accusations are usually leveled by the same people who accuse post-structuralists of being ahistorical. Well, some people may get more angry at being reminded of their own ignorance, but they should probably read Roman Jakobson, certainly no flaming post-structuralist.

Discussions of attempts at a definition of irony are often associated with the themes of vertiginousness and of falling. Irony starts you spinning and makes you fall. But rather than taking on this naturalizing and psychologistic explanation of irony by its effects as part of a preliminary characterization, we should keep in mind that this psychological interpretation itself conceals a potent theological moment. Hermeneutics as a theological discipline comes into existence because we are fallen, and F. W. Schlegel, Benjamin, and de Man, in this respect, are the inheritors of Pascal. In the cases of Schlegel and Benjamin, their preoccupations with religious matters are well documented. In the case of de Man, we are left with a rumor, which, in and of itself, is not irrelevant. It is perhaps no accident that there are still (entirely groundless) rumors of Paul de Man's late religious conversion floating around. It is even more interesting that such rumors exist at all, given that they are entirely unfounded, and therefore represent some kind of pure desire. We are left to ask what it is in de Man's postwar criticism that might leave a kind of underground impression of religious commitment.

The would-be scientific approach of those who assert that Paul de Man always said the same thing, but otherwise, collapses understanding and explanation into an almost paranoid version of a theology, a theology that attributes a divine intention *to the other end*. It cannot even be justified as a methodological working hypothesis of the kind de Man speaks of making in respect of the text of Rousseau.[17] When de Man asserts, for example, that he himself always needs to lean on another text, because he doesn't have the inventive power, say, of a Derrida, what is this but the most calculated of dialectical maneuvers, of the self-professed slave against the master? De Man needs other texts and thus has an encounter with an other; Derrida has only auto-erotic experiences with his own text, he doesn't need an anterior text, something to criticize, an anaclitic object choice. De Man has heteroerotic experiences while Derrida masturbates. Lest anyone think that this is a terrible exaggeration, and that I am performing a terrible misreading of a complimentary gesture, they should read the footnote in *Blindness and Insight* (see the epigraphs to this essay) which has to do, precisely, with de Man's clinamen from Derrida and his desire to *state* it. (An entire and very productive account could be written on the words "to state," "desire," and "statement" in the text of Paul de Man.)

De Man is at pains not to sacralize Rousseau in ways that those who are trying so hard to sacralize de Man fail to imitate, even as they imitate the gesture of thinking that what de Man means when he speaks thus of Rousseau is to attribute to his text a kind of infallibility *in re*. For the shift we have already sketched out above, and which can be seen to have taken place over the course of the seventies, roughly speaking, this tendential shift from an emphasis on figural language to an emphasis on para-figural or non-tropical, grammatical language, works with our remarks here on the divestment of the sign of its interiority, of its image (sound image or mental image) in the following way.

Tropes, classically conceived, involve transports of sense from one signifier to another. This is the most classical sense of metaphor. In this way, the critical language of tropes still speaks of displacements of *meaning*; it still speaks the metaphorical language of the twofold, *recto–verso* unity of the sign. There is an outward manifestation and a more hidden correlate, the cognitive side of things. The grammatical non-tropes mentioned above, allegory included, do not participate in this language of transport

---

[17] See de Man's "Interview with Stefano Rosso," now reprinted in *RT*. This interview is not devoid of a certain amount of violence in respect of what de Man says about the relation between his own text and that of Derrida.

of a sense or of a meaning. They are employed virtually always as marks of disruption of such transports.

Yes, this is even and especially the case for allegory. Allegory, as we think of it here, is not a trope for Paul de Man. It is a grammatical form in which a certain number of disjunctions can be shown to be taking place. As a form, it *shows* these disjunctions. When de Man comes to dwell in and on the allegorical form, he dwells on these disjunctions, and not on a more typical sense of the allegorical as having to do with personification (although as long as personification is discussed as grammatical personification, de Man's discussions can account for this as well and do not leave such discussions behind). The necessity of allegory as a name, not only for the object of de Man's later concerns, but for his essays themselves, is this necessity that the form show itself, that it be capable of being read off – that is to say, legible – as form.

De Man takes up allegorical form as a way of incorporating a coded language of intention (the allegorist's intention). But, in taking it up, he dwells on what the structure of that form tells us about the ruination of that intention. It is the little *tableaux* embedded in de Man's essays – Hegel's personal fault, Pascal's apparent inauthenticity, theory's recording of language's failure to be a model language – that make for their double narrative. In speaking this allegorical language, a language of intentional writing, these essays set up a plot which the structure of the language *as read* then delivers unto ruination. This double plot accounts for the desire, in reading de Man, to make *his* statement about allegory turn into the one place where sign and meaning would converge. But this is an impossible desire, a desire the accomplishment of which is the ruination of his own statement. To read de Man well, the one thing we should not do is to try to make him say only what he means. This would be to reduce his statement to that of the intention of the naïvely didactic allegorist, the teacher who was always right and never wrong.[18]

My insistence on a change of emphasis in de Man's work is thus intimately linked to his shift of emphasis from tropes to non-

[18] The best commentary on this paradox of de Man's statement is Hans-Jost Frey's "Undecidability," in *Yale French Studies* 69 (1985): *The Lesson of Paul de Man*, ed. Peter Brooks, Shoshana Felman, and J. Hillis Miller (New Haven: Yale University Press, 1985).

tropes, that is to say to the shift from emphasis on transports of sense, whether abusive (catachrestic) or not, to disruptions in the relation between signifier, or mark, on the one hand, and signi-fied, that is to say meaning or sense, on the other. We should add here that one of the strengths of pointing out this tendential shift in de Man's work has to do with the ability to counter an objection that might be raised to his and to my own project.[19] This objection can be summarized as follows.

Inasmuch as you and de Man consider reading, once the first incision into a text has been made, to be an activity that works at the level of the signifier considered as bracketed from its signi-fied, you are involved in a fallacy. For, following upon the Saussurean figure, you cannot have the one without the other, and this is precisely what comes with Saussure's figure of the *recto–verso*. Your methodological hypothesis thus involves you in a blatant misunderstanding of the word "signifier."

To this I respond: The image of the sign, as the unity of signifier and signified, has held us captive and enthralled up to this point, and our newfound emphasis on non-tropical terminology should allow us to abandon the conception of the twofold character of the sign altogether. For our purposes, it is a holdover, a vestigial relic of Saussurean ideology – in the most eighteenth-century sense of that word – which is unnecessary for our purposes, and *a fortiori*, by virtue of our need to respond to this very objection, counterproductive and contraindicated. This image has held us captive. Whatever new word (let us retreat to the value of this more neutral word "word") we choose, whether it be "word," "mark," "grapheme," or any of the other awkward and available candidates, let us caution against investing it with any sense of the interiority that seems to inhere, for historical reasons, in the word "sign," and in its breakdown products, those drugs still in our bloodstream, "signifier," "signified."

Furthermore, it is not so much that I am reading something after the fact into Saussure, something that was not there already

[19] I often wondered why nobody ever bothered to ask these questions; but being, I thought, on my own ground, I also felt more than a little bit shaky about the use of a certain Lacanian language which I dared to use anyway, thinking that according to what I knew of it I had a hunch that I was saying something both correct and precise. I have felt my suspicions – and hopes – to be confirmed upon delving into Jean-Claude Milner's *For the Love of Language*, trans. Ann Banfield (New York: St. Martin's Press, 1990).

– depending on where one draws the limits of the *cordon sanitaire*[20] around Saussure's text. While the twofold character of the sign and the thesis of its arbitrariness may be the most celebrated shibboleths of what we have today as the *Course*, we now know of the other Saussure, the Saussure of the anagrams.[21] I will not rehearse the now legendary and hallucinatory aspect of Saussure's private obsession, but summon the matter only for the purpose of calling attention, again, to the prison of the number two, of the signifier-signified relation.

The man who gave us the twofold character of the sign also has two faces. In the front of his store his heirs sell the book the father never wrote, the legendary foundation stone of modern linguistics; while in the back the grandchildren play games with letters and phonemes. In front, Science with a capital *S* comes to linguistics with the ability, via the thesis of the arbitrariness of the sign, to bracket reference and to study language, which has no phenomenal reality as such, as existing full-blown, all at once, and having its own anorganic laws. In back, the older the poems of the West get, the more clearly they turn out to be exact declensions of the divine name. That is to say, the less and less arbitrary and the more and more motivated they become by virtue of a certain kind of slavish devotion to the divine theme-word, the greater and greater the rigidity of their reference, and the closer and closer they come to what might be described as an ultimately theological rigidity of reference.[22]

The anagrams, for all that and as Saussure discovers them, are not really all that threatening to any desire to make the form of language and its meaning coincide perfectly. Rather than entailing some bizarre, perhaps monstrous principle of disruption, the idea that behind the matrix of the visible text – Lucretius, for

---

[20] An expression coined by Proust's father. See Lewis Galantière's introduction to Marcel Proust, *Swann's Way* (New York: Modern Library, 1928), vii.

[21] See Jean Starobinski, *Les Mots sous les mots: Les Anagrammes de Ferdinand de Saussure* (Paris: Gallimard, 1971), translated by Olivia Emmet as *Words Upon Words* (New Haven: Yale University Press, 1979).

[22] Is "god" a rigid designator? According to everything I say between these covers, I should think so. In the case of the anagrams, however, the older texts refer ever more rigidly to the *name* of god – let us be clear on that. The pervasiveness of the theological as a force in the newer analytic metaphysics is astonishing, because so unhistorically commented. See Kripke's *Naming and Necessity* (Oxford: Blackwell, 1980). For a meditation that moves in the same direction but in a different vocabulary, see Jacques Derrida, "Comment ne pas parler – dénégations," in *Psyché*, as well as his *Khôra* (Paris: Galilée, 1993).

example – there is the legible hymn to Aphrodite to be read only reinforces the greatness of the auratic urn of ancient poetry as the bearer of the noblest and most classical craft. The truly threatening possibility would only exist in the case, itself scarcely imaginable, of a text that would be found to have a hypogram which would not appear in the matrix in other than morcellated form, that is to say where the name beneath the text turned out to read as something different from what the text *said* at the level of its direct statement.

This is the same paradox involved in the matter of an analysand's set of associations upon a manifest element of a dream leading to the latent content. For the idea that we can get to the writing on the wall – to use Lacan's appropriation of the biblical figure – is an image that manifests the desire that there be a final *meaning*, that there be *one* true meaning, in a *word*, in *one* word. Thus even this possibility of a hypogram that would not even be a theme-word, because it would never appear as manifest content in a text, still assumes that there is *a* word there to be found, rather than just the meaningless and statistically random static of errant phonemes.

(Ir)reversibility: event and regression
1. vulgar time versus textual time

Let us now approach a very short moment in a long and rambling lecture, the theme of which is the relationship of Schiller to Kant's *Critique of Judgment*:

We saw what the juxtaposition between Schiller and Kleist does, and we saw the way in which Kleist takes you back in a way to certain of the more threatening Kantian insights in terms of Schiller. Or you would find a play like that between Schopenhauer and Nietzsche, the way in which Nietzsche – not just the Nietzsche of *The Birth of Tragedy*, but the later Nietzsche as well – acts critically in relation to Schopenhauer and, I would say, "de-Schillerizes" and "re-Kantizes" what Schopenhauer has been saying. Or, I would even suggest, to take a name which isn't purely German, that something like that could be said to go on between Heidegger on the one hand and Derrida on the other; so that the reading that Derrida gives of Heidegger, in which Heidegger would play the role of Schiller, Derrida would then appear as being closer to Kant, in a kind of similar critical examination of a certain claim for the autonomy and the power of the aesthetic which is being asserted in the wake of Schiller, but not necessarily in the wake of Kant. (*AI*, 131)

What is the most striking event that takes place in this passage? It is not the list of names as such. Nor is it the notion of literary history as a movement of critical-reading-as-destruction, the way in which the later reader, Nietzsche, two or three times removed from the original text in consideration – here the text of Kant – makes a critical move by reestablishing or recanonizing the original text as a monument from which the intervening texts – Schiller, Schopenhauer – are regressions. The intervening, regressive texts are not the ruination of the original text, or ruins subaltern to its stability, outhouses; they are in fact the cheap mortar and plaster which have been used to shore up the edifice of the *Urtext*. But as such they cannot approach any fundamental tensions, which are still hidden in the foundations. It is only the critical excavation of the later readers that can make the whole thing resound in its trembling, solicit it, thus making the layers of cosmetic impasto fall away.

This is not new to this text of Paul de Man. What is new is hidden in the last examples in the list of names. They are not quite German. And what is it to be German? It is not only to be Kant, or Schiller, or Schopenhauer, or Nietzsche. Here, it is to be a literary historian. (Walter Benjamin, whose name ranks equally with that of Heidegger in any discussion of the topos of criticism as destruction, was also not quite German.)[23] What is striking about the last reader-writer or writer-reader couple is the shock of an apparent temporal inversion. Heretofore we have had a very nice sequence of writers and readers: Kant, Schiller, Schopenhauer, Nietzsche. Each one comes after the other, in terms of sequence, in terms of the texts in question, in terms of their commentary on each other's texts.

Now what do we have? We have the relationship of Heidegger to Derrida conceived of oppositely, inserted into this sequence as its deliverance and destruction. A literary historian reads this, and looks up and says: No, de Man has slipped up! It is the opposite! Clearly he means to say that Derrida reads Heidegger the way all

---

[23] Here we must also ask about the relation of the German to the American. The birth of Comparative Literature as a discipline in America after the Second World War could not have taken place without the intervention, in one way or another, of Erich Auerbach, Ernst Robert Curtius, Leo Spitzer, and René Wellek, who, for our purposes, count as German here. Walter Benjamin was and was not a German. He certainly was not assimilated into the German academy.

the others do, in sequence, in a line. But this is not what Paul de Man says. He says that Heidegger reading Derrida is the same kind of error as Schiller reading Kant. Or Schopenhauer reading Kant. And furthermore de Man is putting himself, in this lecture, in his very performance, in the position of Nietzsche-as-undoer here (less of a surprise: now everyone has an anchor for their rage, they can pinpoint it). How can this be? Is there some justification for this?

What is at issue is not this sequence, but sequence itself; what we might call the irony or the violence of sequencing. De Man is writing here not of vulgar–temporal sequence, but of what we might now want to call textual sequence, textual time as opposed to vulgar time. There is an event, let us call it the occurrence of the Kantian text; and then there is the regression away from this event in the form of a history of interpretation of it, and which then tries to include the primary event in a history, even as the outset of that history. Primary sequence and secondary sequence: vulgar time or textual time. And these can flip, as the chi that holds the figure Kant is to Schiller is as Heidegger is to Derrida flips, cata-strophically, as Derrida would say,[24] into the figure Kant is to Schiller as Derrida is to Heidegger.

The first figure is temporal; the second figure is historical. That is: The first figure puts things into a narrative, which some may call historical; but the second, in its very shocking inversion, brings to the fore a textual structure which, de Man wants to claim, is irreversible, and is thus truly historical. It is not a question of influence here, of any interpsychic battle transmuted into an intertextual strategy. It is not a relation that depends on any phenomenal occurrence of Martin Heidegger's eye scanning Jacques Derrida's text, the text of a postcard from Derrida, for example. It is a relation between texts, pure and simple. Impure and in fact very difficult to work out.

The problem is always that as soon as one calls one's interpreta-tion text-oriented, that is to say oriented toward reading – if not towards the reader – one must tell both stories simultaneously, even in the "one must" of this sentence – and therein lies the inherent possibility of confusion. Which story am I telling right now, the story about how I told the story or the story about what

---

[24] See his *Des tours de Babel*, now in *Psyché*.

really happened? And are we (not) simply rehashing the plot-story distinction in yet another of its wearying permutations? No. And here we see again the double plot of de Man's allegories: the attribution to the text of an intention which the reading delivers unto ruination. But now what I must do is to show how this kind of analysis is generated within the reading of single text, in order to explain a verbal structure there, and to show that it is not a matter of my own willful arbitrariness.

Event-regression
2. the thematic scar

We are all thematic readers with a guilty conscience.[25]

It is going to take some time and effort to show how what I have just sketched out rather programmatically can be seen to operate all over in de Man's text, and in the texts he reads there. For reasons that can only become more clear as our walk proceeds, I take as my example a series of texts that take Proust as an example, and not simply as one example among others. These texts were published over the time from 1969 to 1982, and thus cover the period during which de Man's use of a consciousness-oriented vocabulary, loosely associated with Poulet and the Geneva School, gives way to a more rhetorical and performative vocabulary, at once older and more original.

That de Man should have chosen the example of Proust on being solicited to write an essay that was in its first version part of a Festschrift for Georges Poulet is not at all surprising. There is nothing to write home about in the fact of the occasion for this essay.[26] What is interesting is that the gratuitousness of the occasion of this essay inserts it into a chain of de Man's essays which bring forth passages from Proust at crucial moments. This chain could be said to begin with the epigraph to the first edition of *Blindness and Insight*,[27] itself rather gratuitously made into the only deletion between the first and second editions, the text of which reads, "Cette perpétuelle erreur, qui est précisément 'la vie.' –

---

[25] A remark attributed to Paul de Man in the early eighties, no doubt apocryphal.

[26] See Paul de Man, "Proust et l'allégorie de la lecture," his contribution to *Mouvements premiers* (Paris: José Corti, 1972).

[27] New York: Oxford University Press, 1971.

Proust." It proceeds into the essay on Poulet in *Blindness and Insight*, toward the end of which we can read the following paragraph:

A far-reaching change of the temporal structure results from this. The *instant de passage*, the decisive importance of which has been so strongly in evidence, now turns out to create a disjunction within the subject. On the temporal level, this disjunction takes the form of a sudden reversal from a retrospective to a future-oriented attitude of mind. However, the dimension of futurity that is thus being engendered exists neither as an empirical reality nor in the consciousness of the subject. It exists only in the form of a written language that relates, in its turn, to other written languages in the history of literature and criticism. In this way we can see Marcel Proust clearly separate a past or a present that precedes the act of writing from a future that exists only in a purely literary form. Proust mentions certain sensations or emotions that will only become important in retrospect when these same events will recur as part of an interpretative process. "If, in the *Recherche*, the hero's experience is already over at the time that the novel begins, the knowledge of this experience, its meaning and the use that can be made of it remain in suspense until the end, that is to say until a certain event has taken place that makes the future into more than just the point of arrival of the past, but into the point from where the past, seen in retrospect, gains meaning and intention."[28] In Proust's case, we know exactly what this decisive event was: the decision to write *A la recherche du temps perdu*, to pass from experience to writing, with all the risks this involves for the person of the writer. The explicit decision of Marcel Proust recurs in each writer; each one has invested his future existence once and forever into the project of his work.   (BI, 98–99)

Several things which will be important to de Man as a critical writer already stand out in this apparently rather banal paraphrase of Poulet. The topic sentence of the paragraph introduces the notion of disjunction, the full deployment of which we will see shortly. This disjunction is related to the matter not of an instant in time, of a narrative – but an instant that is marked by the engendering of that narrative: this *instant de passage* is the one that results in the writing of passages, passages that begin, as de Man reminds us in the essay on Proust itself, shortly down the line, "plus tard, j'ai compris . . ."

---

[28] This figure has become the dominant of much twentieth-century literature. I think of Gabriel García Márquez, of Borges, and of Italo Calvino's *Palomar*. If I mention Calvino's book in particular, it has to do with its explicitly allegorical character as a description of contemporary literature itself. Calvino's novel is one of the best *critical* studies of twentieth-century literature available.

The disjunction operated in the instant of passage is the disjunction between what we should rightly call – barely interpolating a vocabulary that will manifest itself shortly, but ultimately will also be seen to take its keynote from the text of Proust – the phenomenal self of the writer and the materiality of his text. The play between past and future of which we have already spoken in reference to the construction of critical narratives, in the relation between the texts of Kant and Schiller, for example, is already involved in the primary literary narrative itself. It is not imposed by the critic from the outside. The instant in question, seen, in the literary narrative, becomes the model for critical work.

The literary text is the becoming model for the intention of the critical text – even if the literary text never gets there and the critical text only brings it there by virtue of a certain destructive violence. This comes to explicit statement in the unsurprisingly didactic last sentence of de Man's paragraph on Poulet, where Proust explicitly becomes a model text, for his decision "recurs in each writer." But given the movement of the paragraph, which has already asserted that the passage in question is a passage over the instant of which the writer moves from a left-behind phenomenal self to the construction of the text (a text that now, as the very result of this passage, enters into relation with "other written languages in the history of literature and criticism"), we can now say that the decision of Marcel Proust occurs or recurs in every *reader*, inasmuch as it is the writer-reader who inserts his writing, by virtue of its being written down, into a or the history of writing – which, taken as a history, is a history of reading. The full force of this insertion of the literary text into a history could be said to take place in the use of the verb "to recur," instead of the verb "to occur." What occurs, in an instant, is immediately and retroactively inserted into a series in which it recurs: the ecstatic character of the instant becomes a moment in a story about languages and literatures.

But note how this moment of recurrence *occurs*. Recurrence, the fact that writers are readers, thus also critics, occurs in a sentence in which the example of a single writer, Marcel Proust by name, is generalized into "the explicit decision of . . . each writer." The particular, in being made into the exemplar or model, is inserted into the series of which it is the model or type, which series has a name, literature or writing. Here is the apparently inescapable moment of allegoresis in de Man's writing. How "natural" that it should proceed from a paraphrase of a critic whose work is so singularly taken up with the phenomenology of the reading process as a structure of reader-author and reader-narrator identification.

To move on to our own words, this last sentence of de Man's paragraph, with its concluding *moralité*, has to be a sentence in which a singular, existential term is broadened into a universal statement. What started out, to use the language of logic, as a statement involving the existential quantifier, has become a statement with a universal quantifier.[29] The allegory of reading called "Reading (Proust)," in *Allegories of Reading*, will thus take as its constant pedal-point the failure of a model of some universal, abstract entity or process like reading to account for the structure of a singular text to be read, here Proust. The scar born by the allegory will be that of never being able to leave behind the fact of this inescapable predicament of logic, a predicament engendered by having made a universal out of a particular, a universal that no longer is capable of containing the particular within itself.

Now we can move on to "Reading (Proust)" by moving away from Poulet, as de Man does at the very beginning of this essay, the first two sentences of which forge the next link in his and my chain:

George Poulet has taught us to consider, in *A la recherche du temps perdu*, the juxtaposition of different temporal layers rather than the unmediated experience of an identity, given or recovered by an act of consciousness (involuntary memory, proleptic projection, etc.). The specificity of Proust's novel would instead be grounded in the play between a prospective and a retrospective movement. This alternating motion resembles that of reading, or rather that of re-reading which the intricacy of every sentence as well as of the narrative network as a whole constantly forces upon us. Moreover, as Poulet describes it, the moment that marks the passage from "life" to writing corresponds to an act of reading that separates from the undifferentiated mass of facts and events, the distinctive elements susceptible of entering into the composition of a text. This occurs by means of a process of elision, transformation, and accentuation that bears a close resemblance to the practice of critical understanding. The intimate relationship between reading and criticism has become a commonplace of contemporary literary study. (*AR*, 57)

---

[29] But we know, since Frege, that, unlike existential statements, universal statements do not posit the existence of the objects to which they might pertain. To give the ubiquitous example, the statement of the attributes of god that lists all his perfections and that includes existence as such a perfection does not materially imply the existence of the entity, god, thus described.

This abstract of the preceding essay makes explicit what I stated in my remarks above on the essay on Poulet, namely that the process of Proust-writer becomes, by virtue of a kind of inbuilt re-scanning, the activity of the critic. The image of Proust behind this paragraph is not that of the man dipping a madeleine into tea, but that of the insomniac in the cork-lined room who spent all his time up to the moment of his death editing his own text, and whose posthumous editors have continued with the same process.

It is this shift in emphasis from the image of Proust-writer to that of Proust-reader that allows de Man to shift his focus from that of the intention of and at text production to that of reception – and all of this is still interpolated under the sign of what George Poulet has taught us. But now it is a question of moving from what Poulet has taught us to what Proust's novel teaches us, forces upon us, which is the task of considerably greater complexity that de Man attempts in the next paragraph:

What does *A la recherche du temps perdu* tell us about reading? I approach the question in the most literal and, in fact, naïve way possible by reading a passage that shows us Marcel engaged in the act of reading a novel. This procedure in fact begs the question, for we cannot *a priori* be certain to gain access to whatever Proust may have to say about reading by way of such a reading of a scene of reading. The question is precisely whether a literary text is *about* that which it describes, represents, or states. If, even at the infinite distance of an ideal reading, the meaning *read* is destined to coincide with the meaning *stated*, then there would in fact be no real problem. All that would be left to do would be to allow oneself to be brought nearer to this ideal perfection by taking Marcel for our model. But if reading is truly problematic, if a nonconvergence between the stated meaning and its understanding may be suspected, then the sections in the novel that literally represent reading are not to be privileged. We may well have to look elsewhere, in Marcel's erotic, political, medical, or worldly experiences to discover the distinctive structures of reading, or we may have to go further afield still and use a principle of selection that is no longer thematic. This circular difficulty should not, however, prevent us from questioning the passage on actual reading, if only to find out whether or not it does make paradigmatic claims for itself. The uncertainty as to whether this is indeed the case creates a mood of distrust which, as the later story of Marcel's relationship with Albertine makes clear, produces rather than paralyzes interpretative discourse. Reading has to begin in this unstable commixture of literalism and suspicion.　　　　(*AR*, 57–58)

From here on in we are going to have to move ever more slowly, for, despite the claim to approach the question "in the most literal

. . . and naïve way possible," the contortions of this paragraph reveal this naïveté to be a surface calm. The very move from Poulet-as-teacher to Proust's-text-as-teacher is not a simple one. Given that the full force of the work collected in *Blindness and Insight* has to do with the relation between critic and literary text, or between text and commentary, the dismissal of the critic in favor of the attribution of a certain didactic moment to a literary text is not at all easy. Under what aegis do we apostrophize a novel and ask it to tell us about reading? We can see how we have already begun to legitimate this procedure by making the act of the author himself into a critical act; and thus we can already attribute a certain critical moment to his own text.

However, in order to choose a passage to focus in on from thousands of pages, we are going to have to make some kind of intervention, a choice. And what does de Man do? He chooses a passage in which the narrator, Marcel, *reads*, a strategy that thus "begs the question" by pragmatically presuming that a passage that describes reading is going to turn out to be *about* reading. Instead of saying that this begs the question, we could say it forecloses the question; for this strategy would close down the distinction between writer and narrator, thus eliminating any possibility of the anagnorisis, of the recognition which structures the book. De Man's clarity on this point allows us to shed the illusion of all naïveté, and forces us immediately to a more general question: "precisely whether a literary text is *about* that which it describes, represents, or states." I presume that the distinction between these three verbs can be taken to occur between the first two and the third. The caesura of thought between "describe" and "represent," on the one hand, and "state" on the other, is the same as that between grammar and logic on the one hand, and rhetoric on the other. The cut is clear and clean and occurs, uninterrupted, from "Semiology and Rhetoric" through "The Resistance to Theory." Describing and representing are the kinds of things we expect from narratives; but what is stating, and what would it be for a literary text, or any text, to state something?

We can approach this question in the most naïve and literal way possible and say that stating, as opposed to describing or representing, would be the text's performative dimension in pronouncing on anything at all, whether it be its own composition, the nature of reading, etc. Thus *statement* would belong to the real: it is trauma.

And it is a trauma followed hard upon by the outbreak of the conceptual or of the theoretical, by which the subject shelters itself against this trauma. We get an indication that the semantic value of "statement" here is laden with the register of the speech act, of the fact of something's being said over and above what is being described, constatively, in the said. The text says more, states more than it knows, where knowing here would be taken in the sense of contents capable of being described or represented.

Perhaps we shall be offered further clues in what follows. The statement that even in the case that it be guaranteed – and who could make such a guarantee and how? – that the book was about what it says it's about already seems to presume an "infinite" task, a kind of divine activity. And we haven't even approached, except by preterition, the kind of predicament we will be in as readers if we cannot assume *this* possibility. A reader working *sub specie aeternitatis* might not be so badly off; but where does that leave *us*? The very fact that literature exists, that there are linguistic entities about which we even have to ask this question, because the elaborateness of their codes tells us that they do not simply denote at the level of degree-zero signification, should tell us that we are in the worse-off situation. God would be the very name for such a kind of understanding in the last instance, the name for the agency who can say what he means and mean what he says, or, in this case, close the gap, in reading, between denotative and connotative, or better yet, between constative and performative speech, between describing and stating.[30] We think we are in a narrative, therefore, about our own fall from grace, a fall that could be redeemed "at the infinite distance of an ideal reading."

But we are not god, and furthermore, by virtue of what has already been said about the way in which the existence of something called literature calls the possibility even of theological conflict resolution into question, it's not a given that god would be in such great shape, either. In the best-case scenario, we could let the narrator lead us down the garden path, and simply be attentive to what he tells us, what he "states" – in a more conventional sense of this verb. "But if reading is truly problematic," if this is what the

[30] Far from being a Derridian topos, this idea can be traced back to Longinus. On this matter, see Neil Hertz, "A Reading of Longinus," in his *The End of the Line* (New York: Columbia University Press, 1985).

existence of literary language tells us – "if a nonconvergence between the stated meaning and its understanding may be suspected," – and we have already done as much – "then the sections in the novel that literally represent reading are not to be privileged," or perhaps we should rather say, trusted.

What is it, and how is it, that literary language can put a mote even into the eye of god? The next sentence is truly ironic – not simply because it speaks of looking elsewhere, but because the kind of nonconvergence revealed in the examination of the possibility of simply reading about reading would not guarantee for us that there would be any kind of more successful dream book that would satisfy our needs for practical interpretation. So it isn't a matter of looking for another code to be translated by a manual of reading as an act of decoding. For the assertion-in-hypothesis of the impossibility of this code's being granted by the access of direct statement precludes the possibility of reading's being stably accessible through another thematic. If we don't know what reading is from reading about reading, then we would not know how to decode any other code that would tell us what reading is or would be. So we're back to zero.

But what does de Man mean by "a principle of selection that is no longer thematic?" The answer is crucial, and relatively clear, if banal. The idea of a principle of selection that would no longer be thematic would be that of a principle of selection made on the basis of sheerly linguistic criteria. One would have to resort to tracking signifiers (and *not* words, for words, at least non-syncategorematic ones, would still be assimilable to themes, although *names* would be a borderline category) in a procedure that would resemble indexing and that would not be able to tell us anything about anything except the marks thus being tracked. Thus the idea of a principle of selection that would no longer be thematic operates as a kind of contradictory dream, for it would not be a principle that would allow us to choose a text in any way that would be *meaningful*.[31]

For clearly, as is the case in this paragraph in de Man, one is

---

[31] This discussion parallels the analysis of the becoming theme of the other – and hence, of its neutralization *as* other – for consciousness in Levinas, in whose work the trace appears as trace only as the nonintentional residue which cannot be thematized by consciousness. We are very close to the de Manian notion of the materiality of the signifier here.

always making a choice, as a reader, of a passage that represents some specific topic, some specific concern, and then focusing or zooming in on it with a tool kit assembled from whatever vocabularies we use when we have decided *what piece* of language is to be thus examined. This is manifested in the foreclosure of all the rather difficult speculation that takes place in the next sentence, where a kind of pragmatic concession is made: "This circular difficulty should not, however, prevent us from questioning the passage on actual reading, if only to find out whether or not it does make paradigmatic claims for itself."

In the context of this essay on Proust, it would not be enough to demonstrate that de Man was not simply going for the passage about reading because, in the context of a reading aimed at the heart of phenomenological criticism, it would be an even stronger point to be able to show the disjunction between *logos* and *lexis* operating at *this* moment, a moment of reading, more than at any other. For the stakes here are higher and more sharp than at the more conversational moments we are used to from de Man's other essays, where his rhetoric attempts to soft-pedal precisely what stares him, and us, his readers, in the face. Toward the beginning of "Semiology and Rhetoric," for example, when he turns from the preliminary reflections – longer than usual here, for "Semiology and Rhetoric" is a program essay – to what could be called a series of exemplary mini-readings, we encounter the following sentences:

> These remarks should indicate at least the existence and the difficulty of the question, a difficulty which puts its concise theoretical exposition beyond my powers. I must retreat therefore into a pragmatic discourse and try to illustrate the tension between grammar and rhetoric in a few specific textual examples. (*AR*, 9)

The retreat into the pragmatic forestalls having to name the "circular difficulty" encountered in "Reading (Proust)." It is a kind of cutting. And it is smarter than any kind of long and wearying full-blown critique of empiricism would be, and can be used to justify such a basic retreat from deductive demonstration. It is smarter because less deluded about the possibility of a full-blown, systematic critique being leveled on the grounds of a singularity, a real, a literary text. Sentences like these, read over and over again, in their differing and occasional permutations, call attention to themselves as laws of form, and, more specifically, as laws of the de Man-essay form. They renounce totality by regressing from the rigor of the concept at the moment when the philosopher would say: "What do you mean? Please give me some general account of why it is that the linguistic predicament you claim to find exists, then, if you like, move on to the examples, or even, perhaps, leave the examples out."

Another example of this knot inflects the matter in a different and very important fashion. On the second page of "Pascal's Allegory of Persuasion," after the rehearsal of the preliminaries – a general statement of the *recurrent* difficulties of defining allegory as a symbolic mode, we encounter the following, apparently rather innocent sentences:

> In order to try to to progress in the precise formulation of the difficulty, I turn to what I find to be a suggestive example, one of the later didactic texts written by Pascal for the instruction of the pupils at Port-Royal. The text . . . remained unpublished for a long time, but did not pass unnoticed . . . It has since been mentioned by most specialists of Pascal and has been the object of at least one learned monograph. The text is entitled *Réflexions sur la géometrie en général; De l'esprit géometrique et de l'Art de persuader* . . . It is an exemplary case for our inquiry, since it deals with what Pascal calls, in the first section, "l'étude de la vérité" or epistemology and, in the second, "l'art de persuader" or rhetoric. (*AI*, 52–53)

I cite from this entirely banal paragraph in order to watch the full panoply of its excuses. We have just been learning to be suspicious of de Man's analyses of little "didactic" occasion pieces. De Man loved to read clichés and to twist them out of all possible recognition from the point of view of the tradition.[32] He never read a non-canonical text. His move was always to go for the heart of canonical texts by taking their most apparently banal moments and twisting them out of the legibility imposed upon them by the canonizing history of their reception. Obviously, it would not have been possible to deploy such a strategy over a corpus about which nothing had been written. As far as debates about the canon are concerned, de Man was the most conservative of readers. This is how he shoved his choices out of the way.

Having moved through our previous examples, it is as though it is not enough for him simply to say that he is choosing this text for its obvious thematic import (in the case of this moment of this

---

[32] This practice comes quite close to the notion of "twisting out" ("herausdrehen") in Heidegger's *Nietzsche*, as well as to the last lines of Paul Celan's late lyric, "Unlesbarkeit" (*GW* vol. II, 338).

essay on Pascal we do not have to confront the issue of the first choice or cut so quickly, so the fact that this is a thematically dictated choice should not, at first read, bother the virgin reader of this essay, who doesn't know all of de Man's wiles). He has to go on with a list of names and facts and dates in order to reassure us that this text is Pascal's Pascal. Even though it long remained unpublished, it exerts a force over contemporaries and future commentators, all of the ones who know their stuff and show it in mentioning it. Its character as a didactic text means that it should be relatively perspicuous; for if its aim is to teach, it should be free of paradox, except, of course, where it might be forced up against the limits of its own logic. The choice, de Man is saying, is not my choice. It is overdetermined not only by theme, here, but by the history of reception of this text.

So much for a cataloging of all the excuses that are supposed to make us not look too closely at the structure of this particular choice. It is presented as self-evident. But let's look only one paragraph further down, to see how historical determination or overdetermination is treated once a choice of text to be read has been made:

> The argument of the *Réflexions* is digressive, but not at all lacking in consistency. If it indeed reaches dead ends and breaking points, it does so by excess of rigor rather than for lack of it. That such breaking points are reached, however, cannot be denied. Recent commentators have valiantly tried to patch up the most conspicuous holes by attributing them to historical indeterminations characteristic of Pascal's time and situation. In a text that is as historically overdetermined as this one . . . the temptation is great to domesticate the more threatening difficulties by historicizing them out of consciousness. Even after this operation has been performed, some anomalies remain that pertain specifically to the nature rather than the state of the question. (*AI*, 53–54)

In short, we can lean on historical (over)determinations in order to make a choice of text by presenting that choice as having already been made for us; but once the choice is made, any reference to data outside this text in order to help explain problems within it is out of the question. In a truly Pascalian and dialectical argument such as de Man's, it is no reproach to point out that he can use the same form of argumentation for exactly the opposite goal on the same page. In the first case, where it is a matter of isolating the object of study, the historical determinations are used in order to delimit the object, to make it stand out, to make it show itself by showing how it already stands out to a *Textkenner* such as he. But once it stands out, it does so as a prior-constituted object *against* its background, and has to be treated as though it has an inside and an outside, the latter being irrelevant to any further and closer study.

In this particular anamorphosis of what I am trying to point out, rather violently, as a kind of formal rule about de Man's argumentation, the difficulty – of where to jump into the circle of relevance and of how to get out of it when your methodology wants to discard relevance – has been resolved by an extraordinarily elastic use of historical contextualization, whose rule could be stated as follows: Pre-selection occurs by the overdetermining, agglomerative evidence of the tradition – even if sometimes negatively (if we focus on what was previously avoided); but closer analysis itself must bracket such totality in order to take account of its object.

"Historicizing x out of consciousness" is an anamorph of another extremely important locution in de Man that occurs toward the very end of *Allegories of Reading*: "In fiction thus conceived the 'necessary link' of the metaphor has been metonymized beyond the point of catachresis, and the fiction becomes the disruption of the narrative's referential illusion" (*AR*, 292). What is it to historicize something out of consciousness, to excuse oneself for not reading it, but to do so as Rousseau does in his guilty, *ex post facto* interpretation of his own uttering the name "Marion?" The metaphorical enchainment of the text is disrupted by this seizing on something that is contiguous, thus also contingent, in the narrative context. The metaphorical chain of the fiction is disrupted by the violence of a positing metonymy, but a metonymy that is a catachresis because it produces something – a name – out of nothing, as a para-divine excuse. A reading that reaches for extra-textual determinations in order to account for problems encountered in reading a text is one that avenges itself, or expiates itself on the first object available. Thus de Man is a theologian of the name.

But let us come back to "Reading (Proust)": one of the things that is so remarkable about all of these passages – in which the necessity of making a choice is made, not made, or made in being pushed aside – is the way in which this move from the outside to the inside of the text is structured as a move from a kind of helplessness and passivity to activity: the elaboration of this predicament being *"be-yond my powers, I must retreat"* [my emphasis]; *"*[a]ll that would be left to do would be *to allow oneself to be brought* nearer to this ideal perfection by taking Marcel for our model" [my emphasis]; the general tone of a situation in which critics try "valiantly . . . to patch up the holes" and to "domesticate the more threatening difficulties."[33] I suspend my consideration of what is named as a circular difficulty in this paragraph, in which the self-conscious-ness necessary to any reading of reading is made explicit in its very failure, in order to move beneath the line separating the text from the notes and to consider in detail what is by far the most signifi-cant note in all of *Allegories of Reading*, and which occurs two pages after we have begun to read in this unstable commixture of lit-eralism and suspicion.

Necessary linkage

Similar figures, often polarized around systems of light/dark and inside/outside, are so frequent that they could be said to make up the entire novel. They occur from the first sentence, which has to do with light and dark, truth and error, wake [*sic*] and sleep, perception and dream, and which turns on a literalization of the fundamental epistemological metaphor of understanding as seeing. One of the most interesting examples, also involving Giotto, occurs in the later part of the novel, in a passage from *La fugitive*, during Marcel's visit to Venice, in the company of his mother, after Albertine's death.[34] Gérard Genette quotes the passage as an example of diegetic metaphor, metaphors [*sic*] in which the selection of the vehicle is dictated by the proximity of a detail that happens to be present in the narrative context. The blue color of the backgrounds in the Giotto frescoes at the Arena in Padua are [*sic*] said to be "so blue that it looks as if the radiant daylight had crossed the threshold in the company of the visitor, and would have housed for a moment its pure sky in the coolness of the shade, a pure sky hardly

---

[33] I recur to Hertz, "Lurid Figures." I think that this analysis could be extended profitably to take account of the gigantomachy at the end of "The Resistance to Theory" – an essay remarkably free of the use of examples analyzed in any extended fashion, the dizzying and difficult "Hyperion falling" episode toward the very end being the notable exception.

[34] A comment on Neil Hertz's "Lurid Figures" (in *RMR*) and "More Lurid Figures" (in *diacritics* 20:3 [Fall 1990]): There is something weird going on in the attempt to deal with the death of Paul de Man by converting him, in the fullest and simultaneously Schreberian sense, from the role of the stern Father into that of the ambiguously threatening (not good enough?) Mother.

darkened by being rid of the golden sunlight, as in these brief moments of respite that interrupt the most beautiful days when, without having seen a single cloud, the sun having turned its eye elsewhere for a moment, the blue of the sky softens and turns darker." The comparison of the two blues (Giotto's background and the sky) stems indeed from the proximity of the previous narrative setting in the phrase "having traversed the garden of the Arena in full sunlight" and can thus legitimately be called a diegetic metaphor. But it is clear that more is at stake in the passage. The initial situation is very similar to that of the section we are dealing with, since the positive valorization of coolness and shelter (as marked, for instance, by the negative connotations of the word "débarrassé" which characterizes the full light as undesirable) indicates that the metaphor attempts a reconciliation of such incompatible polarities as hot/cold, inside/outside, light/dark, as well as nature/art. For the light of art, which is devoid of natural warmth and therefore potentially devoid of life, to be like nature, it must be able to borrow, by analogy, the attribute of warmth from the sun without losing its desirable coolness. Natural light has to cross the threshold of its specular representation; this illusion is convincing enough since at least some natural light, however shaded, has to penetrate into the building for the frescoes to be visible. The burden of the passage is therefore not so much to inject warmth into art as to inject coolness into nature; otherwise the symmetry of the totalizing chiasmus could not come about. Hence the necessity for an analogical description in which the heat of the sunlight would not be incompatible with a degree of coolness. What makes the passage remarkable and takes it well beyond Genette's model of a reconciled system of metaphor and metonymy (of "liaison" and "marriage"), is that Proust refuses to avail himself of the simple natural analogy that immediately comes to mind and goes out of his way to insist that the cool darkening of the sun is *not* caused by a cloud. The sentence "le soleil ayant tourné ailleurs son regard" thus becomes pure nonsense from the naturalistic point of view that the logic of the passage, structured as a nature/art dialectic, demands. The implications are far-reaching, not only for Genette's model of happy totalization, but for the entire notion of tropology as a closed system. Such systems depend on the necessary link between the existence and the knowledge of entities, on the unbreakable strength of the tie that unites the sun (as entity) with the eye (as the knowledge of the entity). The sentence "the sun having turned its eye elsewhere" is therefore, from a tropological point of view, the most impossible sentence conceivable. Its absurdity not only denies the intelligibility of natural metaphors but of all tropes; it is the figure of the unreadability of figures and therefore no longer, strictly speaking, a figure.[35]   (*AR*, 60–61)

---

[35] For a comprehensive prospect of this mote in heaven's eye, see Andrzej Warminski, "Prefatory Postscript," in his *Readings in Interpretation* (Minneapolis: University of Minnesota Press, 1987).

The bulk of this long note is devoted to de Man's version of Derrida's "La Mythologie blanche."[36] In both we are told the story of the metaphor-which-is-not-one that is left out when the rest of the figures of a given text are accounted for by a formal system of nicely crossed chiasmata. There is always a leftover: here it is the positing, the im-position of the eye upon the sun. This imposition gives rise to a figure out of nowhere, and can thus be read, at the end of the note, as the one figure that brings all the others into being. But given its own sublime non-origin, it also gives the lie to the rest of them as *natural* figures of representation. This one cannot be seen, it can only be read – and, in being read, it demands that the others be read, rather than seen, as well.

But, at the same time, the relation between Nature and Art in this passage is about the taming of the Gaze, such as Lacan describes it.[37] Inside the Chapel, the paintings tame the gaze, and this act of taming has to be injected back into nature, which is exactly what Proust does when he gives an eye to the sun. What I mean by "the Gaze" here is not the human gaze, which is not what Lacan means, but precisely the nonlocalizable gaze that is so threatening to the subject precisely because it comes from everywhere, not just from one point.[38] The aspect of *contemplatio mortis* here is present by virtue of the subject's being threatened by its own disappearance by the Gaze's very presence; hence the need, apotropaically, to tame it.

And it would be all too easy to produce a gender-centered reading of this passage, a reading de Man begs and a trap he sets as soon as he brings the "erotic" to the fore, in the paragraph cited further above, as the first elsewhere we might look for another thematic entrance to the novel. We could take up this clue, combine it with the death of Albertine and the presence of the Mother, and read this mutilation of the sun along the same lines Freud and Bataille read Schreber. And the link to desire could and should be made via the *concupiscentia oculorum* that must accompany the positing of an eye. But my desire is not there. It is better to

36 In *MP*.
37 In "Qu'est-ce qu'un tableau?," in his *Les Quatre concepts fondamentaux de la psychanalyse* (Paris: Seuil, 1973).
38 This is rather like the moment when Rilke's beheaded torso speaks and says "For there is no place that does not see you. You must change your life." You must change your life because death is everywhere and waiting, and there is no time to lose.

keep trying to account for other strangenesses in de Man's passage.

"For the light of art, which is devoid of natural warmth and therefore potentially devoid of life . . ." Who is saying this? Whose voice has entered here? Up to this point, we have been sheltered by the voice of an authoritative, if somewhat stentorian critical narrator, who has been making some technical observations concerning his predecessor. But the figure of the stern father has now laid down the law. The restatement of the figural needs of the text is accompanied by an apodictic and totalized *moralité* about what art is. Art is devoid of warmth and potentially devoid of life. Certainly we have left the realm of the organic, and the piety of its unities, behind. This is *meditatio mortis*.

Are we not in the hands of a moral critic here? The presupposition that we are would entirely change the way in which we read the modality of the verbs in what follows: "For the light of art, which is devoid of natural warmth and therefore potentially devoid of life, to be like nature, it must be able to borrow, by analogy, the attribute of warmth from the sun without losing its desirable coolness." How are we going to read the "must" in the sentence? What is its status? No matter how this question may be answered by the following sentence in de Man's text, this modal verb cannot remain uncontaminated by a certain moral imperative: it must do x, even if we can suspect, having some foreknowledge of the way in which these things work, that it will not be able to do so. The fulfillment of the moral law thus turns out to be the paradigm of the yoking of necessity and impossibility to which we have become so accustomed in so-called theoretical or so-called deconstructive discourse.

Who wants to be rid of rhetoric? Whose side is the one who is speaking on? After the sentence about the light of art, it is not really easy to give this voice a name, except perhaps the allegorical name of Saint Paul, the Moralist. The moralist speaks in shoulds and woulds and cans and cannots. He tells us what this passage needs to do but cannot do, tries to do, fails to do, and so on.

And there is something about the "necessary link," or its absence. Within the confines of this essay it appears in this note for the first time, although by the bottom of the next page it is already first a "relational link," then a " 'necessary link' " again, already in quotation marks. This is to say that above the footnote line, it appears for the first time in quotation marks, cited from the footnote.

But whence this necessary link? It is from the passage in Combray under consideration above the line. I call my reader's attention to the "entire passage," which I cite, not from this essay, but from "Semiology and Rhetoric," the introductory, programmatic essay in the same book, which was first published in a more extended version[39] just after the publication of the French version of the Proust essay in the Poulet Festschrift:

> It was hardly light enough to read, and the sensation of the light's splendor was given me only by the noise of Camus ... hammering dusty crates; resounding in the sonorous atmosphere that is peculiar to hot weather, they seemed to spark off scarlet scars; and also by the flies executing their little concert, the chamber music of summer: evocative not in the manner of a human tune that, heard perchance during the summer, afterwards reminds you of it but connected to summer by a more necessary link: born from beautiful days, resurrecting only when they return, containing some of their essence, it does not only awaken their image in our memory; it guarantees their return, their actual, persistent, unmediated presence. (*AR*, 13)

Here is the "necessary link." It is the "more necessary link" of the flies to the summer, rather than the contingency of a human tune that might be heard during that season. The "necessary link" turns out not to be a metaphor, but a metonymy. Let us take a moment to see where this "necessary link" occurs again between the same covers. In the last essay of the book, on what is almost the last page of "Excuses (*Confessions*)," de Man is trying to account for the structure of the act of language by which the cowardly Rousseau saves himself and accuses a poor, helpless maid, Marion, by uttering the noise of her name when confronted with the theft of a ribbon by the mistress of the household in which they are both employed. He has described the character of Rousseau's speech act as the production of a pure fiction, a meaningless sound that Jean-Jacques uttered, and which de Man realizes was taken for a sign invested with semantic and referential weight, rather than for a trace having none:

> What makes a fiction a fiction is not some polarity of fact and representation. Fiction has nothing to do with representation but is the absence of

[39] In *diacritics* 3:3 (Fall 1973).

any link between utterance and a referent, regardless of whether this link be causal, encoded, or governed by any other conceivable relationship that could lend itself to systematization. In fiction thus conceived the "necessary link" of the metaphor has been metonymized beyond the point of catachresis, and the fiction becomes the disruption of the narrative's referential illusion. (*AR*, 292)

Now let us remember that, in the passage from Proust that praises metaphor over metonymy, it is in fact a question of the choice between two metonymies, two relations of contiguity: that of the relation between the flies on the one hand and the music on the other to the summer – the first as more necessary and the second as more contingent. The fiction, in our case the subordinate clause "le soleil ayant tourné ailleurs son regard," is metonymized beyond the point of catachresis, not because catachresis is not present, but because of the willful refusal to do anything other than make the structure of the passage like the one we have been dealing with depend on an absolute construction, a fiction, something arbitrary and contingent. It is the very structure of this contingency, as something that will effect all texts, with which de Man ends his footnote – back, as we are, in the system of the sun and its undoing. "Necessary link" turns out to be the necessary link that ties together *Allegories of Reading*, from "Semiology and Rhetoric" through "Reading (Proust)" and into "Excuses (*Confessions*)." "Necessary link" is the law of construction of *Allegories of Reading*.

The way in which this passage reassures itself that it is doing the right thing in talking about the scene of Marcel reading the reproductions of the Giotto frescoes is by repetition or recurrence. We know we made the right choice in reading reading because, at a much later moment in the novel, we come upon the Giottos again. The same strategy frames the last essay in *Allegories of Reading*, "Excuses (*Confessions*)," where de Man's task is not so much to explain the significance of the validity-in-gratuitousness of Rousseau's uttering the name or sound "Marion," but to account for the fact that at a much later date he (Rousseau) has to come back to the episode because it still bugs him. It bugs him because, as a reader of his own text, he is in the same position as any other reader, and he himself mistakes the pure gratuitousness of his own excuse – its only excuse as an excuse – for a referential moment. Both of these essays take repetition as their starting point, what tips the reader off that something is up.

Starting out from the mechanical aspect of repetition, however, their relation is even more profound. In that essay on Rousseau, as in the footnote I am discussing here, it is a matter of the critique of the notion of tropology as a closed system (the system of Rousseau's autobiographies rather than of Proust's novel). In the essay on Proust, this shows itself as a critique of formalism we have been witnessing. In the essay on Rousseau, the point of departure has to do with the examination of the referential moment built into political and autobiographical texts, and the way in which this referential moment is built into the structure of the texts in question.

In the text on Proust, the formal system is shown to open out in the parabasis of a pure catachresis that cannot be explained from within the text considered as a set of tropological substitutions. In the text on Rousseau, the catachrestic moment is the utterance of the name, its own kind of "diegetic metaphor," or metonymy, given that the utterance takes place in a scene in which Rousseau stands accused before the bearer of the name Marion. "Le soleil ayant tourné ailleurs son regard" and "Marion" function analogically as the speaking-asides in which the fabric of the text is rent by the brutal imposition of a fact that cannot be accounted for by a structural model, although the Rousseau essay is considerably complicated by virtue of the fact of that text's being assigned to a genre, that of autobiography – arguably to a certain extent also the case with Proust – in which the speaking aside sets up the reading that accounts for its referential illusion.

In both essays the claim that such a singular disruption is propagated over the entire text and could be said to engender it is strongly present. In "Excuses," we find, among others, the following indices: ". . . what can be said about the interference of the cognitive with the performative function of excuses in the *Fourth Rêverie* will disseminate what existed as a localized disruption in the *Confessions*" (*AR*, 290); and, shortly thereafter, "[t]he implications of the random lie in the Marion episode ('je m'excusai sur le premier objet qui s'offrit") are distributed, in the *Fourth Rêverie*, over the entire text" (*AR*, 291). The "necessary link" can be made in many other ways, as is always the case with overdetermination, whether by tracking the signifier "necessary link" from its first appearance in the Proust essay to its use as a piece of the apparatus of poetics in the "Excuses" essay, or by discussing the relationship between the way in which the name Albertine ties the figural non-trope of anacoluthon in our note and in the Proust essay as a whole (1979) to "The Concept of Irony" (1976), where the same Albertine appears for the same purpose. The name anacoluthon is the figural correlate for the structure of irony considered as permanent parabasis both in "The Concept of Irony" and in "Excuses" (1977), where the reference to Schlegel's formula is pervasive.

There is yet another dimension of the encounter between these two essays and what I am trying to stage here. Genette's version of sex is informed by what I might call a vulgarized Lacanian moment:

Dans cette voie les choses ne peuvent aller plus loin que de démontrer qu'il n'est aucune signification qui se soutienne sinon du renvoi à une autre signification: touchant à l'extrême la remarque qu'il n'y a pas de langue existante, pour laquelle se pose la question de son insuffisance à couvrir le champ du signifié, étant un effet de son existence de langue qu'elle y réponde à tous les besoins. Allons-nous serrer dans le langage la constitution de l'objet, nous n'y pourrons que constater qu'elle ne se rencontre qu'au niveau du concept, bien différant d'aucun nominatif, et que la *chose*, à se réduire bien évidemment au nom, se brise en le double rayon divergent de la cause où elle a pris abri dans notre langue et du rien à qui elle a fait abandon de sa robe latine (*rem*).

(Along this way things cannot go any further than to demonstrate that there isn't any signification supported except by reference to another signification: touching at the extreme the remark that there is no existing language for which the question of its insufficiency to cover the field of the signified is put, it being an effect of its existence as language that it covers all such needs. As we go on to insert the constitution of the object in language, we will only be able to assert that [this constitution] is only to be found at the level of the concept, certainly different from any nominative, and that the *thing* [*chose*], in order to be reduced clearly to the name, is broken into the double and divergent ray of the cause, where it has taken shelter in our language, and of the nothing [*rien*] to which it has fled from its Latin dress (*rem*).[40]

Here we see the elaboration of the notion of the signifying chain as a set of metaphors. But Lacan is smarter than Genette and understands that there is a gap between the signifying chain and the absence, the nothing, of castration, of the object from which the

---

[40] Jacques Lacan, "L'Instance de la lettre dans l'inconscient ou la raison depuis Freud," in *E*, 498; my translation.

chain sets out, in its detachment, and towards which it attempts to move. Castration, for Lacan, is a name for the kind of catachrestic disruption I have been trying to understand in this essay; and it shows itself everywhere along the signifying chain as a disruption that can be seen at all points. It manifests itself in the paragraph just cited in the breakup of the nominative *causa* into its objective, accusative matter, the "nothing" that stands in, in Old French, for the name of the masculine member. The dress (*robe*) comes off to reveal the wound of the scar of castration. The imposition of a missing penis on the mother's body is the catachrestic positing of the first figure. The thing inquires back into its cause, the nothing from which it is severed. Sexual anxiety as a motive for interpretation is a thematic that permeates "Reading (Proust)" and "Excuses (Confessions)" more than any other essays by de Man.

The nonexistent cloud, the "natural metaphor," now an artistic device – that is, the gaze of the sun – turns out to have the same function, in the novel, that the name "Marion" has for the autobiography. Such is the gaze of the name. This is why "The sun must bear no name, gold flourisher, / but be in the difficulty of what it is to be."[41]

The past not recaptured, or "the figure of this circularity is time"

Everything which fell under the scrutiny of his words was transformed, as though it had become radioactive.[42]

He was one of us
only, pure prose.[43]

At this point we must go and see where Proust ends up in the text of Paul de Man. Toward this end I now move on to "Sign and Symbol in Hegel's *Aesthetics*," one of de Man's most ambitious later essays. The opening statement of this essay concerns the topos, familiar to the reader of the later de Man, of the incompati-

---

41 Wallace Stevens, "Notes Toward a Supreme Fiction," in his *The Palm at the End of the Mind* (New York: Anchor, 1971).
42 Theodor W. Adorno, "Walter Benjamin," in his *Prisms*, trans. Samuel and Shierry Weber (Cambridge, MA: MIT Press, 1981), 229.
43 Robert Lowell, "Beyond the Alps," in his *Life Studies* (New York: Vintage, 1959), 3.

bility between the aesthetics and the poetics of literature. He begins with an apparently personal note, something to soften up the large hall at Harvard, where the prodigal son returns to receive many guests:

There is something bleakly abstract and ugly about literary theory that cannot be entirely blamed on the perversity of its practitioners. Most of us feel internally divided between the compulsion to theorize about literature and a much more attractive, spontaneous encounter with literary works. Hence the relief one feels whenever a method of literary study is proposed that allows for a measure of theoretical rigor and generality (and which is therefore, to speak from an academic point of view, teachable) while leaving intact, or even enhancing, the aesthetic appreciation or the potential for historical insight that the work provides.   (*AI*, 91–92)

The ironic combination of the use of personal language to describe theoretical predicaments in this essay begins here. The task of the essay itself will be to explain this ambivalence in a reading that moves over apparently unconnected texts in the Hegelian corpus, to move the explanation of ambivalence from a personal to a theoretical level. This goal is present from the very beginning in the mode of the hypothetical, just as it was in the Proust essay ("But if reading is truly problematic . . ." [*AR*, 58]), and the task before us appears at the end of the first paragraph from which I have already cited: "If it is indeed the case that a difficulty exists between the aesthetics and the poetics of literature and that this difficulty is inherent in the matter itself, then it would be naïve [again, the naïve, TAP] to believe that one can avoid or dodge the task of its precise description" (*AI*, 92). We shall see that the entire essay moves from the personal statement – "most of us feel" – to the impersonality of the general statement about that which it is naïve to believe one can avoid.

The moment of selection is presented in a tone at once blithe and overwhelming:

For reasons that have to do with this particular occasion but hardly stand in need of a less personal justification, Hegel's *Aesthetics* offers perhaps the most arduous challenge to such an enterprise. Nowhere else do the structure, the history, and the judgment of art seem to come as close to being systematically carried out, and nowhere else does this systematic synthesis rest so exclusively on one definite category, in the full Aristotelian sense of the term, called the aesthetic. Under a variety of names, this category never ceased to be prominent in the development of Western thought... Whether we know it, or like it, or not, most of us are Hegelians and quite orthodox ones at that ... [T]he name "Hegel" stands here for an all-encompassing vessel in which so many currents have gathered and been preserved that one is likely to find there almost any idea one knows to have been gathered from elsewhere or hopes to have invented oneself. Few thinkers have so many disciples who never read a word of their master's writings. (*AI*, 92–93)

The law of the Master extends to cover each particular, each one of us, its subjects, inasmuch as we speak the language we speak – or, more simply, inasmuch as we speak. Given the steadily mounting stream of totalizations, it becomes impossible to argue with this paragraph, and to do anything but to go on and read Hegel with our guide or model de Man. Given that our particular selves are all contained therein, it would behoove us to go there and to find out who we are. Hegel is the great novel that records all of our experiences as readers and as thinkers in a systematic fashion. What could be more tempting, or more compelling, especially if it reveals something to us about the "compulsion to theorize" with which we began? The universalizing structure of Hegel's thought will provide us with the machinery necessary to move forward from "this particular occasion" to the most overarching and far-reaching truths about the way things work.

Precisely because of this capacity of the System to subsume all particulars within the concept, it could only be the case with Hegel that the selection of the text to be read presents us with no problem of choice, but simply with a problem of recognizing the truth of the way things are. There are no gyrations to go through about whether the choice of text will get us where we want to go; for the choice has already been made at such a level that only an idiot, one whose particular orneriness did not live up to the dignity of the teacher, could do otherwise. So Hegel is the name of the name that is not, cannot be simply one name among others. "Hegel," in fact, may not coincide with the empirical person of that name, for it is clear from the last sentences in de Man's paragraph that "Hegel" is an allegorical name, a particular name that fulfills a universal function. If there were some kind of nonconvergence between Hegel and "Hegel," then this might serve as a very appropriate example of the allegorical structure de Man will spend this essay elaborating, and which his properly philosophical reader will be unable to recognize.

The next matter of discussion has to do with the definition of the term "symbolic."[44] On the one hand, the term "symbolic" refers to one of the three particular periods of art in the Hegelian scheme of things (symbolic, Hellenic, Romantic); on the other, it also refers to a linguistic structure that could be said to define the structure of what we call art itself. In the light of the second sense, de Man offers us a translation of the famous dictum that art is "the sensory manifestation of the Idea" as "the beautiful is symbolic." Inasmuch as the symbol represents not the arbitrary relation to its content that characterizes the sign, but rather "the concrete interpenetration of meaning and form," we can, according to de Man, assimilate the function of art to the more general, symbolic realm.

But there is a small problem, a check on our progress, for Hegel's own judgments about art fail to link up with his own evaluations of the art of his time:

Hegel's *Aesthetics* thus appears to be, traditionally enough, a theory of symbolic form. Yet a disturbing element of personal inadequacy in Hegel himself seems to prevent the tradition of the *Aesthetics*'s interpretation from resting content in this assurance. For one thing, next to the familiar-sounding assertion, which we think we easily enough understand, that art partakes of the beautiful and is therefore a sensory manifestation of the idea, stands, in the same text, Hegel's more disturbing statement that art is, irrevocably, for us a thing of the past. Would this then mean that the sensory manifestation of the idea is no longer accessible to us in this form, that we are no longer able to produce truly symbolic forms of art? And is it not something of an irony of literary history and a concrete disavowal of Hegel that he declared art to have ended at the very moment that a new modernity was about to discover and to refine the power of the symbol beyond anything that Hegel's somewhat philistine taste could ever have imagined? (*AI*, 93–94)

What follows upon this is a recitation of the way in which this apparently personal fault in Hegel, revealing itself as it does in "Hegel," has prevented readers from Gadamer to Adorno, and on to Adorno's student and de Man's colleague, Peter Szondi, from seeing the relation between this apparently personal judgment on Hegel's part and what he has to say about the nature of language. The moment from this discussion I should like to retain is Peter

---

[44] De Man approached this problem of the double register of the word "symbolism" twenty years earlier in his "The Double Aspect of Symbolism," now in *RC*.

Szondi's expression of this disappointment, which de Man cites a few pages later:

> When Proust compares a moon which is already visible in daylight to an actress who has entered the theater well before making her entrée on the stage, and who, not yet made up or dressed, merely watches her fellow players, then we may well ask if it is legitimate, in a case like this, to distinguish between the abstract and the concrete, between meaning and image. The secret meaning of such comparisons must be sought in the discovery of analogies, of correspondences – the very *correspondances* which Baudelaire celebrates in his famous poem. To the poetic outlook they appear as the guarantee of the unity of the world ... One can certainly not reproach Hegel for his inability to notice such correspondences (although they do not appear only in modern poetry), but one cannot deny that it is his inadequate conception of the essence of language which is the cause of his failure.[45]

De Man's citing of almost an entire page of passages (in the course of a fourteen-page essay) from Peter Szondi, in order to emphasize that Hegel's genre theory is a disappointment, has to be about something else. In fact it is about the entrée of the example of Proust into de Man's argument here, like the actress in the simile cited by Szondi. For the importance of Proust as an example can only, in fact, become evident at the end of de Man's essay, when once again it will be a matter of emphasizing the material character of Giotto's treatment of the Allegories of the Virtues and Vices at Padua. And it is hardly an accident that the passage de Man chooses to cite from Szondi has to do with the moon, the only heavenly body other than the sun visible during the height of day, and one that is visible in reflecting the sun's light – just as the actress in question *watches* her fellow players as though from off-stage, and just as the sun turns its eye elsewhere in the passage with which we have been concerned above.

De Man cites Szondi not so much as an example of contemporary critics' plaints about Hegel, but in a criticism of Szondi's having been seduced by an aestheticizing language that uses the language of Proust's symbols to complain about Hegel, when in fact the example he cites represents the very concrete interpenetra-

---

[45] Cited by de Man (*AI*, 95) from Peter Szondi, *Poetik und Geschichtsphilosophie*, vol. I (Frankfurt-on-Main: Suhrkamp, 1974), 396 (Paul de Man's translation). I have commented on Peter Szondi's "untimely death" (*AI*, 94), a locution that strikes a personal note uncharacteristic for de Man, in my afterword below.

tion of meaning and form, the doctrine of the symbolic, of which Hegel speaks. The point of what is about to come in de Man's argument is that Hegel's theory of the sign or the symbol is, rather than being simplistic, too subtle and sophisticated even for a critic such as Szondi to get it. And inasmuch as Szondi's reference to Hegel's "inadequate conception of the essence of language" unquestionably refers to Heidegger via this very locution, de Man's disappointment at Szondi's disappointment with Hegel is a statement of the insufficiency of the language of essence itself in respect of language. For language to have an essence, whether meaning (as connotative or denotative), metaphor, or whatever, would be to make the word "language" participate in the language game of symbolic revelation, of depth, that de Man decries as the very ideology of the aesthetic and to which he constantly refers.

Now de Man's own argument starts in earnest. The problem is, bluntly stated, a very classical one: how to make sense of the coexistence, within Hegel's text, of the two propositions: (1) that art is the sensory manifestation of the idea, which de Man has already pre-translated as "the beautiful is symbolic"; and (2) that art is a thing of the past. How will our Paul be able to reconcile the spirit of Hegelianism, "the sensory manifestation of the idea," with the apparently more contingent letter of Hegel's text, "art is a thing of the past?" In order to show the more profound and necessary link between these two statements, we are going to have to go far afield from the *Aesthetics*, says de Man: "The answer to this question takes us on a circuitous route, first away from and then back to the *Aesthetics*, a route on which I only have time to point out some stations in an itinerary that is not, I am afraid, an entirely easy walk" (*AI*, 95).

I am afraid that I am only going to make that walk even harder. In an essay the headnote of which tells us that it has left intact the traces of its occasion as the Renato Poggioli Lecture in Comparative Literature at Harvard, we might not be surprised to learn that there is only one sentence deleted between the typescript and the published version of the essay. The sentence in question follows the one just cited and reads: "But I trust you don't expect from me to take you on anything but an arrid [*sic*] journey" ("Sign and Symbol," typescript, 8). The "circuitous route" takes us not only from a later Hegel back to an earlier Hegel and back again, but back to the Proust essay. This constant quilting motion, which moves back and forth, likens the structure of Proust's novel as a story of anagnorisis or recognition to the structure of the Hegelian text, which thus becomes the novel of the concept. The word "stations" of de Man's sentence, following in the same register, refers, of course, to the Giotto panels of the Life of Christ that stand over the Allegories of the Virtues and Vices in the Chapel. The "arid" (besides reminding us of the heat of the sun when crossing the Garden so as to seek shelter in the Chapel) takes us forward to the end of de Man's essay, to the barren ("kahl") character of allegory, as de Man glosses Hegel's treatment of it. But its misspelling takes us to the realm of Arrid Extra Dry, that is to say, to advertising, where we presently go:

Hegel's assertion that art belongs unreservedly to the order of the symbolic is made in the context of a distinction between symbol and sign that in the realm of art does not seem to apply . . . Hegel offers a characterization of the sign which stresses the arbitrariness of the relationship between the sensory component necessarily involved in any signification and the intended meaning. The red, white, and green flag of Italy bears no actual relationship to the color of the country which, as seen from the air, is predominantly ochre in color; only very naïve children are supposed to be cute enough to be amazed that Italy actually does not have the same uniform color it has in their atlas. The symmetrical obverse of this situation is that of Roland Barthes reflecting on the naturalization of the signifier in his analysis of an advertisement for spaghetti, in which the white pasta, the red tomatoes, and the green peppers are so irresistably effective because they convey, at least to the non-Italian, the illusion of devouring, of interiorizing the very essence of *italianité* – and very cheaply at that.   (*AI*, 95–96)[46]

Advertising works by infantilizing us, by turning us all into naïve children. (Naïveté again.) The characterization of the sign as arbitrary is extremely important for de Man, because it implies the power of the sheer negativity of a consciousness that has linked together the signifier and the signified, thus using the raw material of the signifier for its own purposes in effacing some properties of the signified (and, by the inevitable ideological move, the referent) in order to stress others – in the very same manner that Proust's

---

[46] This example (from Roland Barthes, "Rhetoric of the Image," in his *Image-Music-Text*, trans. Stephen Heath [New York: Hill and Wang, 1977]) also comes up in an essay from the early seventies on Roland Barthes. See de Man, "Roland Barthes and the Limits of Structuralism," in *RC*.

narrator is free to relate himself to the objects of his fancy of reading or not, in the same way that Proust's composition is like the process of selection and elision of the critic. The sign is thus "something great" because it testifies to the power of consciousness to remake the world in the world of signification with these powers. The sign is great, we could say, because of its testimony to man's fiction-making capacities, because of its ability to lie. In more technical terms, the sign testifies to the ability of the subject that uses it to link together subject and predicate at will, and to pass such links off as necessary links.

"Arbitrariness" here has the full force of the sense of calling a willful person arbitrary, in the sense of an arbitrary and therefore despotic leader.[47] It is no accident that Fichte's name occurs in the course of this discussion, for this is precisely the characteristic of the Fichtian dialectic, according to de Man, wherein the self is posited in a thetic moment of pure catachresis, after which point it has properties attributed to it by predication. De Man comments this in "The Concept of Irony," where we also encounter Schlegel's discussion – itself presented by de Man as a gloss on Fichtean metaphysics – of irony as "unbedingte Willkür," unconditioned arbitrariness. "Albertine" is also a prominent figure there. The choice of the example from Barthes is dictated not only by de Man's fascination with it – the idea of eating Italy when sitting down to supper is a household joke *chez* de Man – but also from within the Hegel corpus itself, as when we learn, in de Man's response to Geuss, that "national banners" are for Hegel an example of the great arbitrariness of the sign (*AI*, 188).

But how is this subject constructed for Hegel? We have to leap back yet again, to the first volume of Hegel's *Encyclopedia*, to the "Preliminary Notion" of his "little" *Logic*, to find the answer. De Man glosses Hegel thus, with the following *Zusatz* of his own:

The thinking subject is to be kept sharply distinguished from the perceiving subject, in a manner that is reminiscent of (or that anticipates) the distinction we have just encountered in the differentiation between sign and symbol. Just as the sign refuses to be in the service of sensory

---

[47] See in this light de Man's analysis of Pascal on "Justesse, Force," *AI*, 67–68, and, for source material, Erich Auerbach, "The Political Theory of Pascal," in his *Scenes from the Drama of European Literature* (Minneapolis: University of Minnesota Press, 1984).

perceptions but uses them instead for its own purposes, thought, unlike perception, appropriates the world and literally "subjects" it to its own powers. More specifically, thought subsumes the infinite singularity and individuation of the perceived world under ordering principles that lay claim to generality. The agent of this appropriation is language. "Since language," says Hegel, "is the labor of thought, we cannot say anything in language that is not general" . . . Thus the sign, random and singular [that is, arbitrary, TAP] at its first position, turns into symbol just as the I, so *singular* in its independence from anything that is not itself, becomes, in the general thought of logic, the most inclusive, plural, general, and impersonal of subjects. (*AI*, 97)

Here I am compelled to make a rather sententious utterance about the somewhat famous or infamous pair of pages that follow this moment in de Man's text, and which lay out his reading of Hegel's dictum "ich kann nicht sagen, was ich nur meine," a sentence de Man comes to translate, in several stages, as "I cannot say I." This passage tends to provoke either a sense of wonder and of a bravura performance or else of ridiculousness and contempt. The point is, once the argument – which for Hegel is a fact – has been stated, that what can be said can only be said in the realm of the general, then these pages are, argumentatively speaking, super-erogatory. They constitute a provocation disguised as a pedagogi-cal tableau. The matter of importance is the conclusion drawn from the demonstration, and the gap between it and my own conclusion about why these pages are here.

The sign turns into a symbol because what it *says* is said immediately in the realm of the universal, leaving all particularity behind. Thus it would function in the way that symbols do in their movement from concrete instantiation to universal meaning. The blank positionality of the signifier "I" turns immediately into the "rudderless signification" of "Pascal's Allegory of Persuasion" (*AI*, 59) in the loss of its determination in and through (the passage of) time, in fact, in the very movement from one instant to the next.

This point is hardly radical or original. It is simply a restatement of a Hegelian topos that we know in our time through the dissemination it has achieved in the Jakobsonian notion of the shifter, the syncategoreme that depends for its referent on its spatio-temporal position in discourse. (In this century, the only person stupid enough – or maybe smart enough – to have erected an entire metaphysics on getting this wrong is Bertrand Russell, in his *Philosophy of Logical Atomism*. Let us remember that the generation of British philosophers against whom Russell revolted was composed largely of British neo-Hegelians, such as Bradley; and that Russell chooses exactly this moment in Hegel to depart from his teachers and to erect his scientistic epistemology. In Hegelian terms, Russell is an idiot. But idiocy – smart idiocy – is what one needs to carry off a strong reading of Hegel.)

The thing of import for us here is that the Hegelian topos that the word "I" cannot reveal anything particular – that when I say "I," I say what every I has it to say – gives us the intertext for all the kinds of bizarre jokes to which we have heretofore been exposed about any kind of personal failure on the part of the philosopher to live up to the dignity of his calling and to speak in the realm of the concept. Thus "I" is a symbol that is cut off from its sensory token. According to the Hegelian axiom, it cannot be anything else. What is most intriguing, and what drives the mor(t)alistic tone not only of this essay, but of so much of de Man, is that, once again, the example he cites in his pseudo-demonstration is about something else, it is about the conjunction of language ontology with a kind of ethics:

> Certainly, since the validity of thought resides in its generality, we cannot be interested, in thought, in the private, singular opinions of the thinker but will expect from him a more humble kind of philosophical self-forgetting. "When Aristotle," says Hegel, "demands [from the philosopher – de Man's interpolation] that he live up to the dignity of his calling, then this dignity consists of his ability to discard particular opinions . . . and to leave things to be what they are in their own right." When philosophers merely state their opinion, they are not being philosophical. "Since language states only what is general, I cannot say what is only my opinion [so kann ich nicht sagen was ich nur meine]." *(AI, 97)*

What we have here is the yoking together of the realms of language ontology and ethics around the topos of *singularity*.[48] This is where the novelty of de Man's argument lies, although perhaps he himself does not realize it. It is not possible to decide here whether the theory of the positionally blank pronoun has

---

[48] All the work of Emmanuel Levinas inserts itself here in this battle with Hegel as to whether an ethical relation with the singular can be maintained. But in order to put up the fight, Levinas has to mount a critique of the entire notion of manifestation, of the sensory manifestation of the idea. The other, for Levinas, is recuperated by any egology as soon as one begins to speak the language of manifestation.

been invented to exemplify or to justify the dignity of philosophical statement; or whether it is somehow rather the opposite, that the facticity of the linguistic utterance as necessarily universal has motivated this crucial philosopheme. Is what is here asserted as a linguistic truth dictated by the ideological cliché of who the philosopher is – the one who speaks the truth of the concept, of the general – or vice versa? A turn to the corpus of Aristotle might shed contextual light on the decision, but it would not resolve our question, which is, properly speaking, apodictic.

Only the posing of this question can help us to situate the argument of this essay between the now wildly ironic business at the beginning about the theorist's "compulsion to theorize" and the last sentence, where the *moral* of the story turns out to be "[n]o wonder that literary theory has such a bad *name*, all the more so since the emergence of thought and of theory is not something our *own* thought can hope to prevent or to control." (*AI*, 104; emphasis mine).[49] What is asserted in the conjoined ethical and logical modalities combined in the "kann nicht" of "ich kann nicht sagen, was ich nur meine," "I cannot state what is only my opinion," is the necessity and the impossibility that the universal aegis of the law extend to cover all its singular subjects.

I illustrate this point, in an ironic mode, with a story. Once I was standing in the Greyhound bus terminal in New Haven, when a man approached the counter to buy a ticket to Atlantic City. After the transaction, he turned to the sales clerk and asked her, "Say, can I smoke on that bus?" She responded: "Well, that bus goes through the State of New York, and there's a law that there is no smoking permitted on buses in the State of New York, so I guess you can't smoke on the bus." To which the traveler responded: "Have you *seen* that law? I mean, have *you* *seen* that law?" The moral law covers me inasmuch as I speak; thus ethics is the art of speaking well. But I can always keep my own counsel. Or can I?

"Kann nicht" is a very interesting expression, for, depending on emphasis, it can mean two radically different things, that I can *not* do something and that I *cannot* do something. This manifests itself in the crucial distinction in English between "can not," which is

---

[49] It is surprising that Jacques Derrida does not really thematize the double register of the epistemological and the ethical in the context of this essay, since he has had so much to say about this conjunction elsewhere. See "Mnemosyne," in his *Mémoires pour Paul de Man*.

ambiguous, and "cannot," which is not ambiguous and belongs to the order of necessity. The point I am trying to make here is that in the sense that Hegel recalls Aristotle, the "ich kann nicht sagen, was ich nur meine" shades off into a kind of "ich darf nicht sagen, was ich nur meine," "I am not allowed to state what is only my opinion." But there is no doubt, in the context of the beginning of the little *Logic*, on which side Hegel's sentence falls, that is to say in the field of logical necessity. Still, the reference to Aristotle undoubtedly brings in the ethical dimension, which thus cannot be dismissed.

We still have quite a way to go on our arid journey, our barren (*kahl*) road back towards the name of allegory. For the next section of de Man's essay brings us back to the matter of the "circularity" to which we have been recurring, and, ultimately, to Proust's commentary on Giotto. De Man concludes his statement of this whole section of his argument thus, by moving from the structural impossibility of particular statements of his experience to the necessity that the Hegelian system forget this impossibility in order, lumbering like a jumbo jet, to get off the ground:

Thus, at the very onset of the entire system, in the preliminary consideration of the science of logic, an inescapable obstacle threatens the entire construction that follows. The philosophical I is not only self-effacing, as Aristotle demanded, in the sense of being humble and inconspicuous, it is also self-effacing in the much more radical sense that the position of the I, which is the condition for thought, implies its eradication, not, as in Fichte, as the symmetrical position of its negation but as the undoing, the erasure of any relationship, logical or otherwise, that could be conceived between what the I is and what it says it is.[50] The very enterprise of thought seems to be paralyzed from the start. It can only get under way if the knowledge that renders it impossible, the knowledge that the linguistic position of the I is only possible if the I forgets what it is (namely, I), if this knowledge is itself forgotten.

The way in which the passage we are reading . . . forgets its own statement is by describing the predicament it states, which is a logical difficulty devoid of any phenomenal or experiential dimension, as if it were an event in time, a narrative, or a history. At the beginning of the paragraph, after having apodictically asserted that the act of thought predicates generality, Hegel adds, as if it were a word of caution, that

50 This very gap is of course what makes psychoanalysis possible. De Man, unbeknown to his auditors at Harvard, had already (in 1976) given a treatment of the moments in the text of Fichte to which he alludes here. The text is "The Concept of Irony," in *AI*.

these assertions cannot, at this point, be proven. We should nevertheless not consider them, he says, as his own opinions ... but should take them to be facts. We can verify these facts by way of the experience of our own thought, by testing them, trying them out upon ourselves. But this experimentation is only accessible to those "who have acquired a certain power of attention and abstraction," that is to say, who are capable of thought. The proof of thought is possible only if we postulate that what has to be proven (namely, that thought is possible) is indeed the case. *The figure of this circularity is time.* Thought is proleptic: it projects the hypothesis of its own possibility into a future, in the hyperbolic expectation that the process that made thought possible will eventually catch up with this projection. The hyperbolic I projects itself as thought in the hope of re-cognizing itself when it will have run its course.

(*AI*, 98–99, emphasis TAP)

The Hegelian topos of trying thoughts out upon ourselves has fueled philosophical thought well into our own time. Theodor Adorno's *The Jargon of Authenticity* could not exist without constantly weaving in and out of it. Nor could a thinker apparently as far removed from Hegel or Adorno as Roger Caillois.[51] Then there is Kierkegaard: "Abraham cannot be mediated; in other words, he cannot speak. As soon as I speak, I express the Universal, and if I do not do so, no one can understand me. As soon as Abraham wants to express himself in the universal, he must declare that his situation is a spiritual trial [*Anfægtelse*], for he has no higher expression of the universal that ranks above the universal he violates."[52]

But I have emphasized the sentence in which the knot of opacity of this passage is concentrated. The figure here is not a trope, for we cannot call anagnorisis, recognition, or narrative tropes as such, for they do not involve substitutions, but displacements (although, in fact they may promise substitutions – full Being for empty being, for instance). This is the meaning of speculation, in thought as in the marketplace. The recourse to the figure of projection confirms this: thought, here, is a little object a.

– In the absolutely technical sense that thought here is the name for the object that is thrown out by the subject that then returns, the opacity of the object, its material character – which is not an instantiation, being the incarnation of the knot of impossibility

---

51 See his *The Necessity of the Mind*, trans. Michael Syrotinski (Venice, CA: Lapis Press, 1990), 4.
52 *FR*, 60. That this moment in Kierkegaard is tied up with the sublimity of *horror religiosus* will have to be meditated elsewhere.

that stands at the nexus of formation of this thought, of this object. Lacan's insistence, developed out of a happy encounter with Winnicott, that the child's grasping of the first object – perhaps its image in the mirror – is a *méconnaissance*, a miscovery, flows from the same knot of necessity and impossibility that de Man has been discussing in Hegel, namely that this is not a cognition or recognition of the truth, but rather, as a positing, in occurring, is true. For before its event, which is the positing of the subject (though not in idealist terms) there is nobody there to cognize or to recognize anything. This moment is the marking of the child's insertion into the symbolic order; but the moment occurs as a trauma, as a first encounter with the real. De Man's innovation is to insist that this kind of encounter does not merely stop at the moment this first encounter *happens*, but in fact is re-encountered, re-mis-experienced, at all points of encounter with the real along the way.[53]

Narrative, the telling of a story, of a history, depends upon the possibility of being able to *incorporate* event, occurrence, happening into a system of tropological substitutions in which the initial *happening* appears to be (as in the subordinate clause, "le soleil ayant tourné ailleurs son regard") apparently merely another moment in the story. I use the word "incorporation" most advisedly, for what de Man shows is that this attempt at recuperation will always fail, will never be able to assimilate the foreignness of this foreign body, which will function like a foreign word.[54] The "logical difficulty" functions like a catachresis in the structure of the narrative.

Time, like irony, is the name we give to the fact that what the narrative, or the theory of narrative – for our purposes, these are the same here – tries to interiorize as a moment within itself, is incorporated and thus perpetually re-encountered as a scar that will not heal. Every moment of the narrative that ensues from, happens upon this event will somehow bear its mark. The origin itself may be a pure riddle, but the story that sets out from the origin will be riddled by this riddle, which can be read at every moment along the way. The figure of this circularity is time. Time

---

[53] We shall see this shortly, for it is the very reason why Marcel, in his encounter with the Giottos, describes them as having "une étrangeté saisissante."
[54] "German words of foreign extraction are the Jews of language" (*MM*, English, 110). Elsewhere, Adorno refers to foreign words as silver ribs inserted into the body of language.

is the name we give to this permanent scar inflicted upon consciousness, at and as its outbreak, by its encounter with the real. The illusion, or, as de Man puts it here, the forgetting, consists in the belief that through time time will itself be neutralized or redeemed, that we can escape from its predicament once we begin to speak. "Hegel" turns out to be the name of a novel, a theory of narrative, of the novel, that, like Proust-writer, "is the one who knows that the hour of truth, like the hour of death, never arrives on time, since what we call time is precisely truth's inability to coincide with itself" (*AR*, 78):

One understands the necessity for the mind to shelter itself from self-erasure, to resist it with all the powers of the intellect. This resistance takes a multitude of forms, among which the aesthetic is not the least efficacious. For it is not difficult to see that the problem can be recast in terms of the distinctiveness between sign and symbol. As we saw, the I, in its freedom from sensory determination, is originally similar to the sign. Since, however, it states itself as what it is not, it represents as determined a relationship to the world that is in fact arbitrary, that is to say, it states itself as a symbol. (*AI*, 100)

The I, inasmuch as it would pass itself off as a sign by virtue of its own arbitrary proclamation of its relation to its experiences as predicates, can only do so by saying itself, proclaiming itself, as an empty universal. Thus, in saying – the universal – what it is not – a gathering of particulars – it represents itself as in a determined relation, when in fact its relation is rudderless, arbitrary. Thus it passes itself off as a symbol. A kind of totalization occurs here, in respect of the sign, inasmuch as the linguistic sign can do aught else but speak in the realm of the general. But, in doing so, it loses any claim to link its individuality up with the realm of the general in which it speaks. In the logical sense it is pure universal, cut off from any existential statement. The I, as a symbol that says what it does not mean – I itself rather than I myself – is, like evil, in a formulation of the early Benjamin that de Man cites incorrectly (he substitues "allegory" for "evil") at the end of *Blindness and Insight*, the non-being of what it represents.[55]

---

[55] I thank Andrzej Warminski for recalling to me that the actual subject of this last predicate is not "allegory," but "evil." See Walter Benjamin, *The Origin of German Tragic Drama*, trans. John Osborne (London: New Left Books, 1977), 233. The German texts of these sentences are to be found in Walter Benjamin, *Gesammelte Schriften*, ed. R. Tiedemann and H. Schweppenhäuser (Frankfurt-on-Main: Suhrkamp, 1972–80), vol. I, 406.

In the other and simultaneous register of de Man's essay, that which I have called the ethical, we might borrow another formulation close by in Benjamin's text, and say that what takes place in allegory is "the faithless leap toward resurrection," where resurrection here would equal a past successfully interiorized, hence recaptured, capable of being redeemed or played back.[56]

De Man's point here is echoed, again under the sign of the name Benjamin, when he says, responding to a question from Meyer Abrams after his lecture on "The Task of the Translator":

[T]heorization, the theorization of language, is initially and fundamentally a part of language . . . That there is no poetry without criticism of poetry, and that the two necessarily involve each other. I give this the merest name "theorization." The theorization is inherent in language. A language which would not be – and this has nothing to do with common and ordinary language: there's nothing more theoretical than the language on the street, than the common language which . . . The only people who believe that there is language that is not theoretical are professors of literature. They are the only ones who think . . . If you ask the people, they know that language is theoretical, that language is always, and that language is constantly – with the people, whoever that is. If you get popular uses of language, they are highly, infinitely theoretical, they are constantly metalinguistic, they constantly turn back upon language. Or if you see what mass manifestations of language, or mythologies are, they are always highly theoretized. The notion of separating theory is a very understandable, nostalgic move in our profession, I'm afraid . . . I think so, I'm afraid. (*RT*, 102)

The topos explic(it)ated here can be said to date, for our purposes, from Hegel's newspaper polemic of 1807 entitled "Who Thinks Abstractly?,"[57] a question which Hegel answers by saying that it is the language of the street that best represents abstract thinking, because it has all sorts of assumptions about the identity of subject and predicate in standard statements; whereas philosophers always, in asking questions of essence, ask about the concept. What de Man operates in the passage above is an ironic reversal of

---

[56] Already the notion of playback here enters the realm of another great Benjaminian topos, that of mechanical reproduction. These days, so many people seem to talk about "redemptive reading." I do not know what this means, but I do know that if people are trying to do it, they misunderstand rather dreadfully the "faithless" aspect of Benjamin's statement.

[57] See *Hegel: Texts and Commentary*, ed. and trans. Walter Kaufmann (New York: Anchor, 1965), 113–18. The German text is to be found in G. W. F. Hegel, *Jenaer Schriften* (Frankfurt-on-Main: Suhrkamp, 1970), 575–81.

the Hegelian topos for the purpose of making a pedagogical point about the ideology of literary aestheticism in the academy. He does not take the same, rather disturbingly proto-populist position whenever it is a question of addressing a literary–journalistic audience. Thus the fundamental thought which de Man links up between the *Encyclopedia* and the *Aesthetics* can be seen to operate in a text that dates from the year of the publication of the *Phenomenology* itself, the novel in which, says de Man, this truth of language is forgotten so that the story of the mind can be told.

We have yet to account for the scriptural reconciliation of the two dicta, "art is the sensory manifestation of the idea," and "art is a thing of the past," which de Man projected so hyperbolically as the goal of his demonstration at and as and from its outset. What is involved is a kind of differently inflected restatement of what has already come around the topos of Hegel's distinction between interiorizing memory, *Erinnerung,* and the faculty of inscriptional memory, thinking memory, *Gedächtnis.* The language of *Erinnerung* is what I call the naïve language of the symbol, the language that correlates memory with the *expression* of words in which the essence of memory is contained. It is a version of both the affective fallacy and of the intentional fallacy, in the sense that it is the idea that somehow memory inscribes the particular experience of a subject that can be read and thus interiorized by a reader as thought or experience. One should be careful here, for the unenunciated but crucial distinction between the intentional fallacy and the affective fallacy, as they are stated by Wimsatt and Beardsley in the essays of these names, has to do with the fact that while the former concerns text production (the meaning of the text is the manifestation of the *author's* intention), the latter concerns reception (the meaning of the text is the *reader's* emotive reaction). For my purposes, though, since both essays treat fallacies of meaning – whether it is put there by the author or invested by the reader – I can treat them together as examples of the topos of interiorization. It is only a matter of being clear about which end of the author–reader circuit is making the deposit and which the withdrawal.[58]

The language of interiorization has its concomitant, in contem-

---

[58] See William Wimsatt and Monroe Beardsley, "The Intentional Fallacy" and "The Affective Fallacy," in William K. Wimsatt, *The Verbal Icon: Studies in the Meaning of Poetry* (Louisville: University Press of Kentucky, 1954).

porary poetics, in the notion of actualization,[59] that reading somehow is related to the process of actualizing a set of experiences that remain potential in their inscription in the literary text. For Hegel, this type of activity is to be distinguished from the imageless verbality of thought, which has its power in thinking in signs, not in symbols; signs that represent, in their arbitrariness – let us not forget to recall – the very power of the mind over the sensory.

De Man puts forth Hegel's distinction between *Erinnerung* and *Gedächtnis* somewhat apodictically, leaving it to his readers to piece together the fact that the reason why thought belongs to the faculty that treats signs has to do, precisely, with the greatness of the sign, namely that it testifies (the figure is not inappropriate) to the power of thought to be free of determination, or just free. Thought has to depend on the sign and not on the symbol so that it can think and project other than what is the case, a sentiment that will inspire not only Feuerbach and Marx, but also Mallarmé.

(And the best commentary on the relation between the labor of the negative in Marx and Mallarmé remains Maurice Blanchot's "Literature and the Right to Death." Here one should pay attention to the element of *parody* that serves as the link between the way in which Blanchot tells the story about what one does to material elements of the world in order to build a stove and what one does to material elements of the world in order to write a book, where he lists these elements as "paper, ink, the state of the language." The problem of the materiality of the text in the work of Paul de Man could be elaborated starting out from a clear statement of the way in which "the state of the language" does not belong to the world in the same way that pen and ink do. In order to approach this knot we would have to explain the peculiarity of the way in which the words belonging to the registers of "phenomenal" and "material" function in de Man's text. "Material" does not necessarily belong to the same register as "materiality"; for in the case of the passage in Blanchot to which I allude, pen, paper, and stove are all phenomenal entities in the world, that is to say, they are all accessible to cognition, because they are material. The non-phenomenality of language patently is not material in this sense, and yet the word materiality in de Man relates to the act

---

[59] See de Man's commentaries on Riffaterre and Jauss in *RT*.

of positing or inscription, the evenemential character of the occurrence of texts.)

The crucial fact of the distinction between *Erinnerung* and *Gedächtnis* comes home in the all too lapidary sentence, "Memory [*Gedächtnis*] effaces remembrance (or recollection) [*Erinnerung*] just as the I effaces itself" (German interpolations mine, *AI*, 102), which means that the arbitrariness of the power of thought, which is correlated with the power of the sign over the "material, phenomenal" (*RT*, 10) world (which can also be the "material, phenomenal" aspect of the sign taken as a thing in the world, as de Man does in the passage in "The Resistance to Theory" from which I have just cited), effaces the "necessary link" of symbolism, of metaphor, that obtains in the intentional–expressive (ideological in de Man's sense) view of language. The sign effaces the referent just as the I as an empty universal effaces the particular meaning of any individual I as soon as the pronoun is uttered. De Man himself goes on to clarify this:

The faculty that enables thought to exist also makes its preservation impossible. The art, the *technê*, of writing which cannot be separated from thought and from memorization can only be preserved in the figural mode of the symbol, the very mode it has to do away with if it is to occur at all.   (*AI*, 102)

In order to think, we have to be able to link and unlink predicates from subjects at will, arbitrarily, thus doing away with any supposedly natural, symbolic view of language. Now he can conclude his argument:

We can now assert that the two statements "art is for us a thing of the past" and "the beautiful is the sensory manifestation of the idea" are in fact one and the same. To the extent that the paradigm for art is thought rather than perception, the sign rather than the symbol, writing rather than painting or music, it will also be memorization rather than recollection. As such, it belongs indeed to a past which, in Proust's words, could never be recaptured, *retrouvé*. Art is "of the past" in a radical sense, in that, like memorization, it leaves the interiorization of experience forever behind. It is of the past to the extent that it materially inscribes, and thus forever forgets, its ideal content. The reconciliation of the two main theses of the *Aesthetics* occurs at the expense of the aesthetic as a stable philosophical category. What the *Aesthetics* calls the beautiful turns out to be, also, something very remote from what we associate with the suggestiveness of symbolic form.   (*AI*, 103)

It is in the context of this passage that we can now reread such pronouncements as "no poetry after Auschwitz," or "after Auschwitz, poetry only on the basis thereupon." These statements represent the aesthetic, that is to say historical, narrative conclusions of the narrative of the history of art that is one current of the *Aesthetics* as the forgetting of the linguistic, apodictic theory of the symbol and that such dicta inscribe as part of a history. The sign has to be the model for art; for how else is one going to conceive of art as not being sheerly mimetic, a conception which would be the only recourse if one were not to base a theory of art on the purported naturalness of the symbol, instead of the sign as an act of thought?

It is at this point that de Man reveals his *coup de grâce*. He cites a passage about art that is art because it treats its symbols as signs, and the passage has to be, of course, Proust's commentary on Giotto:

Before dismissing [so-called unaesthetic art, TAP] as simply, or merely, ugly, one should perhaps bear in mind what Proust has to say in *Swann's Way* about symbols, which, unlike metaphors, do not mean what they say. "Such symbols are not represented symbolically [*le symbole (n'est) pas représenté comme un symbole*] since the symbolized thought is not expressed but the symbol represented as real, as actually inflicted or materially handled [*puisque la pensée symbolisée (n'est) pas exprimée, mais (le symbole représenté) comme réel, comme effectivement subi ou matériellement manié*]." This symbol that is not symbolic is much like the theory of the aesthetic which, in Hegel, is no longer aesthetic, like the subject which has to say "I" but can never say it, the sign which can only survive as a symbol ... Such signs, says Proust, may have a special beauty, "une étrangeté saisissante," which will be appreciated only much later, at a degree of aesthetic and theoretical remove so advanced as to be always "of the past" and not our own. [brackets unmarked by "TAP" in original]

The passage in Proust from which I am quoting deals with Giotto's allegories of the Vices and of the Virtues in the frescoes of the Arena Chapel at Padua. If we then wonder, as we should, where it is, in Hegel's *Aesthetics*, that the theory of the sign manifests itself materially, we would have to look for sections on art forms which Hegel explicitly says are not aesthetic or beautiful ... Allegory ... is dismissed as barren or ugly (*kahl*) ... Compared to the depth and beauty of recollection, memory appears as a mere tool, a mere slave of the intellect, just as the sign appears shallow and mechanical compared to the aesthetic *aura* of the symbol or just as prose appears like piecework labor next to the noble craft of poetry ...

Allegory, says Hegel, is primarily a personification produced for the sake of clarity, and, as such, it always involves a subject, an I. But this I, which is the subject of allegory, is oddly constructed. Since it has to be devoid of any individuality or human specificity, it has to be as general as can be, so much so that it can be called a "grammatical subject." Allegories are allegories of the most distinctively linguistic (as opposed to phenomenal) of categories, namely, grammar. On the other hand, allegory fails entirely in its purpose if one is unable to recognize the abstraction that is being allegorized; it has to be, in Hegel's words, *erkennbar*. Therefore, specific predicates of the grammatical subject will *have to be* enunciated, despite the fact that these specifications are bound to conflict with the generality, the pure grammaticality, of the "I" ... What the allegory narrates is, therefore, in Hegel's own words, "the separation or disarticulation of subject from predicate [*die Trennung von Subjekt und Prädikat*]." For discourse to be meaningful, this separation has to take place, yet it is incompatible with the necessary generality of all meaning. Allegory functions, categorically and logically, like the defective corner-stone of the entire system.   (*AI*, 103–4)

So many things are made to coincide here that we should suspect a massive snow job. Since when have metaphors meant what they said? Well, evidently since metaphor was proclaimed as the necessary link between sign and meaning, when it was thus – metonymically – praised over the contingency of metonymy by Proust. We get a trace of the materiality of the sign in Proust's description of what allegories are like. In allegory, according to the literary text, which serves as the non-defective cornerstone of the understanding of the prosaic, "magisterial" lecture notes of the philosopher's pupils or slaves, thought is expressed as a sign, as inscribed. But it is up to the beholder to make or to be mystified by the "necessary link" that he or she will have to make in order to understand how the word relates to the image, to select the specific predicates of the allegorical subject which are intended to express the thought materially. Allegory is thus a controlled "calligraphy, not a mimesis" (*AI*, 51), for the thought which it is supposed to express is nowhere available to cognition.

The futurity implied in the understanding of such signs aims at a future perfect: someday I will know enough to have understood the meaning. But this hyperbolic projection acts as though it were not based on a fundamental problem, namely that of the failure of the arbitrary sign ever to be linked up necessarily with its meaning. For allegorical discourse to be meaningful, a subject has to be stripped of its qualities so that only the didactically useful ones will stand out. And this necessity is also joined by another one, namely the fact that allegory's thus being the pure manifestation of the intention of its artificer will make this intention, which is not accessible, the key to any successful decoding. The specificity that the creator of allegory would accord to his or her lesson fails to attain the specificity of that lesson, even though – or because – the very vehicle constructed for the purpose is constructed so as to be as general as possible. Thus described, allegory considered in its form, and as pure form, relates the disconnection of subject from predicate.[60]

This problem obtains just as well in the relation between text and commentary. For what commentary does is to try to select relevant aspects of a text in order to comment upon them, thus to try to state clearly the lesson of the text. But at the same time, thus trying to force a text to have a lesson may in fact utterly falsify the text; and so what one should rather do is to explain the particular ways in which any given text operates so as to avoid being reduced to that lesson and to allow it to remain a singularity. Even in this last sentence I have had to resort to a personification, to attribute intention to the intentionless – language – in order to tell my story.

In the case of "Sign and Symbol in Hegel's *Aesthetics*," I have shown how not only the conceptual apparatus of the essay, its rather profitable stringing together of Hegelian themes, but also its ironic tics centered around the allegorization of the name "Hegel," all lead toward the naming of allegory as a kind of master name for the form in which clefts at the heart of systematic thinking can be shown to undo it from the inside. It is not a matter of performing an operation upon Hegel's text; it is rather a question of discerning a specific pattern – in this case, allegory – and then of being able to read many texts for the anamorphoses of that pattern. It is a matter of recognizing the truth, the insistence, or the repetition. The intention of de Man's allegory is to move from a statement of apparently contingent truisms to the showing of the formal necessity of those truisms.

Before closing our critical inquiry into "Sign and Symbol in

---

[60] Proust and Hegel come together in another place, and it is also a place whose topos is that of the *name* (See *RT*, 9). Consider the way in which the name "Theory" functions in "Sign and Symbol in Hegel's *Aesthetics*," albeit in a negative mode.

Hegel's *Aesthetics*," I must not default on a promise I have been making for some time about the *locus princeps*. De Man was not only fascinated by the earlier Benjamin. The words "aura" (de Man's emphasis), the relations drawn between *Erinnerung* and *mémoire involuntaire* on the one hand and *Gedächtnis* and *mémoire voluntaire* on the other (Bergson via Proust), the emphasis on a certain notion of modernity as involved with a theory of the past that cannot be recaptured – all of this takes us in the direction of Benjamin's "On Some Motifs in Baudelaire," where the aura appears in its disappearance, Proust meets Bergson, and a reading of modernity as the loss of the capacity for experience of all but shock all appear. Such, in fact, are the "correspondences" of de Man's essay. "Sign and Symbol in Hegel's *Aesthetics*," a dry and barren essay about theory, turns out to be one-half of at least one more *symbolon* within de Man's corpus, "Anthropomorphism and Trope in the Lyric" (in *RR*). Both texts are written under the word-cloud of this same name: Benjamin.

And the word-cloud of "*aura*" appears here because things that have an aura are things that *come back*. They come back because, instead of having been perceived in consciousness, they went directly into the unconscious. That which has an aura – had it been perceived – could only have been assimilated by consciousness as a trauma. It would have been an experience too singular to be experienced. So instead of entering the theatre of consciousness as a perception, only to flicker away into nothing, it gets registered in the mechanical, thinking memory of the unconscious as a singularity, as a real, as the mark of a shift in the symbolic order. The aesthetic is the name we use to describe objects that have an *aura*. Far from being objects of disinterest, these are the very objects of ultimate investment precisely because the aura itself is the shadow of their having been experienced – but not in a direct perception – as trauma. There is *trauma* in *aura*. It is thus that the aura of Benjamin's "On Some Motifs in Baudelaire" hovers over both "Sign and Symbol in Hegel's *Aesthetics*" and "Anthropomorphism and Trope in the Lyric," for it is in that essay that Benjamin develops the relation between the two forms of memory and the Freudian dictum (which pervades Freud's text from 1895 until 1925) that consciousness arises only to the exclusion of laying down a memory trace.

Rudderless signification

Then I read her the lesbian scene from Proust. Asja grasped its savage nihilism: how Proust in a certain fashion ventures into the tidy private chamber within the petit bourgeois that bears the inscription *sadism* and then mercilessly smashes everything to pieces, so that nothing remains of the untarnished, clear-cut conception of wickedness, but instead within every fracture evil explicitly shows its true substance – "humanity," or even "kindness." And as I was explaining this to Asja, it became clear to me how closely this coincided with the thrust of my baroque book. Just as the previous evening, while reading alone in my room and coming across the extraordinary passage on Giotto's *Caritas*, it had become clear to me that Proust was here developing a conception that corresponds at every point to what I myself have tried to subsume under the concept of allegory.[61]

In "Pascal's Allegory of Persuasion," an essay that dates from the same period as the one on Hegel just discussed, we can see elements of our same set of problemata appear. In the essay on Pascal, de Man again chooses a text that is itself about scission and division, and is itself divided into two parts; the motivation behind geometric reasoning, and the art of persuasion in general. It is a text about names and things.

Geometry is a superior code because it operates only with nominal definitions, and thus should be able to keep house within its own province. Nominal definitions are definitions in which a naked name is clothed only with predicates carefully attributed to it so as to insure the proper functioning of an axiomatic system. But, at the same time, this system cannot be enunciated without recourse to words it cannot define from within its own sphere, such as "motion, number, and extension" (*AI*, 56). This is the kind of move which is taken for granted, in our time, in discussions of formal systems. But what fascinates de Man about Pascal's difficulties in having to resort to real definitions, definitions of thing, in his demonstration, is *not* the fact that this takes Pascal away from the self-policed world of pure definition, but that the move towards real definition, towards the reliance on the real at

---

[61] Walter Benjamin, *Moscow Diary*, trans. Richard Sieburth, ed. Gary Smith, in *October* 35 (Winter 1985), 94–95. It is virtually impossible that de Man would have known this passage. Benjamin's diary was not published until 1980; de Man was writing on Hegel at that time and had already published his first commentary on the passage from Proust in 1972, then again in 1979.

the heart of the otherwise purely verbal order, is taken as the very ground of the formal system:

[I]f primitive words possess a natural meaning, then this meaning would have to be universal, as is the science that operates with these words; however, in one of the sudden shifts so characteristic of Pascal . . . this turns out not to be the case. "It is not the case," says Pascal, "that all men have the same idea of the essence of the things which I showed to be impossible and useless to define . . . (such as, for example, time). It is not the nature of these things which I declare to be known by all, but simply *the relationship between the name and the thing*, so that on hearing the expression *time*, all turn (or direct) the mind toward the same entity [*tous portent la pensée vers le même objet*]." Here the word does not function as a sign or a name, as was the case in the nominal defintion, but as a vector, a directional motion that is manifest only as a turn, since the target towards which it turns remains unknown. In other words, the sign has become a trope, a substitutive relationship that has to posit a meaning whose existence cannot be verified, but that confers upon the sign an unavoidable signifying function. (*AI*, 56)

We should not at all be surprised to see de Man go for the figure of the sign itself as trope. But something else is going to have to emerge from this; for noticing that something is structured like a trope itself tells us very little. The really tense moment in de Man's demonstration comes shortly afterward:

The interest of the argument is, however, that it has to reintroduce the ambivalence of definitional language. The synecdochal totalization of infinitude is possible because the unit of number, the *one*, functions as a nominal definition. But, for the argument to be valid, the nominally indivisible number must be distinguished from the *really* indivisible space, a demonstration that Pascal can accomplish easily, but only because the key words of the demonstration – indivisible, spatial extension (*étendue*), species (*genre*), and definition – function as real, and not as nominal, definitions . . . The language almost forces this formulation upon Pascal, when he has to say: "cette dernière preuve est fondée sur la *définition* de ces deux *choses*, indivisible et étendue," or "Donc, il n'est pas de même genre que l'étendue, par la *définition* des *choses* du même genre." The reintroduction of a language of *real* definition also allows for the next turn in the demonstration, which, after having separated number from space, now has to suspend this separation while maintaining it – because the underlying homology of space and number, the ground of the system, should never be fundamentally in question. There exists, in the order of number, an entity that is, unlike the *one*, heterogeneous with regard to number: this entity, which is the *zero*, is radically distinct from one. Whereas one is and is not a number at the same time, zero is radically not a number, absolutely heterogeneous to the order of number. With the introduction of zero, the separation between number and space, which is potentially threatening, is also healed. For equivalences can also be found in the order of time and of motion for the zero function in number: instant and stasis (*repos*) are the equivalences that, thanks to the zero, allow one to reestablish the "necessary and reciprocal link" between the four intraworldly dimensions on which divine order depends. At the end of the passage, the homogeneity of the universe is recovered ... But this has happened at a price: the coherence of the system is now seen to be entirely dependent on the introduction of an element – the zero and its equivalences in time and motion – that is itself entirely heterogeneous with regard to the system and is nowhere a part of it. The continuous universe held together by the double wings of the two infinities is interrupted, disrupted *at all points* by a principle of radical heterogeneity without which it cannot come into being. Moreover, this rupture of the infinitesimal and the homogeneous does not occur on the transcendental level, but on the level of language, in the inability of a theory of language as sign or as name (nominal definition) to ground this homogeneity without having recourse to the signifying function, the real definition, that makes the zero of signification the necessary condition for grounded knowledge. The notion of language as sign is dependent on, and derived from, a different notion in which language functions as rudderless signification and transforms what it denominates into the linguistic equivalence of the arithmetical zero. It is as sign that language is capable of engendering the principles of infinity, of genus, species and homogeneity, which allow for synecdochal totalizations, but none of these tropes could come about without the systematic effacement of the zero and its reconversion into a name. There can be no *one* without zero, but the zero always appears in the guise of a *one*, of a some(thing). The name is the trope of the zero.   (*AI*, 58–59)

The " 'necessary and reciprocal link' " makes Pascal into a Proustian, or vice versa, and the trace of the lexicon of permanent parabasis we encounter in the emphasized piece of language "disrupted *at all points*" makes this passage sound much like the treatment of de Man's absolute construction of Proust, or of the I that functions like "the defective cornerstone of the entire system" in Hegel. (And Benjamin's statement above that Proust's gloss says exactly the same thing which he was trying to say in his remarks on allegory in *The Origin of German Tragic Drama* reinforces the link between de Man's own considerations on allegory and the work of the early Benjamin. De Man's discussion of Benjamin's "The Task of the Translator," in its preoccupations with disjunction – things having in common only that they do not resemble that from which they arise – and death, proclaims itself openly as a text about allegory, a fact that has gone entirely unnoticed. Thus it is a text "about" his earlier self.)

But there are also the multiple senses of zero. Once again we are in the realm of the linguistic encyclopedist Jakobson ("zero degree," the unpaired signifier, the signifier that is not binarily opposed, of which the name is perhaps the perfect example – unless of course it is opposed to the thing it names, which is not a part of the linguistic system). But we are also and most important-ly at the very opening of Hölderlin's great poem, "Mnemosyne," of which the first lines read:

> Ein Zeichen sind wir, deutungslos,
> Schmerzlos sind wir und haben fast
> Die Sprache in der Fremde verloren.[62]

Rudderless signification, a sign without signification: At the moment de Man is discussing the very privation of reference, the word that signifies nothing, we are hurled against a most over-bearing reference, even if "the target toward which it turns [has] remain[ed]," to this point, "unknown." For Paul de Man was obsessed with this one poem of Hölderlin, a poem he comments explicitly in "Wordsworth and Hölderlin,"[63] and in his introduc-tion to Carol Jacobs's *The Dissimulating Harmony*,[64] but also alludes to in many places where he is perhaps not even aware that he is glossing it. In "Dialogue and Dialogism," we find the sentences:

The radical experience of a voiced otherness as a way to a regained proximity can indeed be found as a dominant theme [note the Jakob-sonian diction again, TAP] in Levinas and to have at least a submerged existence in Heidegger. One can think of the lines of Hölderlin, "Seit ein Gespräch wir sind / und hören können voneinander" as a common ground. (*RT*, 110)

Now, these lines are most emphatically *not* to be found in "Mnemosyne," perhaps the only poem in which a conversation cannot take place, but in another poem, "Friedensfeier." But what

---

[62] Friedrich Hölderlin, *Werke und Briefe*, ed. Beißner and Schmidt (Frankfurt-on-Main: Insel, 1969), vol. I, 199–200.   [63] Now in *RR*.   [64] Now in *CW*.

is indeed remarkable is that de Man attributes them to "Mnemosyne."[65]

For Paul de Man, Hölderlin *was* "Mnemosyne." But the lines which have left the deepest and most numerous traces all over his later essays come in the following section of the poem, where Hölderlin writes "Lang ist / die Zeit, es ereignet sich aber / das Wahre," a sentence de Man himself translates and discusses as "What is true is what is bound to take place" (*CW*, 221).[66] From then on in, it's the true all the way: "One willingly admits that truth has power, including the power to occur . . ." (*RR*, 242); "The truth is all around us . . . the truth is what happens, but how can we be certain to recognize the truth when it occurs?" (*AI*, 99). The reference is pervasive; it is the permanent parabasis of de Man's later writing. What are we to do with this pervasive if implicit importation of Hölderlin into America?

What is striking and telling about de Man's citation of this single verse from the proverbially late poem of the poet going mad, this extremity of the lyric voice, is the way in which he cites it as an isolated moment, virtually always entirely out of context (when he discusses "Mnemosyne" directly in "Wordsworth and Hölderlin" he does not discuss this line), as a gnomic utterance to be cited as a revelation about revelation. He cites the poetic text as holy writ – to paraphrase de Man's own critique of Heidegger in his early "Hölderlin's Exegeses of Heidegger" – by not citing it, by inverting it *in actu*: *das Wort sei mein Heiliges*.

The truth of occurrence about this word of the occurrence of the true is that it is performed simply as a coup, without anything that could really be called a gloss, in the explicit sense, at all. This master word insists by its very persistence, not by being thematized, but rather by being repeated in a series of deformations, which however leave the *locus princeps* intact. Positing – happening, occurrence, the true – is posited. The final excuse for what comes to be written is that there is no excuse.

It is as though the very power of this verse to be cited as so simply, utterly, and banally authoritative achieves all of its power

---

[65] In the first published version of the essay in *Poetics Today* 4:1 (Spring 1983). The mistaken attribution of the lines was corrected invisibly – over my protest – during the correction of the page proofs of *RT* in the spring of 1986.

[66] In the margins of the German text occur the words "das Echo."

by virtue of the fact that it never comes to utterance as citation, as the word of a poet, as a poem. Rather, it is posited as a real, as a singularity. It is only thus that it can attain the level of the true, something of the order of a kind of axiomatic statement, a cliché, a banality, like any of the hypograms found by Saussure – or Riffaterre, for that matter. It is possible to interpret this verse from Hölderlin as a kind of restatement of the ground of poetics in some kind of adherence to the Heideggerian discourse of the *Ereignis*; but that would be to rob the simplicity of de Man's move of its power by making it dependent on a kind of inheritance of a philosopheme that is scarcely one anyway.

From the point of view of de Man's text, it would destroy the power of the violent simplicity of the gesture. From the point of view of the thinker – who at this moment really is no longer a philosopher, in the sense that what he, Heidegger, is trying to convey, does not adhere to any kind of conceptual content – it would be to falsify the thought by giving it content, something that the evenemential character of what Heidegger says, in the word *Ereignis*, does not have.

But what is *not* repeated is the verse that follows in Hölderlin's poem, "Wie aber Liebes?", "But what about love?" In the midst of the thought of the man who was, by his own statement, drawn into the "compulsion to theorize" by the movement of the very thought he was trying to track, how are we to talk about love in the text of Paul de Man? The very question is at first glance nothing less than shocking. How can we imagine it? What kind of love can it be?

Concern for repetitions

Car le jour où il y aura une lecture de la carte d'Oxford, la seule et la vraie, ce sera la fin de l'histoire. Ou le devenir prose de notre amour.[67]

What are we up against here? What's love got to do with it? Toward the end of the first section of "The Rhetoric of Temporality," in the context of a comparative discussion of Wordsworth and Rousseau, there occurs the following passage:

---

[67] Derrida, *La Carte postale de Socrate à Freud et au–delà* (Paris: Aubier-Flammarion, 1981), 127, card dated 2 October 1977.

In the world of the symbol it would be possible for the image to coincide with the substance, since the substance and its representation do not differ in their being but only in their extension: they are part and whole of the same set of categories. Their relationship is one of simultaneity, which, in truth, is spatial in kind, and in which the intervention in time is merely a matter of contingency, whereas, in the world of allegory, time is the originary constitutive category. The relationship between the allegorical sign and its meaning (*signifié*) is not decreed by dogma; in the instances we have seen in Rousseau and in Wordsworth, this is not at all the case. We have, instead, a relationship between signs in which the reference to their respective meanings has become of secondary importance. But this relationship between signs necessarily contains a constitutive temporal element; it remains necessary, if there is to be allegory, that the allegorical sign refer to another sign that precedes it. The meaning constituted by the allegorical sign can then consist only in the *repetition* [de Man's emphasis] (in the Kierkegaardian sense of the term) of a previous sign with which it can never coincide, since it is of the essence of this previous sign to be pure anteriority. The secularized allegory of the early romantics thus necessarily contains the negative moment which in Rousseau is that of renunciation, in Wordsworth that of the loss of self in death or in error.[68]

(*BI*, 207)

The purity of the anteriority at issue is the past that can never be recaptured because it is a past that was never present, the same past that we encountered above in de Man's reading of Hegel. We recognize the "sequential and narrative" character of allegory (*AI*, 51) here, with the anomalous and flirtatious Saussurean "signifié" thrown into the midst of this rather standard, romantic, critical vocabulary in order to indicate that what we are dealing with is an interpretation of the metonymy of the sequence of discourse itself as allegorical.

Allegory tells a story. The only way in which the relation between the sign and meaning is not decreed by dogma has to do with the fact that in the creation of modern, secular allegory, de Man wants to remark the displacement of emphasis onto the temporal disjunction of the allegorical form itself, its poetics; rather than simply, we could say naïvely, to use that form in order to try to make some clear statement of meaning.

[68] Arne Melberg has started to map out the matter of "*Repetition* (in the Kierkegaardian sense of the term)" in his article of this title in *diacritics* 20:3 (Fall 1990). See also my "Abraham: Who Could Possibly Understand Him?" in Niels Jørgen Cappelørn and Hermann Deuser, eds., *Søren Kierkegaard Studies* 1 (Berlin: de Gruyter, 1996).

But in order to glean something of love let us see what kinds of things our Paul has to say, at moments, about repetition. They are never merely repetitious. We start, as always, by going backwards. Just before his death in 1983, in the preface to his *The Rhetoric of Romanticism*, de Man writes, speaking of that gathering together of essays written over a period of thirty or so years:

I would never have by myself undertaken the task of establishing such a collection and . . . I confess that I still look back upon it with some misgivings. Such massive evidence of the failure to make the various individual readings coalesce is a somewhat melancholy spectacle. The fragmentary aspect of the whole is made more obvious still by the hypotactic manner that prevails in each of the essays taken in isolation, by the continued attempt, however ironized, to present a closed and linear argument. This apparent coherence *within* each essay is not matched by a corresponding coherence *between* them. Laid out diachronically in a roughly chronological sequence, they do not evolve in a manner that easily allows for dialectical progression or, ultimately, for historical totalization. Rather, it seems that they always start again from scratch and that their conclusions fail to add up to anything. If some secret principle of summation is at work here, I do not feel qualified to articulate it and, as far as the general question of romanticism is concerned, I must leave the task of its historical definition to others. I have myself taken refuge in more theoretical inquiries into the problems of figural language. Not that I believe that such a historical enterprise, in the case of romanticism, is doomed from the start: one is all too easily tempted to rationalize personal shortcoming as theoretical impossibility and, especially among younger scholars, there is ample evidence that the historical study of romanticism is being successfully pursued. But it certainly has become a far from easy task. One feels at times envious of those who can continue to do literary history as if nothing had happened in the sphere of theory, but one cannot help but feel somewhat suspicious of their optimism. *The Rhetoric of Romanticism* should at least help to document some of the difficulties it fails to resolve. (*RR*, viii–ix)

This is a cruel paragraph, and I am not talking about the split infinitives, which, combined with the wonderfully awkward northern European syntax, make the most gruesome of double binds (following Bateson and Laing I use that word in the least trendy and the most technical sense) into the last and most graceful and charming flourish of a dying man. What is the legacy that is being left to us younger scholars by the evil grandfather we would rather forget by historicizing him out of consciousness, to use the wonderful figure he himself invents and/or repeats (one is never sure)?

The fate of youth hangs suspended in the irresolution as to whether the failure of the elder was necessary or contingent. Here, the refuge taken, the pragmatic moment I have already discussed at length, is the investigation of "figural language." De Man has made an ironic reversal from the position of "Semiology and Rhetoric," where, the theoretical elaboration of the matter being beyond his powers, he retreated into the more naïve, pragmatic encounter with Archie and Edith in front of the television set. The theoretical serves as the refuge from the melancholy spectacle of a sheer agglomeration of readings in the canon of romantic litera-ture. His strategy is dialectical enough to contain both stances. "The Resistance to Theory," filled with retreats of this "earlier" type into handy little examples, was written shortly before the moment of death, of the preface to *The Rhetoric of Romanticism*. But since no reliable temporal scheme of earlier and later can thus truthfully be told, because both positions coexist almost simulta-neously, what is important must be the gesture of the retreat, of taking refuge.

It will never suffice to replace even the attempt at reading a text with excurses into the history of ideas. It is also necessary to recall that, lest one think that this anti-historicism is the result of the lifework of the dying, evil grandfather deconstructor, it is the founding of the discipline of comparative literature in the United States which owes itself to this very rejection of historicism, a gesture by René Wellek to Arthur Lovejoy, in the debate coincid-ing with the founding of the journal *Comparative Literature* as a polemical response to the *Journal of the History of Ideas*. The debate centers around the definition of romanticism, or rather its de-definition. It is most eloquently summed up in 1955 in an article de Man called "The Double Aspect of Symbolism," and which we can read as a kind of abstract (written apparently *in medias res*) of his dissertation in Comparative Literature at Harvard, *Mallarmé, Yeats, and the Post-Romantic Predicament*, submitted in 1960 when de Man was forty-one years old.

In this article de Man reenacts, or rather repeats, the problem of this tension between the attempt to define romanticism as a historical (eighteenth- and nineteenth-century, say) or linguistic (let us call it a heightened awareness of the wiles of symbolic language) phenomenon as the tension inhabiting the very word "symbolism" itself. This word serves not only as a technical designation for a linguistic practice that – as de Man reminds us almost thirty years later, still repeating, in "Sign and Symbol in Hegel's *Aesthetics*" – has its etymology in ancient Greek contract law; it stands as well as the more or less problematical proper name we use for a movement in the history of late nineteenth- and early twentieth-century poetry.

Let us come back to this paragraph of paratext, this preface, failing, as it is, unlike and despite all hope, to fall between our fingers. What is the double bind of this passage? Well, let us admit from this outset that we are dealing with one of the very few moments of autobiographical writing, even if it is scholarly or intellectual autobiographical writing, in and among de Man's texts. (The use of the plural here is a caution dictated by the very topos of melancholic enumeration present in the passsage itself: again, why is it necessary that there be *one* text of Paul de Man?)

We are in a story about the relations between the general and the particular that is being told as though it were a particular, the particular of a particular, part of the history of one Paul de Man – and yet not. I myself would never have undertaken this collection, and yet I confess. What *I* confess is that we are performing criticism, or, as I have called it elsewhere, post-criticism, by anamorphosis, by producing an examination of a single and always singular passage of text by exploding it, as though in an architectural axonometric drawing, to keep with the visual figure and abandon the surgical. (Benjamin sees the two as opposed. The discussion to which I refer, in his "The Work of Art in the Age of Mechanical Reproduction," is the one concerning the relation of the cameraman to the surgeon, where the surgeon is the one who *does not see*, because he pierces the order of what is seen, of what is visible, and the cameraman becomes the surgeon of sight by the metaphorical catastrophe – the figure defined in the context of a discussion of Benjamin because it fits so well with so many of his [later] figures. The cameraman is the surgeon of sight.[69])

Paul de Man's version of repetition in the Kierkegaardian sense sounds, ironically enough, much more like the melancholic stam-

---

[69] An intriguing, if unwitting, commentary on this passage has been provided recently in the film *The Silence of the Lambs* (USA, Jonathan Demme, 1991). For "metaphorical catastrophe," see Derrida, "Des Tours de Babel," in *Psyché*.

mer of what Kierkegaard calls recollection. It is not joyful, but rather manic, compulsive:

And to read is to understand, to question, to know, to forget, to erase, to deface, to repeat – that is to say, the endless prosopopoeia by which the dead are made to have a face and a voice which tells the allegory of their demise and allows us to apostrophize them in our turn. No degree of knowledge can ever stop this madness, for it is the madness of words. What *would* be naïve is to believe that this strategy, which is not *our* strategy as subjects, since we are its product rather than its agent, can be a source of value and has to be celebrated or denounced accordingly.   (*RR*, 122)

The passages surrounding this last moment of "Shelley Disfigured" are laced, more richly than ever in de Man, with a Freudian-Lacanian vocabulary: "Verneinung," "symbolic," "imaginary," real in the sense of the tychic event that is Shelley's drowning. Because this last event does stop the text of Shelley's "The Triumph of Life," in a tychic encounter that cannot be mastered by any repetitive strategy contained within Shelley's own text, the critical narrative repeats in the manner that trauma dreams repeat, according to Freud, in a vain attempt somehow digitally to remaster the experiential analog of a shock that cannot be assimilated. Trauma, the shock of the new, is the strongest way to lay down a memory trace, since any "experience" that would travel along pathways, *Bahnen*, that already exist, evanesces in the theater of consciousness and will leave no trace, since there is nothing new to record. What criticism does is to attempt to understand a literary text, a singularity, a real, a chance and unique event, by introjecting it into a story of which it would be a part. But what we call literary texts are thus because we keep reading them, because we keep trying, and failing, to master the absolute singularity of the events of their constellation.

Criticism, reading, is compulsive. It attempts to control, for it is the activity of a subject, and to cease to control would be to cease to be a subject. What wants to be introjection, interiorization, defusion of the shock of experience, *Erinnerung*, turns out to be a failure, an incorporation, an experience that is forever walled off – understanding – because it never was an experience in the first place.

Love is suspended between the compulsive character of its recollection and a futural dimension of repetition, which is not, however, guaranteed ever to come into being. The absolute anteriority implied by the structure of allegory may project itself forward toward a moment of understanding, whether it is Proust's "later I understood" or Hegel's projection of the spirit's self-recognition over the course of its trajectory. But Kierkegaard's book, *Repetition*, in its alternation of storytelling with parodies of philosophical exposition on the theme of motion – whether it is possible – itself suspends the decision as to the futural status of our task.

It is with a certain amount of fear and trembling that one reads a book such as *Repetition*, whose author changed its ending, very late in the process of composition, from the announcement of the suicide of one of the main characters to the announcement of his marriage. And, given that many traces of the first alternative are left in the book which went to press after the author had decided for the second, the point is not so much to flesh out the implications of these two alternatives considered separately, but rather to ask what it means that they are capable of being supported by the same narrative. Given the ambivalence he writes there about the possibility of *going further*, of movement at all, de Man's remarks on our future, in the preface to *The Rhetoric of Romanticism*, sound disturbingly like the indecision not only of the narrator of Kierkegaard's mock treatise, but of the author himself, as to how the story will turn out. We don't know anything, from Kierkegaard, about what happens after marriage or suicide; and we don't know, from de Man, whether there is any kind of future for the study of romanticism, except for the continuation of the stammering, mournful path of endless enumeration, which can never, even with a moment of cutting, result in a gesture of totalization. And the history of criticism since de Man's own death, considered in this light, can only be considered as a kind of horrified, foreclosive rejection, an anxious scattering of critical subjects, as yet another – predicted – regression away from the severity of the law of the dead Father. The children may try to introject the Father; but he remains in his crypt, incorporated and walled off, yet radiating his effects in the hyperinflated marketplace of the contemporary scene.

Up to this point I have withheld comment on the last utterance of "Sign and Symbol in Hegel's *Aesthetics*," so that I could insert it here, into this moment of my own repetitive series:

We would have to conclude that Hegel's philosophy which, like his *Aesthetics*, is a philosophy of history (and of aesthetics) as well as a history of philosophy (and of aesthetics) – and the Hegelian corpus indeed contains texts that bear these two symmetrical titles – is in fact an allegory of the disjunction between philosophy and history, or, in our more restricted concern, between literature and aesthetics, or, more narrowly still, between literary experience and literary theory. The reasons for this disjunction, which it is equally vain to deplore or to praise, are not themselves historical or recoverable by ways of history. To the extent that they are inherent in language, in the necessity, which is also an impossibility, to connect the subject with its predicates or the sign with its symbolic significations, the disjunction will always, as it did in Hegel, manifest itself as soon as experience shades into thought, history into theory. No wonder that literary theory has such a bad name, all the more so since the emergence of thought and of theory is not something that our own thought can hope to prevent or to control. (*AI*, 104)

Experience is a shade, like the moon in daytime. It shades off into thought in the manner that it tries to recover experience by way of words, a difficulty anybody who has ever tried to write down the memory of a dream upon awakening encounters. It shades off in a forgetting of its own inbuilt structure when it tries to invent a lyric voice in order to overcome the sheerly empty fact that it cannot express its own self in words. The best one can hope for is to have a new experience of the words that are written down; but this experience will never be a sheer repetition of the state of consciousness one was originally trying to describe. Hence the "compulsion to theorize" with which de Man's essay begins and which we find repeated, in other words, at the very end of "The Resistance to Theory":

But the same [avoidance of rhetorical reading] is still true even if a "truly" rhetorical reading . . . could be conceived – something which is not necessarily impossible and for which the aims and methods of literary theory should certainly strive. Such a reading would indeed appear as the methodical undoing of the grammatical construct and, in its systematic disarticulation of the *trivium*, will be theoretically sound as well as effective. Technically correct rhetorical readings may be boring, monotonous, predictable and unpleasant, but they are irrefutable. They are also totalizing (and potentially totalitarian) for since the structures and functions they expose do not lead to the knowledge of an entity (such as language) but are an unreliable process of knowledge production that prevents all entities, including linguistic entities, from coming into discourse as such, they are indeed universals, consistently defective models of language's impossibility to be an model language. They are, always in theory, the most elastic and dialectical model to end all models and they can rightly claim to contain within their own defective selves all the other defective models of reading-avoidance, referential, semiological, grammatical, performative, logical, or whatever. They are theory and not theory at the same time, the universal theory of the impossibility of theory. To the extent however that they are theory . . . rhetorical readings, like the other kinds, still avoid and resist the reading they advocate. Nothing can overcome the resistance to theory since theory *is* itself this resistance. The loftier the aims and the better the methods of literary theory, the less possible it becomes. Yet literary theory is not in danger of going under; it cannot help but flourish, and the more it is resisted, the more it flourishes, since the language it speaks is the language of self-resistance. What remains impossible is to decide whether this flourishing is a triumph or a fall.   (*RT*, 19–20)

"Triumph or a fall" lines up with "to prevent or to control," "celebrate or denounce." Theory is Jupiter, the right-wing, reactive child of the literary Titan, language, because it attempts to control, to translate the idiom, the singular, to kill the singular utterance of the Father and to resurrect it and him as the name of the law. This "fall," the last word, reminds us not only of the preceding passage on "Hyperion falling" (best read in reference to the Pascalian notion I have discussed above of the need for interpretation, hence allegory, as the need of the fallen and as itself the act of falling) but also of the last word of Rilke's Tenth *Duino Elegy*, the underlined happiness we are unable to process because it suddenly *falls*.

Two or three things I know about him, or, the dream of an ideal language

[I]f there were a certain discourse – scientific, for example – such that lack could not find a place there in which to inscribe itself so as to act as effect, the lack would nevertheless *already* be inscribed there, if only because of the need or the demand for *another* language invoked to determine the meaning, the theoretical possibility of this discourse without lack. If a language owes its perpetual failure to this lack, the lack in turn has an obligation to the language to attain within it – through an infinite passage of one mode of saying to another, even if it was not marked in that region of discourse – to attain within that language (scattering there, at that moment, in the moving plurality of a place that is always unoccupied) at the limit, an excess of place – "the word that is too much." It is perhaps this "word too much" that constitutes (while immediately dismissing him) the invisible partner, the one that does not play . . ."[70]

The rhetorical mode of such structures can no longer be summarized by the single term of metaphor or of any substitutive trope or figure in general, although the deconstruction of metaphorical figures remains a necessary moment in their production. They take into account the fact that the resulting narratives can be folded back upon themselves and become self-referential. By *refusing*, for reasons of epistemological rigor, to confirm the authority, though not the necessity, of this juxtaposition, Rousseau unsettles the metaphor of reading as deconstructive narrative and replaces it by a more complex structure. The paradigm for all texts consists of a figure (or a system of figures) and its deconstruction. But since this model cannot be closed off by a final reading, it engenders, in its turn, a supplementary figural superposition which narrates the unreadability of the prior narration. As distinguished from primary deconstructive narratives centered on figures and ultimately always on metaphor, we can call such narratives to the second (or the third) degree *allegories*. Allegorical narratives tell the story of the failure to read whereas tropological narratives, such as the *Second Discourse*, tell the story of the failure to denominate. The difference is only a difference of degree and the allegory does not erase the figure. Allegories are always allegories of metaphor and, as such, they are always allegories of the impossibility of reading – a sentence in which the genitive "of" has itself to be "read" as a metaphor. (*AR*, 205)

Before I touch this paragraph, the last passage of de Man I will cite, I need to provide a reference I come upon over and over again in a piece of writing I often teach. Here is a citation within a citation:

In effect the study of myths poses a methodological problem by the fact that it cannot conform to the Cartesian principle of dividing the difficulty into as many parts as are necessary to resolve it. There exists no veritable end or term to mythical analysis, no secret unity which could be grasped at the end of the work of decomposition. The themes duplicate themselves to infinity. When we think we have disentangled them from each other and can hold them separate, it is only to realize that they are joining together again, in response to the attraction of unforeseen affinities. In consequence, the unity of the myth is only tendential and projective; it

[70] These are "the last words" (omitting a reference to the work of Roger Laporte of which I have more to say below in my essay on Blanchot's *Celui qui ne m'accompagnait pas*) of Maurice Blanchot's "Le problème de Wittgenstein," in the version of that essay published in his *L'Entretien infini* (Paris: Gallimard, 1969). In the first version of the essay published under this title, in the *Nouvelle Revue Française* 11:131 (1 November 1963), there is no such footnote at the bottom of the last page of the essay. I have modified the translation from Blanchot, *GO*, 132.

never reflects a state or a moment of the myth. An imaginary phenomenon implied by the endeavor to interpret, its role is to give a synthetic form to the myth and to impede its dissolution into the confusion of contraries. It could therefore be said that the science or knowledge of myths is an *anaclastic*, taking this ancient term in the widest sense authorized by its etymology, a science which admits into its definition the study of the reflected rays along with that of the broken ones. But, unlike philosophical reflection, which claims to go all the way back to its source, the reflections in question here concern rays without any other than a virtual focus... In wanting to imitate the spontaneous movement of mythical thought, my enterprise, itself too brief and too long, has had to yield to its demands and respect its rhythm. Thus is this book, on myths itself and in its own way, a myth . . .

Since myths themselves rest on second-order codes (the first-order codes being those in which language consists), this book thus offers the rough draft of a third-order code, destined to insure the reciprocal possibility of translation of several myths. This is why it would not be wrong to consider it a myth: the myth of mythology, as it were.[71]

Here is Derrida citing Lévi-Strauss in "Structure Sign and Play in the Discourse of the Human Sciences," Derrida's contribution to the Johns Hopkins colloquium on The Languages of Criticism and the Sciences of Man at which he and Paul de Man met. I take this system of ordination from Lévi-Strauss as a procrustean template onto which I can fit Paul de Man. Allegory, for de Man, fits at the level of Lévi-Strauss's own work at the level of the *Mythologiques*, at the level of the third order. Mythemes are second-order codes built out of the more conventional, metaphrastic structures of language. Lévi-Strauss's mythologics incorporate the mythemes, the second-order codes, into a constellation or arrangement that lays bare their disjunctions and contradictions.

But de Man's ordination system, cited as the second epigraph just above, is different. He says "second (or third)." Why? It is not simply because he considers the allegorical explosion of the text (itself level two, telling as it does the stories of figures and names, level one) as a *superposition* upon the literary text. This would be the same for Lévi-Strauss. The ambiguity of ordination for de Man has to do with the fact that because of the lack of any stable metalanguage, the language of the allegorical-critical falls prey to

[71] Richard Macksey and Eugenio Donato, eds., *The Structuralist Controversy: the Languages of Criticism and the Sciences of Man* (Baltimore: Johns Hopkins University Press, 1970), 257–58.

the same predicaments as the text upon which it superposed, and can thus be taken in turn as a new text to be read, as I do here. The lack of metalanguage prevents the stability of assignment of ordination, of levels, because all language fails to be a model language.

This is why, in the passage from "The Resistance to Theory" cited above, rhetorical readings are theory and not theory at the same time. To the extent that they proclaim something great about their results in the realm of discourse that, like de Man's text on *Julie*, gives us "the paradigm for all texts," they speak the language that resists any grappling with the singularity of any given text. But inasmuch as they would deal only with one text and restrain themselves from any gesture of totalization, they are models only of a single text, replicas that show the cracks of the original, the original that they repeat, word for word. To the extent that they tell a story they are theory; to the extent that they refuse to put a moral at the end of the fable of reading they tell they are not theory, for they do not enable a knowledge of any text other than themselves. In fact, the frighteningly inevitable thing is that they do not allow for knowledge of themselves, for they make themselves into even more impenetrable singularities. It is only to the extent that they are theoretical that they are capable of being taught. But inasmuch as they regress, in the very language of theoretical statement, from commenting only one text and making no other pronouncements (if such a lyrical dream be possible), they cannot be theory. Theory can be taught, but then it is not reading. And a reading taught as theory also is not reading, but the theorization of that reading. This, indeed, is the moment of pedagogical renunciation with which "The Resistance to Theory" begins – and ends.

One can only prepare the way for the encounter with a text; one can but set examples. But examples can always be misread, as I misread them here, by being spliced into new stories with different morals. Every attempt at understanding will be such a misunderstanding, a *méconnaissance* that is, however, inevitable for every subject that reads, necessarily, with its own arbitrariness, in the strongest and most ironic sense.

Reading is the name of a singular event for Paul de Man. It cannot be taught, truly, any more than a narrative of a psychoanalysis can be told or written. (For whom would it be written? As a redundant and not meaningless, but certainly useless memorandum from the analyst to the analysand, or vice versa?) The singularity of every transferential encounter structurally forbids that the knowledge such an account would try to convey be accessible to a third.

And yet: criticism is written, readings are written down as the experiences of subjects with texts; just as case histories are written in order to to teach how psychoanalysis works in the mode of thick description. Thus readings and case histories set up their own monumentalization or reification by those who would teach them – or dismiss them – as dogma. Likewise love is the repetition of a pattern that denies its repetitive, compulsive character, asserting its originarity and originality, like lyrical language, considered as the work of love in remembering the dead. And if one wants to see how someone behaves, watch how he or she behaves with the dead. Watch him or her dance alone, as one does nowadays.

I myself no longer know how to dance.

4

<hr>

❖❖

Because the nights: Blanchot's *Celui qui ne m'accompagnait pas*

❖❖

<hr>

– Oseriez-vous tutoyer Blanchot?
– Laisse cette question à plus tard . . .   (*P*, 27)

A novel is a prose narrative of some length that has something wrong with it.[1]

– Pour faire droit à un autre texte, au texte d'un autre, il faut assumer d'une certaine manière, très déterminée, le défaut, la faiblesse, ne pas éviter ce que l'autre aura su éviter: pour le faire apparaître depuis ce retrait.
                                                                          (*P*, 37)

Introduction

The desire for something completely simple.

This essay is not an essay on Blanchot. It is an essay at *Celui qui ne m'accompagnait pas*. This attempt is noways guaranteed to succeed, and furthermore, I do not know in advance what any criteria of success might look like. In all likelihood, I will not even know after this is written.

For pragmatic purposes (which should be, by this point, entirely suspicious) I will try to keep to four separate divisions within the course of this essay. I call them – all too quickly, but for the purposes of writing some kind of introduction that might help legibility – :

1. *Moaning.*   I use this word advisedly. Here I try to come to

<hr>

[1] Randall Jarrell, cited in the "Noted with Pleasure" section of the *New York Times Book Review*, 6 May 1986.

173

grips with the problems involved in discussing this book. This – my anxiety – is not personal. There are many precautions to be taken in getting off the ground.

2. *Critics: big names on Blanchot.* Here I will try to deal with significant aspects of the commentary that already exists on Blanchot and on this book, and will discuss works by Michel Foucault, Paul de Man, Jeffrey Mehlman, and Jacques Derrida. I try to learn from them, and in general not to explain their insufficiencies, but why their projects are different from mine, what their stakes are in relation to my own.

3. *Intertexts: big names in Blanchot.* I would prefer not to use the word *intertext*, but, as this is a preliminary note for the purpose of trying to help my reader to understand what is no doubt going to be very difficult, both because of the material under consideration and most of all because of my own insufficiencies, I use it anyway. I would prefer to use the word *names*. For here I will discuss the two or three words in the course of this *récit*[2] that are capitalized without falling at the beginning of sentences. I take it for granted that the notion of intertext is highly problematical. I withhold mentioning these names, and the intertexts to which they do and do not point, for a little while longer.

4. *Reading.* No doubt this will be the shortest section of the essay, if I ever get to it. In this part I intend to perform a reading of *Celui qui ne m'accompagnait pas*. This is the essay I have promised, and which originally I intended to write – the *whole* essay – without referring to another single text. As the necessities of dealing with the aspects covered in the three previous sections emerged, I saw that this original desire for a kind of purity was in itself suspicious, mimetic of some aspect of my own object. This does not mean that I have given up the desire to carry it through. The differences between knowing and acknowledging, or between remembering, repeating, and working through, have never been greater. Furthermore, I also acknowledge, now and throughout this essay, that having to take care of the three preceding sections first is a kind of avoidance of this last bit, that is to say of the real matter at hand. Avoidance is resistance in polite company. Usually this taking care of the commentary is just considered to be

---

2 I leave this word untranslated here in order to emphasize the strangeness it has acquired through Blanchot's use of it, as well as to highlight that which the peculiarities of his usage have led to in his commentators, particularly Jacques Derrida, in his *Parages*.

the necessary condition of something called scholarship, but I invite all to consider the possibility that scholarship can be a more or less polite name for *reading avoidance* (which does not presume that we know what *reading*, without the *avoidance*, is). I invite my readers to consider the possibility that my attempt is the very symptom of the anxiety of avoidance.

Of course these hygienic remarks on protocol are provisional. It will be impossible not to have led you already into some kind of reading of the book before I come to what I am demarcating as a reading of it. Something will already have happened. The purity of these distinctions will have been contaminated. And therefore what is indicated in statements of the type "I have not yet begun to read," or "I will never have begun to read this book" is not quite a feint or a gambit, but can be seen as the manifestation of a certain very real, and perhaps somewhat proud anxiety. The anxiety is that I will not, despite the eutrophic proliferation of provisos, *nisi*s, and *caveat*s, have covered my other end – or that I will have covered up the other end of this essay, the reading; that I will have buried it.

In any case I will not be able to keep to these proposed distinctions or divisions between the sections of my essay. So much of this is obvious, but the work of criticism has so much to do with stating the obvious. (I say this here, at the outset, in order to parry the accusation – which in any case I accept – that everything that takes place here only has to do with my fascination with difficulty. There is difficulty here.)

1. Moaning

The desire for something very simple.

And behind every name, a series of names; which is precisely why the name is to be avoided. In this attempt to subvert reference by not referring to it, there is a hoped for escape from the madness of losing track of the references. But in this avoidance there is also the madness, it would seem, of a certain kind of violent suppression or foreclosion of the fear of failing fortitude in keeping one's own story *pure*, only to have the references flood back in. How far is it possible to sustain this purity against the madness that comes when the power of keeping the names away fails?

At this point it is necessary to reconsider the form of the essay in its very pretense at talking about something, in its very aboutness.

As a form of limited scope, it is a crystalline form which, the longer it goes on, risks the exposure of a flaw: if it moves toward the treatise and the tendency of that form to weary and exhaustive summation, it moves toward the abjection of the ever more full recognition of its own lost object. Could not the scope of the investigation have been drawn differently; the range of exploration have included more, or less, or been something completely different (a fact which might have become more evident at some point or other in the middle, when I realized that all along I was writing about something else)? In truth I wasn't, but I can say that something happened in the middle, and the project was transformed. Such an admission is unthinkable in the form of a full-blown study, anathemic to its very attitude toward truth. Thus, the essay is more honest. If it achieves a span, a tension between its beginning and its end, this suspension between what it thought itself to be (about) at the outset and the peripeteia, digression or peregrination that follows *is* its very object. It is in this sense that the essay and the meditation are not coextensive, although not disjunct.

And it also becomes possible to glimpse some affinity between the essayist and the melancholic, the one who is constantly in fear of losing because he has already lost – it, somewhere along the way, even if it was at or before the beginning. So the thematic of melancholy has achieved star status in our constellations of the mental over the past years, as though to pronounce the word and give a name would be of some help in describing the state of where we are now, that is, of having lost it. Whether we say that the consistency of our stories has failed, or that something was left out in the very form of our telling them, these Mahlerian strains produce the lush and purple-verdant tones of so much of our time.

But should we not reconsider melancholy? Instead of being taken up so much as a theme, in the reappearance of the end-of-the-century and millenium discourse so omnipresent today, in the post-post-post (really just the gesture of the *post-* itself), should not melancholy be examined, not at this first, thematic level, of loss-in-idealization of the object, the mourning of the self, but rather be taken up as that very loss of the *right to idealization*? Isn't melancholia – the loss of our selves – at least a double loss, something which eludes the *theme*, because it involves the loss of idealization, of the (realm of the) ideal itself? It appears, like the aura, only in its disappearance. Mourning: one draws back from an exterior object choice, from an investment in the outside world; one forms an ideal image, the interior *eidolon* replacing the exterior object, in and as the scar of its passing. But what if this idealizing mourning had to be mourned?[3] In the morning, at dawn, every dawn, we have to mourn the mourning of the night before.

The desire to write this essay, as I have just said, in other words, without notes. Fitting this *récit* into some history of novels or of stories or of narratives is about as difficult as fitting an essay which would exist, on its own, without notes, into something which is supposed to be this book.

How much will they allow me to get away with?

When will they tell me, no means no?

Critics: big names on Blanchot

From the very beginning, I have wanted this essay to emerge as the most internal kernel of criticism, to be as seamless as Blanchot's little book-bomb itself. To cite only *Celui qui ne m'accompagnait pas* in writing about *Celui qui ne m'accompagnait pas*. After all, that is what disturbs me so much about the book, what attracts me and fascinates me: the commentaries which have made Blanchot Blanchot for us, here, today, for me here, now, are the commentaries that talk about "Blanchot." Geoffrey Hartman, Michel Foucault, Paul de Man, Emmanuel Levinas, Jeffrey Mehlman, Jacques Derrida, Andrzej Warminski, J. Hillis Miller – not just anybody. Not just any names, and not just any names for me. But when it comes to this book, the commentaries fail. There are no commentaries on this book. When it comes to this book the commentaries tend to leap to talking about Blanchot as such, not to discussing the book as such. Ultimately we should have to ask, why replace the biographical Blanchot, whom no one, perhaps even Blanchot, has anything to say about anyway, with another version of a purportedly totalized, ontologically weighted entity, the allegorical "Blanchot?" – But the truth is, we could go on to

---

[3] This is the topos of Blanchot's eloquent pages at the end of *L'Amitié*, a book devoted to his relation to his friend, Georges Bataille. And these pages were echoed rather strongly in early 1984, when Derrida gave the lectures which he published in 1986 as *Mémoires for Paul de Man*.

insist that the displacement to a book, *however one wanted to define the limits of a particular text*, would displace this totalizing gesture only one step further. Formalism is itself the ghost of theology. But, while it is possible to state this, the fact of stating it does not make it any more possible or desirable that we should leave theology, and all its ghosts, behind.

The book is pillaged for citations, for something that will allow its readers to plug it into a discursive field named "Blanchot."[4]

In Levinas and in Françoise Collin, the title of the book is not even mentioned.[5] In Foucault, it is cited more than any other work, but not as a work, rather as part of the Blanchot-as-discursive-formation, where utterances from this book are interposed more prominently, more often, and most significantly and importantly in commentary with words from other books. It is as though words from this book could be cited in order to illuminate ontologico-linguistic commitments that characterize the *œuvre* as a whole. (Here we recognize *in statu nascendi* the attitude which will lead Foucault to cite Beckett at the opening of *The Order of Discourse*, his inaugural at the *Collège de France*, without citing him: the shocking anonymity of the ever more naked voice of Beckett's trilogy.)

Nevertheless, these comments are not to be taken in any way as a derogation of Foucault's essay. In the opening section, "I lie, I speak," Foucault treats the development of Western literature as a *passage à l'acte*: whereas the utterance "I lie" can be treated in a Russellian hierarchy of logical types, and dispensed with by means of the theory of sets which Russell used to dispense with his own paradox, the statement "I speak" cannot be so dispensed with. For inasmuch as what happens in such an utterance is not of the order of description, it cannot be accommodated by any such theory of types, of logical hierarchies of sets in a catalog of states of affairs of simples; because an *act*, or shall we say, an event, or an

---

[4] In Foucault this tendency is so strong that (it could be said) the very notion of discursive formation is the name Foucault adopts to describe what he already finds in his "Blanchot." A reading of "What is an Author?" and of *The Order of Discourse* would bear this out. But my essay is about *Celui qui ne m'accompagnait pas*, and not about "Foucault."

[5] See Françoise Collin, *Maurice Blanchot et la question de l'écriture* (Paris: Gallimard, 1971), Emmanuel Levinas, *Sur Maurice Blanchot* (Montpellier: Fata Morgana, 1975). Brian T. Fitch's *Lire les récits de Maurice Blanchot* (Amsterdam: Rodopi, 1992), is the first book on Blanchot to include a chapter on *Celui qui ne m'accompagnait pas.*

occurrence, is not a *state* of affairs. This is not without relevance to the "cette fois" of the first sentence of the book under consideration, namely *Celui qui ne m'accompagnait pas*: "Je cherchai, cette fois, à l'aborder." For here we are attempting to get ahold of the (in)difference of this time, of each time, in this series which isn't one – which doesn't seem to be, at least at this time, a historical one, in the vulgar temporal sense. It is not vulgarly historical because the history, the story – if there is one in this story – is produced between the moments, in the interval between each "this time" and the other "this time"s. Such is the attraction for Foucault of a book like *Celui qui ne m'accompagnait pas*: names reduced to pronouns allow for extreme quotability, surrounded by a certain seductive mystery.

We could call this mystery *ontospeak*. It is a mystery generated by the denudation of the familiar, the bracketing of the everyday. But the uncanniness of this suspension consists in the fact that it takes place in the very language of the everyday, in its very surroundings. – Not to mention the possibility of deracinated citation for the purposes of the *leçon*, that most Cartesian and classically French of exercises.

Still, Foucault does better:

[The language of fiction] must no longer be a power that tirelessly produces images and makes them shine, but rather a power that undoes them, that lessens their overload, that infuses them with an inner transparency that illuminates them little by little until they burst and scatter in the lightness of the unimaginable. Blanchot's fictions are, rather than the images themselves, their transformation, displacement, and neutral interstices. They are precise; the only figures they outline are in the gray tones of everyday life and the anonymous. And when wonder overtakes them, it is never in themselves but in the void surrounding them, in the space in which they are set, rootless and without foundation. The fictitious is never in things or in people, but in the impossible verisimilitude of what lies between them: encounters, the proximity of what is most distant, the absolute dissimulation in our very midst. Therefore, fiction consists not in showing the invisible, but in showing the extent to which the invisibility of the visible is invisible. Thus, it bears a profound relation to space; understood in this way, space is to fiction what the negative is to reflection (whereas dialectical negation is tied to the fable of time). No doubt this is the role that houses, hallways, doors, and rooms play in almost all of Blanchot's narratives: placeless places, beckoning thresholds, closed, forbidden spaces that are nevertheless exposed to the winds, hallways fanned by doors that open rooms for unbearable encounters and create gulfs between them across which voices cannot carry and that even muffle cries; corridors leading to more corridors where the night resounds, beyond sleep, with the smothered voices of those who speak, with the cough of the sick, with the wails of the dying, with the suspended breath of those who ceaselessly cease living; a long and narrow room, like a tunnel, in which approach and distance – the approach of forgetting, the distance of the wait – draw near to one another and unendingly move apart. (F, 23–24)[6]

No doubt. The Rilkean virtuousity of this passage (reminiscent, in its expansiveness, of the *Sonnets to Orpheus*: except that Blanchot's narratives do not move toward any mournful-triumphant "I am") allows Foucault to get away with this "no doubt." What is it about the no doubt? About what is there no doubt? There is no doubt, Foucault wants to assert: it is the linguistic–ontologic burden of the speech of the desert without subject that is the work of Maurice Blanchot. There can be no doubt that this is what dictates rooming houses, empty rooms, coughs, people who are always dying, as the linguistic vehicles of emptiness that thematize the desertic, rarefied thoughts going on behind them, in the mechanics of the *Sprachontologie*.

Still, in our own terms, this is the macro-grossest thematic reading. We move, in Foucault's essay, from the philosophical predicaments, "I lie, I speak," seamlessly, and float into the rented rooms of the fictions, seemingly seamlessly, no doubt. The formal, linguistic qualities of language, revealed by its having been unchained from The Subject, shake out in terms of bleak and denuded images of the bleak and denuded. These bare rooms, where one hears only a cough, but which one never sees, do, even if only negatively, in *contre-jour*, highlight too the rooms in which one sees everything, and the room from which one sees everything (that is to say the choice of these images presages the structure of Bentham's panopticon, with which Foucault will shortly be so fascinated, and about which he is so eloquent). Too easy, Foucault, too symmetrical.

Why? Because the point is not that these narratives are pure – of names, references, places – they're not. But it is in the law of the narrative that anything proper to this book must come forth in and as its being part of this narrative, and not in citations from *this book* adduced in the course of essays written in response to the

---

6 *Foucault/Blanchot*, trans. Jeffrey Mehlman and Brian Massumi (New York: Zone, 1987), henceforth indicated by *F*, followed by page number in text.

question, who – or what – is Maurice Blanchot? And why do we feel compelled to deal with Blanchot as though he were, somehow, the highest instance of the law available to us in print today?

In the light of what I have called the seamlessness of Foucault's commentary, I must insert this truly adversarial moment of my own argument. For Foucault's is the attempt, by reading across the corpus, to make the kind of ontology without ontology fit in, dovetail with the empty rooms made manifest in the transitions brought about by this obvious, and yet purely seductive, "no doubt."

And yet – am *I* not running after a chimera, the chimera of something even more negatively theological, to borrow an expression from Foucault; am I not looking for a purity even beyond the purity of which Foucault writes, in this my search for the non-thematic? Yes and no. My enterprise is "about" the necessity of the contamination that might be seen "behind" the purity of Foucault's seamlessness, about the necessity of the scar inflicted by him on the text-body of "Blanchot" by the need to make it all dovetail so nicely, for the purposes of such a good lesson, such a good literary essay. The scar, after all, only exists in and by virtue of the act of commentary, of *critique*:

From the moment discourse ceases to follow the slope of self-interiorizing thought and, addressing the very being of language, returns thought to the outside; from that moment, in a single stroke, it becomes a meticulous narration of experiences, encounters, and improbable signs – language about the outside of all language, speech about the invisible side of words. And it becomes attentiveness to what in language already exists, has already been said, imprinted, manifested – a listening less to what is articulated in language than to the void circulating between its words, to the murmur that is forever taking it apart; a discourse on the non-discourse of all language; the fiction of the invisible space in which it appears. That is why the distinction between "novels," "narratives," and "criticism" is progressively weakened in Blanchot until, in *L'Attente l'oubli*, language alone is allowed to speak – what is no one's, is neither fiction nor reflection, neither already said nor never yet said, but is instead "between them, this place with its fixed open expanse, the retention of things in their latent state." (*F*, 25–26)

Again: this time, the *no doubt* is written as "That is why . . ." Never have we seen Foucault as more of a *philosopher* than here: how else could he have articulated everything of Blanchot's corpus to date in these sweeping sentences? And it is as a philosopher that

Foucault has given us one of the greatest essays on Blanchot that ever will have been written, and a great and powerful essay by any standard.

It seems almost as though Foucault never appeared so much in what I am calling his philosophical guise as in his essays on his literary object choices. I am thinking not only of the essay under discussion here, but also of his essay on Roger Laporte's *La Veille*.[7] Laporte's little book, the first in a series, was first published ten years after *Celui qui ne m'accompagnait pas*, and could be considered a reading of it. It contains no "names," only the pronouns "je" and "il," in all their various case inflections and contractions. Whenever an *il* in the book is meant to indicate the *il* of the first sentence, "*Il a disparu*," it is italicized, whether as *il, le, l',* or *lui.* Thus it attempts, by virtue of the disposition of the difference between roman and italic fonts, to harden up the unsaturable ambiguity of the "l" in the first sentence of *Celui qui ne m'accompagnait pas.* "*Il* a disparu," Laporte's first sentence, is a reading of "Je cherchai, cette fois, à l'aborder"; and it is a reading in which the cardinality of the third person is decided in its very emphasis.

While it is necessary to pose the questions above concerning Blanchot's truncated third person, Blanchot will not answer them for us. No reading of his book will allow us to decide the sense of that letter in the first sentence. Laporte's *La Veille* is a steady-state meditation on disdistance and writing, and it deserves to be read. An interesting and fruitful (and truthful) story could be told about it as a regression from the event of *Celui qui ne m'accompagnait pas.*

In Foucault's discussion of words trying to articulate, to bump up against the outside of words, do we not hear an echo of an entire rhetoric of the outside of language, which permeates the rhetoric of Derrida from the preface to *De la grammatologie* and the end of its first section to a moment when, twenty years later and in an interview, he responds to a question about the "il n'y a pas de hors texte" with the response that all he has ever been trying to do is to elaborate the limits of language, to speak *about* the outside of language?[8] Here the rhetoric of the outside, which we want to

---

[7] Paris: Gallimard, 1963. It is now republished as the first part of *Une vie* (Paris: POL, 1985). Foucault's essay appeared in the *Nouvelle Revue Française* 130 (October 1963), under the title "Guetter le jour qui vient."

[8] See the interview with Derrida in Richard Kearney, *Dialogues with Contemporary Continental Thinkers* (Manchester: Manchester University Press, 1984).

discuss structurally, as it were – of the structural recourse to the outside – shakes out into the thematics of radical provisionality. This recourse to the outside comes out as a kind of wish for a *passage à l'acte*, which takes the form in figures of seeing the light at the end of the tunnel, even if they are brought up with great ambivalence and in order to be denounced as being the very dream of the inside: the dream of the zone as the very fiction created by the system as the system's very anchor or navel. Here this thought of the outside touches upon the rhetoric of the "if only I had the time," of the "this would require a much more thorough analysis," which structures Derrida's entire work, even in that work's very anxiety of *patience*. Perhaps Derrida's "pas dehors" silently comments Foucault's "pensée de dehors."

It is as a philosopher that Michel Foucault can cite what he himself refers to as a narrative, in this transgeneric game, for its recourse to the philosophical topoi and stakes involved – in order to terminate, at the end of this passage, with a citation from a book where the generic distinctions dissolve, are left, as it were, in their latent state. Yet even so, in this discourse on the end of genres of discourse, Foucault has not found it necessary to plunder "Literature and the Right to Death," or any of the other major, so-called *theoretical statements* of Blanchot that exist, copiously, up to the date of his writing. It is still, for the most part, only the "fictions" that are thus pillaged and plundered.

In my desire for complete honesty (no doubt suspicious, this very rhetoric of confession Foucault spent the end of his life interrogating), I wish to highlight what has already made itself manifest, what has become my own strategy. Instead of performing pastiche, whether more or less successful, upon Blanchot's *œuvre* as a whole, I am trying to lay bare the ground to speak about only this one book, by beginning – as is fitting for an essay, that is to say for an attempt at a (de)monumentalizing discourse – to assess the state of, that is to say, to highlight the limitations of, the commentary. I have to walk myself across the garden in full sunlight, and enter the house through the porch, from the outside, rather than just stand outside the window. I have to work through my own fears about reading avoidance, about the fact that I might never encounter this text, this time, or any other time, by cutting through the midrash that's already there.

Thus I am moving through the commentators in order to strip

myself bare, to get rid of the references in a kind of lutrification; to gird myself for my own encounter with this text I am thus in the course of sacralizing. Furthermore, all of these commentaries – even the recalcitrant ones, like the ever characteristically ornery Mehlman, whom we will encounter presently – themselves treat "Blanchot" with a certain amount of reverence (in the case of the last mentioned, even if under the sign of a powerfully driven negation of desacralization, of saying that he will accompany him by not accompanying). In their acts and thematically, all these critical texts tend to sacralize "Blanchot," to attribute to (t)his text a para-theological power. They tend to sacralize in reverence by sacrificing the reference, the rigidity of the reference to this text, which they all use in the most instrumental sense ("I used him").

I too am reveling, in all this prolegomenal struggle, in my desire to find the holy of holies, the sacred of the sacred, the hyperbologically extreme moment of this corpus itself. On the one hand, I am reproaching Foucault *et al.* for making everything into one thing, something of one piece; I am accusing him of making the language ontology and the thematics of the empty rooms converge. Or at least I am interrogating him on the subject, calling him on it. On the other hand, I am also saying that writing about this book (I am perplexed, constantly, by the need to choose between "fiction," "narrative," "*récit*," "novel," so I'm opting for the simplest and just calling it a book) has to do with my own anxiety and object choices. Why should I allow myself to succumb to the same need to make my anxiety cohere with the need to read, or at the very least, to talk about this book? What about magisterial indifference? The very indifference of Blanchot himself? Certainly it is the calm of this book which generates that anxiety, the fact that there are no anchors – that generates its allure, hence the need to write about it, as well as the concomitant anxiety. This strategy of laying bare the ground is consonant with my own project of discussing the scarred relation between text and commentary, the limitations imposed by the incision of the choice of not how, but where to write. And yet, should this not be the most simple thing, to be carried out with the most blunt and banal tools? (Or do we have no tools, are we avoiding the fact, that not only do we have no tools, but that we have no hands?)

Certainly the commentaries that have mesmerized the Franco-textophile marketplace in the last years are the commentaries on

Death Sentence and on *The Madness of the Day*.[9] I have no inclination to try to produce any more words about these two works, moments of which have been dissected to the point of utterly wearying repetition. Who can take it anymore? Everybody seems to be fascinated by these works in which male narrators write about encounters with female characters:[10]

But what does Blanchot mean by "nulle suite" (nothing that follows)? He appears to mean no further events in his life, no more experiences with other women. On the other hand, he could mean nothing that follows in the sense of "no further written words," such as the words he is in the act of writing.

The French word for "thought" is feminine and therefore is spoken of as "elle," she. This means that there is an implicit identification of N. or J. and "that thought." The invocation of J. and N., the calling to them by saying "Come" or a proper name, ultimately reveals itself to be a narrative prosopopoeia for the performative invocation of a strange "thought" that is the hidden theme of the récit, as it is the theme of all Blanchot's work.

What does Blanchot's thought of the eternal return have to do with prosopopoeia in his work? What returns, in *L'Arrêt de mort* and in Blanchot's work as a whole, even in the criticism, is a situation of close proximity and immense distance involving two persons, a man (the protagonist–narrator) and another, the other in the récits usually a woman ("elle," "la pensée"). These personages approach each other with a movement that is infinitely slow and yet has infinite force.[11]

Let us take up these remarks of J. Hillis Miller. His essay on Blanchot, called "Death Mask," finds its central *theme* in the word *prosopopoeia*, the giving-face to that which doesn't have one – to the dead, to the inorganic, to the anorganic, language. But is this prosopopoeia here? It is time to distinguish the catachrestic act of giving a face from what may be even more monstrous, that is to say giving but one feature of a face – eyes with no mouth, a nose, or, as here, a voice with no eyes – or simply a name. It is time seriously to consider this aspect of the detotalization of aspect in prosopopoeia. These fragments from Miller's pages offer us a

[9] Both translated by Lydia Davis and published by Station Hill Press (Barrytown, NY) in 1978 and 1981 respectively.
[10] Frank O'Hara: "Heterosexuality! You are Inexorably Approaching. (How Discourage Her?)." See "Meditations in an Emergency," in *The Selected Poems of Frank O'Hara*, ed. Donald Allen (New York: Vintage, 1974), 87–88.
[11] J. Hillis Miller, "Death Mask," in his *Versions of Pygmalion* (Cambridge, MA: Harvard University Press, 1990), 189, 193, and 209–10 respectively.

chance to think about issues which go beyond his own essay on Blanchot, and perhaps to move toward our own *récit*.

Why is it that Blanchot's "plots," if such they can be called, involve, typically, a man and a woman? Miller: the man is the man, well you know, the *il*, *il y a* and all that, and the woman is the woman, you, know, *cette pensée*, and all that. Myself: why then is it the case, in the récit[12] which is, pragmatically speaking, *at first blush* the most *abstract* of them all, the one most fraught with pronouns – the one in which there are no proper names except the word "Van Gogh," which occurs once, on page 73, the word "Maelstrom," which occurs once with a capital *M* on page 93, and the words "Sud" and "Oui," which occur in a few places with capitals – why is it the case that in this book, clearly the formal acme of Blanchot's career as a récitologist, there is no "woman?" There are many "elles." These cannot center around the figure of a woman (or, as in the disconcerting and disorienting opening of *Au moment voulu*,[13] as a prolepsis for a woman's name), nor around the expression "cette *pensée*," of which so much has been made, at the end of *L'arrêt de mort*.[14] If these "elles" seem to center around anything, or to take off from anything, it would have to be the word *paroles*. In the space between the last sentence of *Death Sentence* and the strange soliloquy toward the end of *Celui qui ne m'accompagnait pas*, Blanchot the writer has moved from *cette pensée* to *paroles*.[15] And so why is Miller, in a kind of critical masculine protest, compelled to leap from the expression "nulle suite" as an indication of a kind of terminal one-night stand with the feminine, to the idea that this means " 'no further written words?' " This novel could be considered Blanchot's most pared down, his most abstract. It is filled with "pensées"; – or maybe it doesn't contain a single *pensée*, for the narrator's thoughts are part of the story, and we will have to ask about what appears to be the allegorical status of some of the narrative *moves*, which may or may not be thoughts – but there is no "elle" that fades off into a female "personage," as Miller would call "her."

The question is more general, and can be put roughly like this: Why is it that so many illustrious commentators are lured by the seductions of semi-abstraction presented by the – elusive enough –

---

[12] I cease to underline this word. [13] Paris: Gallimard, 1951.

[14] At the end of the second version, that is (Paris: Gallimard, 1971).

[15] A fact noted by Derrida in his "Pas" (now in *Parages*).

female masks, but no one feels compelled to deal with the only one of the récits where both the narrator and his interlocutor are male? – That is, they won't deal with it as anything other than a kind of philosophical–narrative manifesto to be cited in passing, for giving the gist of what "Blanchot" is "about." The feminine pronoun seems to be a cipher for a whole register of seductions from which the commentators cannot escape, inasmuch as they haven't, even as much as the male interlocutor is thus their and my own seducer, from whom I cannot escape. The ease with which the collusion of a female initial shades off into a female pronoun and then into "this thought," "cette pensée," should be suspicious.[16] The recognition of the Mallarméan conceit ('je dis: cette femme'') puts the attention of the male author-figure writing down the female character in a certain historical perspective. But the reading of this book *as this book*, which should not be merely a subsumption of Blanchot – or of this book – into "the tradition," should deal with the question: Why is there no "woman" in this book? Contemporary Blanchot criticism is far from emancipating itself from the mystique of an eternal feminine it itself would criticize roundly in any other critical discourse.

It is all these commentaries on Blanchot's "women" that make *Celui qui ne m'accompagnait pas* into a *hapax legomenon* in Blanchot's corpus, not mine. These commentators are the ones who speak endlessly on the subject, while I, alone in a corner, my head aching, question. My point is: Do you want to talk about the rule, or the exception? I often find that the rule is hidden in the exception.

The power of such a book over a mind given to flying along at the level of the concept is extreme; and the author of this essay is not exempt – on the contrary, obviously I am caught. In this respect it is not such a bad thing to have powerful and illustrious predecessors, if only, in this case, not to read them. Or better: to read them, and just to say no; or, better yet, not quite, yes and no. And here's why:

Quand on considère l'impression d'insuffisance ressentie par la critique littéraire à l'idée de commenter ou d'analyser les oeuvres de Maurice

---

[16] "In the early evening, as now, a man is bending / over his writing table. / Slowly he lifts his head; a woman / appears, carrying roses. / Her face floats to the surface of the mirror, / marked with the green spokes of rose stems." This is the opening of Louise Glück's "Poem," in her *The House on Marshland* (New York: Ecco Press, 1975).

Blanchot, on est d'abord tenté de l'attribuer au radicalisme de l'entreprise de l'auteur. Tout se passe comme si Blanchot écrivait d'un point de vue qui présuppose – sans le révéler – un mode d'analyse textuelle qui, dans sa rigueur, est encore à inventer, reste entièrement "à venir." Comment le critique pourrait-il espérer suppléer, excéder ou même accompagner (Littré: "suivre par honneur, conduire en cérémonie") – un texte qui si clairement englobe le sien? En désespoir de cause, le commentaire dégenère en une imitation, ou pire, en une parodie de son sujet . . . Et pourtant, réfléchir sur ce qui résiste à l'accompagnement chez Blanchot c'est se rendre compte d'un certain délié de ses textes, d'une érosion de leur propre autorité, qui revient à rien moins qu'à une annulation de leur propre statut commes premiers. Comment un discours critique pourrait-il vraiment "pénétrer" un texte qui sape à ce point sa propre intériorité, rallier un mode d'écriture si manifestement distante d'elle-même?

En thématisant un discours potentiel "sur" Blanchot comme un impossible "accompagnement" (Littré: "*Mus*: action de jouer une partie de soutien à la partie principale"), nous avons, on le voit, évoqué l'un des motifs de l'auteur. Et ce qui va suivre, en fait, sera une lecture déviée de Blanchot, un effort vers un discours critique qui, dans son éloignement calculé de son texte "premier," fonctionnera comme *celui qui ne l'accompagne pas*.

(When we consider the impression of insufficiency felt by literary criticism at the idea of commenting or of analyzing the works of Maurice Blanchot, we are first tempted to attribute it to the radicalism of the author's project. Everything happens as if Blanchot were writing from a point of view that presupposes – without revealing it – a mode of textual analysis which, in its rigor, is yet to be invented, remains entirely "to come." How might the critic be able to hope to supplement, to exceed, or even to accompany (Littré: "follow by honor, lead ceremonially") – a text which so clearly encompasses his own? In despair of a cause or a beginning, the commentary degenerates into an imitation, or worse, into a parody of its subject . . . And yet: to reflect on what resists accompaniment in Blanchot is to become aware of a certain unwinding of his texts, of a certain erosion of their own, proper authority, which amounts to nothing less than the cancellation of their proper status as primary.

In thematizing a potential discourse "on" Blanchot as an impossible "accompaniment" (Littré: "*Mus*: action of playing a part in order to support the main part"), we see that we have evoked one of the motifs of the author. And what will follow, in fact, will be a deviating reading of Blanchot, an effort toward a critical discourse which, in its calculated distancing from its "primary" text, will function as *the one who does not accompany*.[17]

---

[17] Jeffrey Mehlman, "Orphée scripteur," trans. Jean-Michel Rabaté, in *Poétique* 20 (1974), 458. English translation mine.

But can one do this? Look at what happens. Effectively, Mehlman has renounced the possibility of commenting directly our book, and, in the very gesture of attempting to manifest strong indifference to it, he contributes to a kind of sacralizing of its power: of that which we cannot speak about, we will pass over by writing the rest of our essay about Rilke and Derrida. Not at all inappropriate for an examination of the state of the Orphic today. But let us look and see what this does to Blanchot, without Mehlman's even having moved past the title of the book.

When in doubt, always cite the *Littré*. In this case, it's a bad move, because the musical side of the definition quickly takes Mehlman and those who would follow him into Rousseau territory, and Mehlman is under the spell of the fact that the revolution in Rousseau studies taking place around him would have it that Rousseau is everything. But it is not a question of *accompagnement* here, nor a question of Rousseau, who is not everything, but of the verb *accompagner*, or, more specifically, of the third-person singular, active, indicative, imperfect form of that verb, *accompagnait*; and if there is a literary figure who is *accompagnait*-ing, it is not Rousseau, but Poe or Poe–Baudelaire.[18] In the course of our story (which is not Mehlman's story) about Blanchot's story, the imperfection of the verb is important, and so is Poe.[19] For the moment, let us just say that if there is another cognate of *accompagner* to be discussed in respect of *Celui qui ne m'accompagnait pas*, it is the word *compagnon*, or *compagne*.[20]

Let us follow in the path of the " 'follow by honor.' " Mehlman's paragraphs are trying to strategize their way out of being phagoc(i)(y)totically vacuolized by a master discourse, that is to say, by everything that might fall under the sign "Hegel." This is why the situation is so dire, why there's all this self-consciousness about writing on Blanchot by (not) accompanying him. And the

[18] In the eighties it is Henry James, then History. In the nineties, Culture.

[19] Concerning what happens to the infinitive when it tilts into its modifications, we have much to say above in "Anamorphoses of Grammar." Let it be said here only that it cannot be taken for granted that limited, conjugated verbs are simply modifications of the infinitive. And furthermore it is no accident that this should come up in a discussion of Blanchot's fictions. Derrida discusses this in "Pas" and elsewhere.

[20] "Notre compagne clandestine" is the title of a remarkable little essay by Blanchot on his friend Emmanuel Levinas, which appeared in a first-rate *Festschrift*. (See *Textes pour Emmanuel Levinas*, ed. François Laruelle [Paris: Jean-Michel Place, 1980].)

"insufficiency felt" lines up with the action of what one is doing in the submissive or passive action of "follow by honor." To have to follow is bad enough, but to have to make obeisance is worse.

Let me reiterate my own plaints about the difficulty of writing on Blanchot, and thus express my sympathy, in this one regard, with Mehlman. After all, I too have been moaning. But the problem is one of form, of the form of moaning. Either you say you are moaning, as I have done, and go on to attempt what appears to be next to impossible, admitting all weaknesses, defects, and insufficiencies along the way; or you act out a posture of sovereign indifference, and trace out what, say, Blanchot has done to Hegel.[21] What you cannot do is to bring up the vocabulary of discipleship and its accompanying resentment (the most Hegelian vocabulary there is) and *then* go on to perform a massive preterition, thus showing yourself up in *feigning* indifference. Preterition is a very dangerous figure, especially when it involves names, and Big Names. The Law of the Father will come down hardest on those who (fail to) speak his many names, especially when the failure to do so is structured as a denegation.

An essay such as mine is a test, and the stakes are very high indeed; for the necessity of finding *something else* to say about *this* book is identified, thus, in the most paradoxical way, with the author's search for his own voice-in-writing. And the conclusions are not at all guaranteed – the reader-writer enters here at his own risk. If one were to produce an interpretation – if *I* were to produce an interpretation of *this* text, which were to lead to some kind of perfect convergence between the philosophical problems which can be read off from its surface and the linguistic structures which (supposedly) support them, then the entire enterprise enunciated from the beginning of this my project would be in jeopardy. And yet – if I do anything other than produce such results, the thematic of all my considerations will not be proven, borne out. I must say these things, but, in respect of this book, I must not. (Sharpen this paradox to the finest point through the white night of this book.) Lest the first person be considered intrusive here, the knee-jerk reaction of rejecting such apparently personal drives should hold

[21] See, for this alternative, Andrzej Warminski's "Dreadful Reading: Blanchot on Hegel," in his *Readings in Interpretation* (Minneapolis: University of Minnesota Press, 1987).

back long enough to see that any reader who has taken seriously the lessons this reader has tried to take seriously must allow him- or herself to be thus affected. This autobiography is everybody's autobiography, where everybody here denotes a certain community of readers (which, it is true, may not – nay, almost certainly does not – exist). And the longer I put off some kind of confrontation, explication, or *Auseinandersetzung* with this *pons asinorum*, the greater the anxiety. Life: every candidate should choose his or her own bridge, a bridge made only for him or her and built by him or her, and jump. I should say now that my confidence in my own being able to carry off this project is weak, and that I know that I have walked into my own trap. This is a spiritual trial, an *Anfechtung*; and, as such, I must proceed to the final test, even if it be the last act.

Celui qui ne m'accompagnait pas is a novel set in a house, with two characters, neither one of whom has a name – although this begs the question as to whether the pronouns "I" and "he" have assumed the status of proper names here (but what is a proper name, at the end of *this* century?) – nor leaves the house. The first voice speaks, but about what the reader doesn't know, *yet*: "Je cherchai, cette fois, à l'aborder." *Aborder*: to broach, to get ahold of, to get on board, to approach, to approach with sexual aim (to try to pick someone up), to get a grip or a grasp on, maybe; but the very difficulty of broaching the subject is the difficulty of getting ahold of the object of the verb of this first sentence, which has been compressed beyond the pronoun into the "I". Who is he, who is she, what is it?

The difficulty of beginning to read this book: one seeks, each time, to get ahold of it. For 174 pages this continues, as though the opening attempt, written "this time," in the punctual preterate, were just another time in the series of attempts, all of which could have been written about in the totally unrelated simplicity of the simple past:

Celui qui ne m'accompagnait pas commence par un événement *d'abord* qui n'est pas un événement et pas un commencement puisque rien n'y a, proprement, lieu: "Je cherchai, cette fois, à l'aborder." L'abord n'est pas un événement originel, et le récit commence par ce faux commencement ou ce faux-pas de commencement. L'abord est encore moins un événement originel (je prends ces mots dans leur sens courant) quand personne,

surtout, n'aborde personne, mais cherche, sans être sûr d'y arriver, à
aborder; ne cherche pas mais dit (récite), maintenant, qu'il chercha, dans
le passé, à arriver à aborder. Chercher à arriver à aborder, chercher la rive
d'un bord, c'est l'insistance de l'é-loignement. Et pourtant, il y a récit,
irremplaçablement. L'aborder n'a pas eu lieu, mais ce non-lieu s'est
produit "cette fois," une fois unique, donc, marquée par un passé simple.
Le désir de toucher au bord a eu lieu: "Je cherchai, cette fois, à l'aborder."
Qu'est-ce qu'avoir eu lieu pour un faux pas? Il a eu lieu, vers l'autre, au
passé. Or ce passé, l'unique fois d'un abord qui n'a pas eu lieu, n'est pas
arrivé à son terme, sa rive, sa marge ou son bord, sa berge (si tu veux bien
entendre ce mot comme de ce qui garde et met à l'abri, par exemple contre
une chute ou une noyade) mais qui, comme mouvement d'aborder, a
toutefois eu lieu, ce passé est repris, sans pouvoir être repris, dans
l'étrange présent, le présent illimité du récit . . .

(*Celui qui ne m'accompagnait pas* begins by an event of approach [*abord*]
which is not an event and not a beginning because, properly speaking,
nothing takes place there: "I sought, this time, to approach it-her-him
[*l'aborder*]." The approach is not an original event, and the story [*récit*]
begins with this false beginning or with this *faux pas* of beginning. The
approach is even less an originary event (I take these words in their
current sense), especially when nobody approaches anybody,[22] but
tries, without being sure of getting there, to approach; does not seek but
says (tells [*récite*]), now, what he sought, in the past, to come to approach.
To seek to come to approach, to look for the shore of an edge [*bord*], is the
insistance of dis-distancing. And yet, there is story, irreplaceably. The
approach does not take place, but this non-encounter [*non-lieu*] is
produced "this time," one unique time, thus, marked by a simple past.
The desire to touch the edge has taken place: "I sought, this time, to
approach it-her-him." For a *faux pas*, what is it to have taken place? It
took place, towards the other, in the past. But this past, the unique time
of an approach which has not taken place, has not arrived at its end, its
shore, its margin or its edge, its shelter (please understand this word as
having to do with what keeps and shelters, against a fall or a drowning,
for example), but which, like the movement of approach, has always
taken place, the past is taken up again – without being capable of being
taken up again – in the strange present, the unlimited present of the
story.   [*P*, 96–97; my translation])

After having read this book, after having tried to get ahold of it, is
it possible to relate the series of attempts to get ahold of it in any
other way – that is in any way other than that of a straight series,
with no relation, really, between the times and the terms, except,

---

[22] Claude Lanzmann, speaking at Yale in May 1986: "*Shoah* is a film in which
nobody meets nobody [*sic*]."

perhaps, the comma? What you remember is the imperfect of the title; but what you begin with is the preterate of the first sentence. How do we move from the perfection of a series of attempts – one assumes them to be failures, or at least incomplete in their completion – to the imperfect, that is to say to the durative and more durable and incomplete incompleteness of what kept happening, of habit? If I sought to get ahold of it *this time*, what had I previously done, been doing?

Derrida has come closer than anyone to reading pieces of *Celui qui ne m'accompaganit pas* in his "Pas," a set of fragments specifically devoted to a discussion of Blanchot's récits. But even here, his project is thus more comprehensive than mine (he wants to talk about the narratives of Blanchot), and mine more comprehensive than his (I want to talk about *one* narrative by Blanchot). Instead of talking about the strange present, I want to speak of the relation between the imperfect of the title, the preterate of the first sentence, and the general imperfection of the narrative that follows.

The desire for something very simple.

In writing about this book, there is the feeling that an infinite number of essays could be written, all of them inadequate; because each and every one would be bound to cover only a small piece of the ground of a small book written in the most tightly controlled of styles. And that the only commentary upon the book would be the reincantation of the book, over and over again, to the point of a memorization that would be able to repeat the entirely fragile – to the point of being problematical – narrative. Or else its renunciation. Gieseking writes in his book on piano technique that the first step in the learning, the playing of any piece of music is the *learning* of it, the memorization of the text.[23] In the case of Blanchot's novel this would be to contemplate a Borgesian madness, to bring Pierre Ménard out of the realm of crystalline fiction and into the world. But there would always be the new anxiety of having left some one or another of the more than dialectical interplays out. How could any reader keep this all in sight, in mind? How could any reader's temporal bandwidth keep the entire sequence in mind, the exploded moment which is the course of this book? This non-

---

[23] See Karl Lehmer and Walter Gieseking, *Piano Technique* (New York: Dover, 1972).

allegory is thus the destruction of all sequence, because at any given moment, from the edge of the first page on, one may ask, what has happened so far? Yet it is impossible to turn back.

Strategies, tactics: how to touch this book? Every sentence is so necessary that citation is impossible, because if one cites, one doesn't know where to begin or to stop. Likewise, paraphrase is useless, for the prose is so terse in its very urgency (is it only urgent for me? how can I make it urgent for everybody else?) that there could be no paraphrase – for one thing, because nothing happens.

An idea: in order to give the reader of this my essay some notion of the difficulties involved, cite all the spoken words between the two "characters" (I should rather call them *persons*, in the grammatical sense) in a given interval of the book, say the first third. Risk the weariness of this exercise; risk shocking readers with the violence of it, with the denudation it performs upon the book under discussion; risk exposing the absurdity, futility and absolute triviality of such a maneuver. Hope that nothing will distract me during this exercise. Hope that the phone will ring and save me from it. Violate the discretion of this book by writing down all infelicities towards it and thus violate all its discretion; admit all failures and admit that, finally, I or one still is not yet off the ground in this attempted reading; that so far this is nothing but a set of epigraphs–epitaphs. This is an essay on epigraphs: in my epigraph is my epitaph, and so on.

[Lui] Mais vous ne l'êtes pas.
[Moi] Je voudrais l'être.
[Moi] Il me semble, qu'en un sens j'ai tout, sauf . . .
[Lui] Sauf?
[Moi] Sauf que je voudrais en être débarrassé.
[Lui] Vous vous en tirez plutôt bien . . . Vous êtes remarquable, vous savez.
(He: But you are not [at the end].
I: I would like to be.
I: It seems to me that in a sense I have everything, except . . .
He: Except?
I: Except that I would like to be rid of it.
He: You make it through OK . . . You are remarkable, you know.)

– This is a silly, mechanical charade which I cannot continue here, so I give up. The idea of looking at how little speaking there is is accomplished, but it is a one-liner. The only pertinent matter would be to discuss whether the direct alternation or stichomythy is constant, or whether it breaks down; whether either of the voices says things to which the other voice has no response before the first speaks again, after no matter how long a narrative interval. And what of speech, the address to the reader, which is not contained in quotation marks? We will have cause to return to this question.

Intertexts: big names in Blanchot

Vincent,[24] and a little bit of Bataille

Emile Benveniste has given postwar French thought so many of its commonplaces that it is hard to underestimate the power of his magisterially banal text in its suggestiveness. When it comes time to write a formal–intertextual history of this time, the two volumes of essays collected together under the title *Problèmes de linguistique générale*[25] will serve the role of the mother lode of theoretical clichés. But there is another text, too, which will help to serve the same function, and it is Marcel Mauss's *Essai sur le don*.[26] These two texts, so different in genre and scope, pack a considerable hypogrammatic punch in French postwar prose.

There is no doubt more than one relation between the two works. In an article published first in the *Journal de psychologie normale et pathologique*,[27] called "Actif et moyen dans le verbe," Benveniste gives a comparative account of the origins of active, middle, and passive voices in the Indo-European language system, the upshot of which we can summarize as follows:

The original diacritical distinction, historically speaking, had nothing to do with activity and passivity. Rather, there were two original diatheses, active and middle, the distinction between which had to do with whether the action of the verb takes place interior to the speaking subject, in which case the verb was a

[24] "Is It or Isn't It? A Van Gogh Languishes in Limbo," read a *New York Times* headline (8 July 1990). The *New York Times* often prints articles about Van Gogh, columns which oscillate between trying to decide whether the self-portrait in the Metropolitan Museum is a fake, or, in the travel section, retracing the great artist's steps through the French landscape, staying at inns near where he stayed, etc.   [25] Paris: Gallimard, 1966.

[26] In Marcel Mauss, *Sociologie et anthropologie* (Paris: Presses Universitaires de France, 1950).

[27] In 1950. It is now to be found in Emile Benveniste, *Problèmes de linguistique générale*, vol. I (Paris: Gallimard, 1966).

middle verb; or exterior to the speaking subject, in which case the verb was an active verb. In respect of this opposition, what we now call active and passive verbs are the same, for whether I say "I hit" or "I am hit," the action of the verb takes place exterior to me. But if I say, "I think," this verb is a middle verb, for, according to historical linguistic accounts, the action takes place within the speaking subject.

Here I want to speak only of one verb, which Benveniste uses as an example of verbs which have both active and middle forms in the *ancien régime*, where activity and passivity are not diathetically distinguished, only interiority and exteriority. This example is the verb "to sacrifice" in Indo-European. If I make a sacrifice on behalf of someone else, in my sacerdotal role, say, the verb will be ridden, riven, struck, written in(to) the old active. But if I sacrifice on my own behalf, the verb will be written in the middle, as though I were performing an activity interior to myself.

This example is odd. It is odd as a case to illustrate the opposition interiority–exteriority; because rather it seems to highlight what we might call the register of oblativity, of gift-giving in general, of the indirect, of the dative. We are in a place where the verbal register seems to be slipping off into the nominal register, where voices are slipping off into the obliquity and the indirectness of cases.

And the sacrifice is not just any thought, much less simply a grammatical paradigm in the manuals. If, in French letters, there is a name attached to this thought, it is the name of Georges Bataille, whose work on theology, on sovereignty – these are to say on Hegel – on eroticism, on death, on general economy, on the theory of religion, and on Van Gogh, is tied up in a network of sacrifices and of gifts, of potlatch, the general economy of what Mauss calls total prestations, of orgasm, of painting, and of the Passion.[28]

In his *Théorie de la religion* of 1948, not published until 1973,[29] Bataille characterizes religion as an activity which takes place around the impossible activity of becoming sovereign in miming the experience of one's own death. How does this everyday and impossible experience take place? Through sacrifice, of course: in the act of sacrifice I kill something else, I enact the substitution of

---

[28] I do not want to insist that it is sacrifice uniquely that ties all of Bataille together, which would be to sacrifice Bataille on my own monotheoretical altar and for my own purposes.   [29] Paris: Gallimard.

the I with the It, I identify with the victim; and through this impossible identification I "experience" my own death. And do not the quotation marks around the verb *experience* here somehow put quotation marks around all experience, if thought through to the end? Bataille, in all of his incomplete scraps of drafts, always thought it all through to the end, or, in not thinking it through to the end, and in making provisions, did better than think it through to the end.

Sacrifice is the name for this nexus of pronominal subreption, or cowardice. It is a very sneaky activity, and its sneakiness reminds us of our finitude, as a symptom thereof. Who, after all, can truly make a "real" sacrifice? There are only two possible answers: god and the suicide. Everything is inside god, whereas the suicide sacrifices his interiority. The cardinal example of the former is called the Passion, and the latter is futile according to the reason of the epicurean dictum that one does not experience one's own death.

The consequences of all these reflections on sacrifice for the attempt to grasp what writing is are substantial. For there can be little doubt that Blanchot's anamorphic take on Bataille's reading of Hegel[30] puts the activity of sacrifice into writing. It is writing that is the sovereign operation for Blanchot. So that, for example, fragmentary writing, "Fragmentaire," read the way in which Warminski reads it, is *Nivellierung*.[31] *Nivellierung*, leveling, is here the act of making observations, remarks, which treat different moments of the dialectic on the same level, while at the same time making the gesture of saying – and quite sincerely – "it is nothing" – both of Hegel and of one's own commentary.

The "comedy" of sacrifice *becomes* writing. But we must be careful to remind ourselves that this is not the comedy of restricted economy, of those whose laughter is as a prop of their power in their observations of the imperfections of others, but the laughter that rips the ground out from underneath the world of the one who laughs.[32] The sudden *peripeteia* acted out in such laughter is what rips the breath away. This suddenness is Bataille's laughter. This

[30] I refer to "From Dread to Language" and "Literature and the Right to Death," in *GO*.

[31] A word Warminski does not use, but which is omnipresent.

[32] See Thomas Hobbes, *Leviathan*, edited and with an introduction by C. B. Macpherson (Harmondsworth: Penguin, 1968, 1981), 125–26. These paragraphs are accompanied by the glosses "Sudden Glory, Laughter," and "Sudden Dejection, Weeping," respectively.

suddenness, the suddenness of the sudden reversal, is the matter of laughter and tears.[33]

Writing, then, is the most serious comedy. At the same time, it is nothing. These activities – sacrifice and writing – are only "cowardly" to the extent that they partake of the *jeu des petits esprits*, in which these motions would be involved in a politics of comparison.

It is enough that I am writing this, and will have written this, but the tone is no accident, either. *Risk* everything, that is the only demand. And write it all down.

I will have written the worst, and the best, essay on *Celui qui ne m'accompagnait pas* – even in all this massive and prefatory avoidance and preterition. – But no one can accuse me of playing a harmless game, of not having taken it seriously. – Or else they can, because I have just given them the words in which to do so; and because the very contaminative structures I have outlined authorize anyone who would do so to do so. Who am I to say whether you should laugh or cry?[34]

It is necessary to ask: Have I not fallen victim to the worst kind of parodic tendencies described and cautioned against by Jeffrey Mehlman above? – Certainly. But that is not all I have done. But I am obliged to do it; to make sure to explain the *necessity* of literature here, and of writing.

On the one hand, I should say that I will not try to make this any more difficult than it has to be; but on the other hand, I want to say that it is not necessarily my choice that will prevail in this matter. And lest it seem that to say that is to give a lame excuse, I should say that on the other hand, I want to make this extremely difficult; to inflict on the reader the difficulty of my writing this in the reading of it; to make it felt; to multiply the reservations, the difficulties.

I had to get rid of the commentaries first, or, shall I say, dispense with them, admit them their just dispensation. Because it is my

---

[33] One in his series of *Lectures on Unknowing* entitled "Unknowing: Laughter and Tears," translated by Annette Michelson in *October* 36 (Spring 1987).

[34] Roland Barthes, in "To Write: an Intransitive Verb?" (in Richard Macksey and Eugenio Donato, eds., *The Structuralist Controversy: the Languages of Criticism and the Sciences of Man* [Baltimore: Johns Hopkins University Press, 1970]) was almost certainly speaking, at the end of his paper, in the final section on the middle voice, about such writing as *Celui qui ne m'accompagnait pas.*

proximal and for the most part to deal with commentaries. It's what I do best.

But then there are the people we call *martyrs*, witnesses, who die – not necessarily by suicide – and whom *we see*, whom we witness as having seen their own death, face to face as it were. With their faces, we give death a face. Claude Lanzmann's film, *Shoah*, puts a contemporary aspect on this, one not unrelated to our concerns here: in his interviews with members of the *Sonderkommando*, the inmates who were charged with the duties of taking people into and bodies out of the gas chambers, Lanzmann's project seems to be to push – and to break through – the limits of identifications that were constantly taking place and at the same time being fore-closed. This performative dimension of Lanzmann's film is legible from the very title sequence – stripped down as it is from the five-or ten-minute displays to which the viewers of narrative film have become accustomed – in the card that bears the title of the film, and a citation from Isaiah, which reads in French: "Et je leur donnerai un nom impérissable," which is rendered in the English subtitles as: "And I will give to them an undying name."

For Bataille, this face of the martyr, or the face that fascinated him in this capacity, is the face of Van Gogh, whose self-mutilation ("I give you my ear, my most passive organ") and suicide can be discussed as attempts at sovereignty, as attempts at identification with the sun.[35] Hence the sunflower: I am a sunflower, I turn towards the sun, I give you the sunflower, which, in my painting turns towards the sun, towards me, in my signature, and towards you, as you look at it, and I will stage an event that will burn all of us in one conflagration, in one holocaust, in one total prestation. "This is what gives Van Gogh's paintings their festive character," writes Bataille in "Van Gogh as Prometheus."[36] The "festive character" is the character of the potlatch, of the miraculous feat of total prestation that takes place there, where the limited or restrained economy of gifts and return gifts opens out into an event where it is not possible to isolate donor, donee, or *don*, or for

[35] I have profited from a reading of Eric Michaud's "Van Gogh, or, The Insuffi-ciency of Sacrifice" (*October* 49 [Summer 1989]); but my difference with Michaud has to do with a certain, more pronominal approach to the problem of sacrificial subreption.

[36] Translated by Annette Michelson in *October* 36 (Spring 1987).

that matter, verb from noun, gift from giver or receiver or giving from being given to.

It is all part of an of *imitatio Christi*: we feed on Van Gogh in the same way that we feed on stories about the Shroud of Turin, except that while the latter has a permanent owner, Van Gogh canvases come up for auction regularly, and often present opportunities for the inflation of the category of the aesthetic itself in terms of the prices they bring. Van Gogh is our icon for the extremity of experience; and as such His Works fetch a high price – this constantly augmented price serving as the very catachrestic figure of expenditure-reified-into-value itself. Can we imagine the burning of a Van Gogh?

Bataille is thus somehow the author of the French law known as *dation*, whereby the inheritance taxes on an estate are settled by the direct acquisition by the state of its share. It is not at all coincidental that this law's most famous exemplum is in the case of the Picasso estate, whereby it is something called art that is thus acquired. Here is one way in which the relation between death, art, and sacrifice shakes out into very pragmatic exchanges indeed, a kind of *habeas corpus* that extends the body of someone called an artist to the body of his work, in and around the death of the artist, whose work is taken in taxes. As Bataille is to Van Gogh, so we should think of Stevens to Picasso, and of David Hockney's elaborations on their relation.

Maelström[37]

En vérité le nom n'est jamais seul.   (*P*, 17)

Late extra. – In central passages of Poe and Baudelaire the concept of newness emerges. In the former, in the description of the maelstrom and the shudder it inspires – equated with "the novel" – of which none of the traditional reports is said to give an adequate idea; in the latter, in the last

---

[37] Reading Steven Shaviro's *Passion and Excess: Blanchot, Bataille, and Literary Theory* (Tallahassee: Florida State University Press, 1990), I do find *one* citation from *Celui*, on page 124, taken from a couple of pages before the end of Blanchot's novel. In fact this one citation is surprising, because there are other indices between Shaviro's sheets that he has not read *Celui qui ne m'accompagnait pas*. Shaviro discusses the word "Maelström" in the context of a discussion of a remarkable poem by Emily Dickinson (and this after a discussion of Poe – and of Mallarmé, but not of Baudelaire).

line of the cycle *La Mort*, which chooses the plunge into the abyss, no matter whether hell or heaven, *"au fond de l'inconnu pour trouver du nouveau."* In both cases it is an unknown threat that the subject embraces and which, in a dizzy reversal, promises joy. The new, a blank place in consciousness, awaited as with shut eyes, seems the formula by means of which a stimulus is extracted from dread and despair . . .[38]

Places whose *names he has never heard*.[39]

On page 93 of *Celui qui ne m'accompagnait pas* occurs the word "Maelstrom" once, capitalized. The word has been a common noun in French, according to the *Robert*, since 1857. It is a word of Dutch origin, although as a proper noun and in its first occurrence it names a current off the coast of Norway. What are we to do with this? The decade of the 1850s produced, among other things, Baudelaire's translation of Poe's story "A Descent into the Maelström," which is printed in the Pléiade edition of Baudelaire's translations of Poe without the dieresis – just as it occurs in Blanchot.

This is a story in which an old fisherman describes to Poe's frame narrator his encounter with a tidally produced whirlpool off the coast of Norway; an encounter which should have resulted in his own death, and which did result in the death of his brother. I highlight several elements of the story which might have some bearing on my story about Blanchot's narrative.

But before we throw ourselves, *à corps perdu*, into Poe, more commentary. What is Derrida's "Pas?" It is not a book; it is not a finished product, nor is it an essay; nor is it an interview. It is a kind of dialogue, ostensibly between a male voice and a female voice. Its ostensible subject is the narratives or fictions of Maurice Blanchot. The male voice addresses the female voice with "vous," the female the male with "tu." There are themes and there are words. The themes, or some of them, are the sea and its neighboring regions (not the open sea, but its *parages*, breakwaters, shores); the ability to say "tu" or "vous" and the relations between this and distance, intimacy; what it means or is to be without a name; the nature of a conversation such as the one being carried on; the differences of genders and genres; passivity, and the night. Words,

[38] Adorno, *MM*, 235–36.
[39] Thomas Pynchon, *Gravity's Rainbow* (New York: Lippincott, 1971). I take these words, with their emphasis, from the first page.

or some of them: *pas, oui, viens, sans, sauf, si, Ent-fernung, é-loignement, tu, vous* – the relations among these.

In its very banality, this description renounces any kind of adequacy. This 100-odd-page-long, free-floating encounter with Blanchot's fictions drowns out any attempt to treat it systematically, as some kind of whole: that is part of the activity of its patience. It is presented as a fragment of work in progress; it could never be finished. Derrida himself had to make some choices (he has discussed the monstrosity, that which is indicated, of his own cutting and pasting operation); and his readers also have to make their own choices, too. In speaking of "Pas," we will have to leave some things out, intentionally or not. We will confine ourselves to remarking some passages, gestures.

"Pas" is now published in a book called *Parages*, whose ostensible subject is the narratives or fictions of Maurice Blanchot.[40] There are three other attempts at essays within the same covers. These deal, more or less, with what we know in English as *Death Sentence* and *The Madness of the Day*. The introduction discusses the years of divagations that lead to this *fascination* (another theme of "Pas"), the fascination that led to this *admiration* (another theme word). Emphasis is another theme, the sparsity of emphasis in Blanchot: also his strange diacritical marks, the lozenges and sets of points that begin paragraphs in some books.

Derrida nowhere discusses the "±±" headers of the opening sections of *L'Entretien infini*.[41] Of these marks, I should say that I have always imagined them as something like the Fregean assertion sign (*Urtheilsstrich*) that accompanies propositions, with all its built-in possibilities of negation, the construction of trees, and so on. But this imagining is just a foil to explore the differences between Frege's sign and Blanchot's. Frege's sign prefaces propositions, that is to say, statements that have truth values. In its barest form, " ⊢" means "it is asserted that," or "it is asserted," followed by the contents of the proposition whose truth is being asserted. Blanchot's mark, the only one of his idiosyncratic marks I will discuss and the one I find the most interesting, has no such easily statable, translatable content.

Let us think about this mark, or about half of it, without its repetition, as it is used in mathematics. There, "±" is used in

---

[40] "Pas" was first published in *Gramma* 3/4 (1976).

[41] Paris: Gallimard, 1969.

formulae to express relations between terms sometimes positive, sometimes negative, depending on the sign of the terms involved in any particular instance of the use of the formula for the solution of an equation. Blanchot doubles this mark as though to say, not "this is either asserted or negated, depending," but "whether this is asserted or negated can be asserted or negated, depending." Depending, the second time, on what? In fact, the reduplication of the sign reduces any dependency irreducibly, for the logic of "whether this is asserted or negated can be asserted or negated" clearly cannot be made to depend on anything, for any dependency imaginable (on external factors, the analogon here of any determination of the equation to be solved) could be, would be neutralized by the other half of the sign. For us, $\pm\pm$ is thus the mark of an absolute construction.[42]

Parages is the only book to date in Derrida's corpus (along with the much smaller in scope *Ulysse gramophone*[43]) to be devoted singularly to an author's narrative fictions. That alone should make it worthy of note. Why Blanchot, after all? Let us take up one of the themes, which I choose here, apparently the least "philo-sophical" of all. I will begin with the waters, the sea, the story of *eaux*. Even before he begins "Pas," this monumental ruin to Blanchot's narratives, Derrida is already concerned with what takes place near the sea, or rather at the seaside. Hence his title, *Parages*:

Car la rive, entendons l'autre, paraît en disparaissant à la vue. Une partie de ce livre, sa note la plus basse, s'appelle *Journal de bord*, comme pour tenir le registre d'une navigation, mais tous les bords, d'un texte à l'autre, sont aussi des rivages, rivages inaccessibles ou rivages inhabitables. Paysage sans pays, ouvert sur l'absence de patrie, paysage marin, espace sans territoire, sans chemin réservé, sans lieu-dit. Non qu'il en manque mais s'il a lieu, *il le faut*, il devra d'abord s'ouvrir à la pensée de la terre comme au frayage du chemin. Page après page, on le vérifiera mais je n'en pris claire conscience qu'après coup, tout paraît attendre ici au bord, et au bord de la mer, parfois tout près de s'y perdre ou de se laisser battre par elle.

---

[42] There has been little if any discussion to date of the relation between the wager in Pascal and the notions of sacrifice (and its subreptions) and sovereignty in Bataille. So much attention has been given to Bataille as a reader of Hegel that other, pre-Hegelian and French and Catholic antecedents have been largely ignored.   [43] Paris: Galilée, 1987.

(For the shore, that is the other, appears in disappearing from view. A part of this book, its lowest note, is called *Border Lines*, in order to hold to the register of a navigation – but all edges, from one text to another, are also shorelines, inaccessible shorelines or uninhabitable shorelines. A landscape without a country [*Paysage sans pays*], opening upon the absence of fatherland, marine landscape, space without territory, without a restricted road, without a local name. Not that it is lacking, but if it takes place, *it has to*, it should first of all [*d'abord*] be opened to the thought of the earth as to the breaking of a path. Page after page, this will be verified, but I didn't realize it clearly until afterward: everything seems to wait here at the edge [*bord*], and at the edge of the sea, sometimes close enough to be lost there or to allow itself to be weathered by it.   [*P*, 15–16; my translation])

Following upon this, we are treated to the opening lines of *Thomas en exergue*, along with the opening sentences of *Celui qui ne m'accompagnait pas*. Why the sea, why the ocean? Let us leave Rilke out of it for the time being: I do not want to go that way.

At the edge of the sea – the site, Derrida wants to say, of so many of Blanchot's narratives – things are ill-defined. Their borders are constantly shifting. There is, after all, fog. But let us think about what Heidegger (whose name is ever present in the diction here) might say. Or rather, let us try to think about what kind of message in a bottle Derrida is sending to Heidegger.[44]

Let us examine some of the implications. Traces remain as furrows in the earth; but waves, *sillages*, and *vagues*, in their very vagueness, disappear, or rather propagate out into a kind of disseminated, almost undifferentiated oblivion. The marks are there, but they radiate out into the almost indistinguishable.[45]

So all roads lead to the sea, at some point or other. But with the sea alone one cannot do much. What is more compelling is the land–sea interface, what takes place in the *parages*. Derrida insists, from his very introduction on, that *Celui qui ne m'accompagnait pas* is a seaside book, beginning, as it does, with the *aborder*:

Le bord, "*la pensée qui l'avait amené au bord de l'éveil*": quitter le bord et rester au bord, dans *Celui qui . . .*, depuis le moment où "je cherchai, cette fois, à l'aborder," énoncé qui se répète et déplace constamment, revient près du bord. La paralyse du bord . . .

---

44 In respect of Derrida's need to locate *Celui qui ne m'accompagnait pas* near the water, I would rather maintain, since we in fact never leave the house (there are those steps taken to the kitchen for a glass of water), that the oceanic feeling of navigation, divagation in *Celui* also refers to *Thomas*.

45 This phenomenalizing reading *is* a parody.

– Le bord qu'il quitte sans le quitter, aborde sans aborder, dans et comme *Celui qui ne m'accompagnait pas*, c'est aussi un bord de mer. Un voisinage caché. La proximité indéterminée, la direction indécidée qu'on nomme, au cours de l'approche, *parages*. L'eau est ici eau-de-la-mer. Au–delà d'elle, le bord, partout. C'est aussi un lac. Au-delà du bord, elle: partout. Elle entoure une île. En elle, on ne marche plus, le pas n'est pas possible. Autrement dit, il s'accomplit dans son impossibilité même, il s'affranchit de lui-même. Faux-pas de la mer. Pas deux pas dans l'eau-de-la-mer.

(The edge, *"the thought which had led him to the edge of wakefulness"*: to leave the edge and to remain at the edge, in *Celui qui . . .* from the moment when "I sought, this time, to approach it," a statement which is repeated and displaced constantly, returns close to the edge. The paralysis of the edge . . .

– The edge he leaves behind without leaving it, broaches without broaching [*aborde sans aborder*], in and as *Celui qui ne m'accompagnait pas*, is also[46] a seaside. A hidden nearness. The indeterminate proximity, the undecided direction that is called, in the course of the approach, *parages*. The water here is the water of the sea. Beyond it, the edge, everywhere. It is also a lake. Beyond the edge, the ocean [*elle*], everywhere. It surrounds an island. Upon it, we no longer walk, pace is not possible. In other words, it is accomplished in its very impossibility, it frees itself from itself. *Faux pas* of the sea. Not two steps in the water of the sea.

[*P*, 106; my translation])

Now why is it, and how can it be, that Jacques Derrida, a man who is so close to so many names, can and does discuss not only the ocean but the lake, without mentioning the Maelström?

I must say, I do not understand this lake. Because I think that the island in question is not in the middle of a lake. It is the island between the shore and the high sea that not only makes for the *parages*, the waters that exist between the islands and the sea, but the peculiarity of the underwater topography of which creates the Maelström, every six hours. For is it not a moral of Poe's story "A Descent into the Maelström," that what is far and away the most dangerous, more terrifying than anything that might take place on the open sea, is very close by, within sight of land? Instead, Derrida refers to the abyss (*P*, 75).

---

46 [Why this "also"? What is it, between these two voices, that it is *also* the seaside? What is being pushed out of sight and out of mind with this "aussi?" It is the violence of the encounter of these two voices, and, I would venture, between these two *male* voices.]

Let us look into the Maelström, the abyss Derrida does not name, and which Poe, Baudelaire, and Blanchot do. "A Descent into the Maelström" is a buddy story, or, as they say in today's lexicon, a story of companions: a frame narrator, an old fisherman, his brothers, and mates and daily companions. The site of the telling is high on a craggy promontory, overlooking the regularly produced, irregular current off the coast of Norway which is known as the Maelström. The old fisherman tells the story of what happened to him from along this vertical axis of the overlook into the abyss, from a perch of which the unnamed narratorial "I" says:

Nothing would have tempted me to be within half a dozen yards of [the precipice's] brink. In truth so deeply was I excited by the perilous position of my companion, that I fell at full length upon the ground, clung to the shrubs around me, and dared not even glance upward at the sky – while I struggled in vain to divest myself of the idea that the very foundations of the mountain were in danger from the fury of the winds. It was long before I could reason myself into sufficient courage to sit up and look out into the distance.   (*CTP*, 127)

Reason here is consideration of the horizon, and it is dictated by and as a defense against the terror – and thrill – of looking into the abyss. The narrator takes his thrill voyeuristically, by contemplating the position of the companion. As these two look off into the scenery, about to witness the regular tidal whirlpool, the fisherman–companion looks off into the distance and gives us the topography:

"Further off – between Moskoe and Vurrgh – are Otterholm, Flimen, Sandflesen, and Stockholm. These are the true names of the places – but why it has been thought necessary to name them at all, is more than either you or I can understand. Do you hear any thing? Do you see any change in the water? . . ."

"This," said I at length, to the old man – "this *can* be nothing else than the great whirlpool of the Maelström."

"So it is sometimes termed," said he. "We Norwegians call it the Moskoe-ström, from the island of Moskoe in the midway."

"Maelström" is a Dutch word, like the nearby "Van Gogh."

The ordinary account of this vortex had by no means prepared me for what I saw. That of Jonas Ramus, which is perhaps the most circumstantial of any, cannot impart the faintest conception either of the magnificence, or of the horror of the scene – or of the wild bewildering sense of *the novel* which confounds the beholder. I am not sure from what point of view the writer in question surveyed it, nor at what time; but it could neither have been from the summit of Helseggen, nor during a storm. There are some passages of his description, nevertheless, which may be quoted for their details, although their effect is exceedingly feeble in conveying an impression of the spectacle.   (*CTP*, 128–129)[47]

What does Poe mean by "circumstantial?" The word, like the observer, could only have circled the vortex. The beholder looks on and conveys no adequate account of what was seen, which account can only be read for some other details. The only certainty is negative. He beheld it; but in the distance of beholding, the sublime character of the situation was somehow lost. Can the trauma of the sight of an ocean which is about to devour everything be conveyed in a description?

And what, after all, about the names, of which there is a momentary yet florid proliferation? If nothing else, you can always orient yourself with toponyms, grasping at whatever barren shrubbery may be growing in the immediate vicinity; in the same way that scholarship can always try to comfort itself with the search for sources and a safe, intertextual anchorage. Why is it necessary to name them, after all, when the list of names is only to be followed by the questions, "Do you hear any thing?" "Do you see any change in the water?" Let us look again into the "Maelström" now, and we will find that

[t]he edge of the whirl was represented by a broad belt of gleaming spray; but no particle of this slipped into the mouth of the terrific funnel, whose interior, as far as the eye could fathom it, was a smooth, shining, and jet-black wall of water, inclined to the horizon at an angle of some forty-five degrees, speeding dizzily round and round with a swaying and sweltering motion, and sending forth to the winds an appalling voice, half shriek, half roar, such as not even the mighty cataract of Niagara ever lifts up in its agony to Heaven.   (*CTP*, 129)

[47] Is it possible that Immanuel Kant was thinking of this very passage in Jonas Ramus when he wrote the famous passage on the dynamic sublime in the *Critique of Judgment*? See de Man, *AI*, 134. For Kant, after all, as for many of the rest of us, his readings are his nightmares. We know that Kant's examples of beauty and sublimity tend to come from things he never saw, but from accounts he read, that is to say, from discourse, travel literature. (This fact has been commented in a more than jocular and all too true way by Benjamin, in his "Unbekannte Anekdoten über Kant," (Walter Benjamin, *Gesammelte Schriften*, 4, 808). To speak, or to write, is not to see.

This proctological (or, should we say, -scopic?) view is further elaborated with more scholarship:

– These are the words of the Encyclopædia Britannica. Kircher and others imagine that in the center of the channel of the maelström [*sic*] is an abyss penetrating the globe, and issuing in some very remote part – the Gulf of Bothnia being somewhat decidedly named in one instance. This opinion, idle in itself, was the one to which, as I gazed, my imagination most readily assented; and, mentioning it to the guide, I was rather surprised to hear him say that, although it was the view almost universally entertained of the subject by the Norwegians, it nevertheless was not his own.

(*CTP*, 131)

So, the Maelström is thought to be an abyss, in the sense that everybody used the word in the seventies. But someone thinks that this is not the case. It is also a kind of black hole that has an event horizon, an invisible radius that cannot be seen but is *represented* by the particle spray it emits, its white-foam halo or aura. The Maelström emits particles. The tropology that links eye to ear to mouth to anus to sun to sunflower is trotted out again. Now we can see, or read, that there is a whole system that links our *names*: Van Gogh and Maelström. Also "Sud." What links Van Gogh to the Maelström is first of all the North–South axis, the geographical verticality of the sublime, another figure of its *altus-altus*.[48]

But for the purposes of our investigations, these visual excurses are prefatory. For what we really must focus our attention on is the word "companion." This is the word, perhaps itself a name, which also surfaces over and over again in *Celui qui ne m'accompagnait pas*. For these purposes, there are other plot lines to be mapped out.

Who is the companion? What is the companion? A companion? A companion is someone you break bread with, someone you fish with, someone to whom you tell, or from whom you hear, a story – someone who can be lost, who can leave you out in the cold, to your own devices. There is no bread in "A Descent into the

[48] For some of the best available today on sublimity and the line of sight, see Hertz, *The End of the Line*. It is at this moment that the north of the province of the Maelström links up with the auroric swirl of the Starry Night, and that the thought of libation in Heidegger (See "Das Ding," in *Vortraege und Aufsaetze* [Pfullingen: Neske, 1954]), as the unifying of the fourfold, links up with the more linguistic question of sacrifice in Bataille.

Maelström," but there are fish. The bread broken seems to be – the story.

In truth so deeply was I excited by the perilous position of my companion, that I fell at full length upon the ground, clung to the shrubs around me, and dared not even glance upward at the sky –.   (*CTP*, 127)

From the first page of the story, the companion is the one who tells the story to Poe's narrator, and on the last, he, the companion, says:

"I was borne violently into the channel of the Ström, and in a few minutes, was hurried down the coast into the 'grounds' of the fishermen. A boat picked me up exhausted from fatigue – and (now that the danger was removed) speechless from the memory of its horror. Those who drew me on board were my old mates and daily companions – but they knew me no more than they would have known a traveller from the spirit-land. My hair, which had been raven black the day before, was as white as you see it now. They say too that the whole expression of my countenance had changed. I told them my story – they did not believe it. I now tell it to *you* – and I can scarcely expect you to put more faith in it than did the merry fishermen of Lofoden."   (*CTP*, 139–40)

At another point in the story they are the "old companions" (*CTP*, 135). The unbelieving companions at the end, with whom one can share perhaps loaves and fishes, but not credible discourse, are the companions of the companion of the narrator, the narrator-companion. In the middle of the story, after the *mise-en-scène* I have related, there is another story of (lost) companions, that of the two brothers who do not survive the encounter with the Maelström, or the story. In the middle of the unexpected storm that drives the boat carrying the three brothers (and their catch) into the whirl-pool, one brother – the youngest – disappears in the very first onslaught, without very much incident, in fact in a clause in a sentence whose major part describes the loss of the mast of the ship. It remains to be told how the older brother – the teller of the story being a middle child – is to be dispensed with.

This is the crux of the story, for it involves a substitution, and a singling out of the one who survives. What we are witnessing is in fact called triage. (And what is this story if not a compulsive repetition of threes and sixes, the Trinity versus the Devil? The half-dozen yards, six hours?) When the brothers – and now there are two – realize that they are headed for the abyss, the teller, our fisherman, is clinging to a ring bolt, and the other, remaining brother to a barrel. This is the situation as it stands when the boat enters the event horizon of the whirlpool:

All this time I had never let go of the ring-bolt. My brother was at the stern, holding on to a small empty water-cask which had been securely lashed under the coop of the counter, and was the only thing on deck that had not been swept overboard when the gale first took us. As we approached the brink of the pit he let go his hold upon this, and made for the ring, from which, in the agony of his terror, he endeavored to force my hands, as it was not large enough to afford us both a secure grasp. I never felt deeper grief than when I saw him attempt this act – although I knew he was a madman when he did it – a raving maniac through sheer fright. I did not care, however, to contest the point with him. I knew it could make no difference whether either of us held on at all; so I let him have the bolt, and went astern to the cask. This there was no great difficulty in doing; for the smack flew round steadily enough, and upon an even keel – only swaying to and fro with the immense sweeps and swelters of the whirl. Scarcely had I secured myself in my new position, when we gave a wild lurch to starboard, and rushed headlong into the abyss. I muttered a hurried prayer to God, and thought all was over. (*CTP*, 136)[49]

Now, having traded places, they are in it. And now, in the calm of the interior of the whirlpool, things begin to happen inside the head of our fisherman, whose terror seems to have given way to the tension of a calm and a silence as though everything had already been destroyed. In fact, even before the final slide and the exchange of grasping hands, the trading of places, a kind of calm had already come upon him:

It may look like boasting – but what I tell you is the truth – I began to reflect how magnificent a thing it was to die in such a manner, and how foolish it was in me to think of so paltry a consideration as my own individual life, in view of so wonderful a manifestation of God's power. I do believe that I blushed with shame when this idea crossed my mind. After a little while I became possessed with the keenest curiosity about the whirl itself. I positively felt a *wish* to explore its depths, even at the sacrifice I was going to make; and my principal grief was that I should never be able to tell my old companions on shore about the mysteries I should see. (*CTP*, 135)

By this point, in the suspension of the natural attitude of terror, which makes all phenomenology sublime, the merry fishermen of the end of the tale are already old, that is to say former, companions. At this point we have to ask whether and why the

---

[49] The reasons Adorno chooses this passage as the epigraph to his dissertation on Kierkegaard (*Kierkegaard* [Frankfurt-on-Main: Suhrkamp, 1962, 1974]) must be pondered in a separate study.

singularity of the companion. What is the law that dictates this, that anything other than one term in the equation must drop out (the younger brother, the plurality of the companion fishermen who cannot assimilate the story, the older brother as well – everyone except Poe's narrator)?[50]

There is this concern with names in this story. Such as Maelström, Moskoe-ström, all the toponyms of which it is said that why they even have names is an enigma. But there is at least another moment of naming. It comes after the fact, and it involves the teaching and learning of the words necessary to tell the story. Now that our fisherman is in the Maelström, holding onto his barrel, his brother at the doomed ring, he is overtaken by a calm, dispassionate attitude, in which he watches the various objects in the vortex around him, and begins to compare their rates of descent, relative to size and shape. The largest sink most quickly, and spherical objects too. The shape that proves most resistant is the cylinder, like the proverbial message in – or, in this case, the label on – the bottle. The old man, companion to the narrator, is the proverbial bottle containing the message.[51]

The Poe–Baudelaire story is a story told *to* the frame-narrator, not *by* the narrator (as opposed to *Celui*, where it is the first person who tells whatever could be said to constitute the story) but by a person whom the narrator refers to more than once as his "companion" (*compagnon* in Baudelaire's version). In this regard it is also significant that the story told in the Poe is that of a person (the fisherman, the narrator's companion) who tells the story of a lost companion (his brother, who died in the same encounter with the Maelström which the teller of the story survived). Whereas in the Blanchot the first-person voice moves through a long monologue over the course of which the voice of the third-person interlocutor-voice, referred to as the companion from a certain point in *Celui* . . . on (*C*, 17) and present from the beginning of the book, disappears in the whirlpool of "paroles."

The Poe–Baudelaire contains a set of markers that clearly identify it as deliberately – more and more deliberately, as we shall

---

[50] If there is a contemporary text of which these same questions must be asked, it is Errol Morris's film, *The Thin Blue Line* (USA, 1988), in which there is a compulsive repetition of brothers – and sisters – who didn't make it, who could not or would not tell the story. In the end, the law of narrative would seem to be: how to kill off your companion.

[51] The message that may or may not arrive in Paul Celan's Bremen Speech of 1958. See Celan, *GW* vol. III, 185–86.

see – written in what we might call, after more than a decade of renewed interest in the subject, "the discourse of the sublime." Not only is it presented as a narrative of having lived through an experience of surviving (what should have been) one's own death, an experience related explicitly at several points as being absolutely incommensurable with any form of telling, with the horror experienced, with narration, description, or credibility, rather in the fantastic manner of the Kleistian.

But also the Maelström of the title belongs to what we might call the Northern Sublime, and is viewed, in the story and during the extended moment of its telling, from a very high peak, overlooking the ocean, a height from which the frame narrator shrinks, as the old man who tells the story of his encounter with the vortex visible at this not quite comfortable distance leans out over a ledge above a gaping precipice, first over the rocks far below, and then the sea and its currents. Here we are in the by now more comfortable (it shouldn't be, but it is, for us, now, let us say, a little bit familiar) topos of the coincidence of the high and the deep. It is comfortable for us because we have heard so much about it; it is a cliché for Poe–Baudelaire because, by the time of their writing, Schiller had already given them a manual for the production of the theatrical sublime. The sublimity of the situation is further enhanced by the textbook Schillerian theme of absolute detachment in the face of one's own imminent death. This is the attitude which allows the fisherman to take the measures that ultimately save his life, and which he tries to explain to his companion-brother, whose inability to overcome his own terror with similarly sublime detachment – thus extricating him from the paralysis of that terror by following our character's example – is what insures his death.

The sublimity of the fisherman's detachment is conveyed even in its very verbal incommunicability. Not only does he not expect Poe's frame narrator to believe him: in the same manner, his companion-fishermen, the ones with whom he breaks bread, with whom he harvests the multiplied loaves and fishes, *everyday*, who fished him out of the drink on that day, disbelieve him. And he is incapable of conveying the calmness that ultimately allows for his own survival, but noways guarantees it to his brother, in words or in signs. Their words are drowned out by the roar of the whirlpool, and the brother cannot, in his terror, be made to understand, or to act on the basis of the actions the fisherman narrates himself as having taken. He cannot imitate, in his terror. He may be a brother, but he is not a *semblable*. Still, in the matter of belief or disbelief, as it is represented in the story, there is a thematized, material trace[52] of the experience which presumably can be read as the sign of having experienced absolute terror: the fisherman's hair has gone from black to white in the course of an afternoon, a fact which presumably his "old mates and daily companions," who fish him out of the water, would recognize. The white hair of the fisherman *represents*, by catachresis, his terror, in precisely the same fashion that the ring of foam *represents* the Maelström, which is, in its depths, unfathomable to the eye.

Discussion of this passage will be the only reference to "the sublime" in this study, which contains so many other indices of the sublime that continual reference thereto would be supererogatory and boring. It seems to be the stamp of our time that we need the classical mechanics of the sublime in order to discuss the fantastic character of all the quantum leaps of our everyday experience. Yet thus, while the discourse on the sublime is more necessary then ever – not only as a formal exercise, figuring out what or if the sublime is, what are its rules, etc., but for the purpose of conveying the shock of horror at what we see in the streets and on television or in the newspapers every day – it may also turn out to be the most dangerous kind of trap. The sublime machine has become our main variety of vanilla soft ice cream (only one flavor).

Thus, in terms of my own diction, I have preferred to avoid this vocabulary, largely out of the fear that my own inadequacy would reduce me, in front of any image or text, to babbling, and saying, Sublime, absolutely sublime! Perhaps, in order to preserve the uniqueness of all the new shock experiences that yet await us, it will be necessary to abandon *the* sublime and to start talking about sublimes with different flavors. There is no longer one sublime. Maybe there never was. But the mode created by Longinus, in his description of previous and more ancient texts, could perhaps no

[52] That the materiality is thematized means that it is not materiality in the strong sense. At the same time, the thematization explains why Poe was so attractive to vulgar, thematic, so-called deconstruction, which never goes beyond the theme, and is thus not deconstruction at all.

longer be elaborated, even paratactically, between the covers of one book, or in one grand speech.

– That is sublime – for Lyotard, say, but not good enough for me, which is why I will not have spoken of the sublime. This uniqueness, which, in fighting it, we have to admit, seems to be an essential characteristic, a gathering trait of the sublime, and must be interrogated much more patiently. It is right that I should come to discuss Derrida's "book" on Blanchot in the context of Poe and of Baudelaire's Poe (there are too many qualifications at issue to do anything other than put those words into what look like scare quotes, but are in fact more like brackets in some textological operation: read the preface to Derrida's disparate gathering, *Parages*).

Is it (not) astonishing that the entire "history" of "reception" of *Celui qui ne m'accompagnait pas*, that is to say, of all the purportedly critical works I have been discussing thus far – none of which, truly, could be said to be an essay on or at *Celui qui ne m'accompagnait pas* – is it not shocking that in a book where the voices do not have *names*, in almost 200 pages of namelessness, in the course of which only two or three words resembling proper names are to be found, that no one would have troubled themselves about this? And this in a book in which the question, theme, or motif of the name is so powerfully broached ("Vous voulez dire qu'il ne doit pas y avoir de nom entre nous?" [*C*, 43; *P*, 93]).[53]

These "names" are Van Gogh, which we have already (mis)treated above,[54] "Maelstrom," and the words "Sud" and "Oui," capitalized, about which we will have had nothing – much – to say. And which I continue to mistreat: while "Van Gogh," has the ring of being a particular toponym, something to tie its bearers to a specific piece of earth, it also rings, perhaps, with the Dutch–Flemish "hooch," or the German "hoch," meaning high, as in "Hochdeutsch." Thus, continuing with our speculations about

---

[53] I might hazard the guess that it is the occurrence of the word *parages* in Baudelaire's translation of Poe that dictates the title of Derrida's book. See Edgar Allan Poe, *Œuvres complètes*, trans. Charles Baudelaire (Paris: Gallimard, 1951). We find there, in these few pages, "parages" (188), "parage" (188), "parois" (195; again, 199).

[54] It is clear enough, from reading the aforementioned essay by Eric Michaud, that Van Gogh himself was accidented by the name of his father, or by the maelstrom in the sky of the starry night.

the provenance of Derrida's title, we would have to say that Derrida's book is *de haute parage*, of high birth, in fact of the highest, *Le Très-Haut*, because it is born of the height itself – and thus, no doubt, of the light, or the maelstrom, of the law. Derrida, son, or grandson of Van Gogh, or Moses, or Freud.

For us, so much is a question of these words, and of how shocking they are, as they float across the page, all of a sudden, like hallucinations, making the reader look back to see if he or she has really seen them, in a sort of reverse scanning. They are shocking because they are so clearly so unassimilable, so inadmissible: no one will go near them. The name is a trauma. Given the pronominal denudation, one should be very careful here; and I am sure of only one thing, that I have not been careful enough.

It is one thing to delay the reading of this book that offers so few *prises* in using the (non-existent) commentaries upon it to say what may look like *n'importe quoi*. It is another to make the more overtly desperate gesture of seizing upon these names in an attempt to write a commentary, when one knows full well that one is grasping at a couple of mirages simply in order to get ahold of something in these rudderlessly deictic and other than pronominally nominally deserted regions.

Certainly, for Derrida, whose *Parages* are named so prominently in Baudelaire's version of "A Descent into the Maelström," these things are astonishing – for one who is so sensitive beyond the simple pragmatics of the name. And furthermore: it is in these waters of the Poe–Baudelaire that there might be found a link between his own title and the waters he seeks to *aborder* in his remarks on why *Celui qui ne m'accompagnait pas* takes place "near" the water, in the "Pas rages" of a maelstrom, for example. "Near," given the fact that Derrida's dialogue, one of his finest pieces of writing to date, is all "about" the near, about proximity, distance, *Ent-fernung, é-loignement*, a whole Heidegger–Blanchot discourse which should not be reproduced here.

Derrida's not picking up on the names in this book is even more astonishing. The Baudelaire–Poe is such a topos for French letters that it could almost be said to be a-topic, to have no place in the sense that it is everywhere; and it is only in this hyperbolic proximity to Derrida, Barthes, and Lacan, among others, that Derrida's not commenting the name "Maelstrom" can be understood, as an effect of his proximity to the text in question.

Therefore, his not mentioning or commenting the names is not astonishing at all, and this goes for the "Van Gogh" as well. His (not) mentioning either one, or his displacement of the Van Gogh situation into another text and another painting is part and postal parcel of the whole problematic of *Ent-fernung* at issue in "Pas."

Reading: the south

Where are we, then?

The desire for something completely simple.

As though to transfer my own fatigue from myself to you, I have amassed all the foregoing. In a sincere attempt to clear the brush and pave the way, I have tried to make way for something like a reading of *Celui qui ne m'accompagnait pas*. I have done this by trying to stake out a map of the difficulties and the pitfalls that await the potential reader of this book; by giving a choosy but nonetheless laborious run-through of some of the commentary at this book in the almost fifty years since its publication, and by adumbrating some kind of relation to the names that occur within it.

Within the bounds of these three tasks (which are not isolated or even merely contiguous, but which run into the same waters, and through each other, like water in water, into the same vertiginous vortices), I have tried to muster all the lessons I have tried to apprehend in textual geometry, in the language games of all the newer newer criticism, and even, perhaps, into post-criticism. In trying to stay in one place, I have ended up running very hard. Any patience I once thought I had has run away with itself – even from before the first word. Now, once again, I am all alone with my monumental ruins, and with this book, still untouched through all my storms and the storms of others, which I have catalogued. My copy has lost its cover.

I am left with the desire for the extreme simplicity of something I have covered up with all my tendencies in the opposite direction. I will not resume, render any more abstract, that which has come before and already. Now I will read *Celui qui ne m'accompagnait pas*. Now I will resume my reading of this book, which has already gone on for too long, not to have touched it, somehow. Watch me tilt, as I seek, yet again, to broach it.

The first page of *Celui qui ne m'accompagnait pas* is enough to drive anyone crazy:

Je cherchai, cette fois, à l'aborder. Je veux dire que j'essayai de lui faire entendre que, si j'étais là, je ne pouvais cependant aller plus loin, et qu'à mon tour j'avais épuisé mes ressources. La vérité, c'est que, depuis longtemps, j'avais l'impression d'être à bout. "Mais vous ne l'êtes pas," remarquait-il. En cela, je devais lui donner raison. Pour ma part, je ne l'étais pas. Mais la pensée que, peut-être, je n'avais pas en vue "ma part," rendait la consolation amère. Je cherchai à tourner la chose autrement. "Je voudrais l'être." Manière de dire qu'il évita de prendre au sérieux; du moins, il la prit sans le sérieux que je désirais y mettre. Cela lui semblait, probablement, valoir mieux qu'un souhait. Je restai à réfléchir sur ce que "je voulais."

(I sought, this time, to broach it [or him]. I mean that I tried to make him understand that, if I was there, I wasn't able, by virtue of that, to go any further, and that in my turn I had exhausted my resources. The truth is that for a long time I had the impression of being at the end. "But you aren't," he remarked. In this, I had to grant that he was right. For my part, I wasn't. But the thought that maybe I didn't have "my part" in sight rendered the consolation bitter. I sought to turn the matter otherwise. "I would like to be." – Manner of speaking which he avoided taking seriously; at least he took it without the seriousness I wanted to put there. Probably that seemed to him to be worth more than an aspiration. I was left thinking about what "I wanted." [C, 7])

What is this about? It seems that two people are talking. There is a first-person voice and a third-person voice. The interlocutor is a third person before he is a second person. The narrator's gender is not yet determined. The third person is masculine. Having translated the paragraph, let us try to remark some of the difficulties attendant to the exercise. Let's face it: we don't have any idea what this is about. Is it a conversation between teacher and student, between friends, between lovers, between analyst and analysand? I leave this matter aside.

The sentence most difficult to translate is the first. What does the "l," the direct object of the first verb, *aborder*, stand (in) for? The succeeding lines steadfastly refuse to determine or saturate it in any way. This *abord* is difficult, if not impossible, to *aborder*. It could, I suppose, be the third-person voice itself, in the sense of *aborder* as to approach someone. (Then this is a kind of pick-up scene.) The *Robert* gives as the first *figural* meaning of *aborder*: "aller à quelqu'un qu'on ne connaît pas, (ou avec qui l'on n'est pas familier) pour lui adresser la parole." Thus the sentence would read: "I sought, this time, to approach him." Already I have veered away from this in my rough translation above, trying to leave the matter as undetermined as possible. We don't know enough yet, and already we can have a certain amount of confidence that even after the most meticulous reading of the book, we still won't. Why, after all, does it have to be either/or? Let it remain both *him* and *it*, to broach and to approach.

But perhaps we have already explained why there is not, at this point, any translation of *Celui qui ne m'accompagnait pas*, perhaps into any (other) language.[55] And these difficulties of translation will only be exponentially multiplied. *Aborder* can also mean to attack, something or someone, in the manner of the sudden. This sentence, then, is an attack. But does it broach anything, does it even gain a grasp on the subject? Certainly it does not do so on the or its object.

These are very plain words. But clearly this is no plain speaking. This is a book written in ordinary language, in the greyness of the everyday. But what it shows us is the bracketed, extraordinary nature of something like the ordinary language of ordinary language philosophy, which was in its heyday on the other shore, across the permanent and almost always turbulent *parages* of the channel, at the time that our book – Blanchot's – was published. What Blanchot's book plays with is the open set of rhetorical effects – drama, citation, and so on – which the ordinary language philosophies (if they ever existed) were trying to bracket in a perennial and hopeless attempt at sanitation, a despairing, always already damage control.

Let's face it: this first sentence is cruel and grueling. It surrounds itself with – nothing.[56] Not even with the rest of the book. Sometimes I sit and think and sometimes I just sit.[57]

– We have not yet finished with the first sentence. The verb is punctual, preterite. Common enough for French narration. Think of how we all learned the simple past in school – in French. But the title is imperfect: force of habit. How are we to construe this? After

---

55 I am still waiting for Lydia Davis's version of *Celui qui ne m'accompagnait pas*, which I have learned is to appear under the title *The One Who Was Standing Apart from Me* (Barrytown, NY: Station Hill Press).

56 Thus, in its ab-solution, it relates to the "±±" discussed above, as well as to the first sentence – if it can be called that – of *Le Pas au-delà*: "Entrons dans ce rapport." (Paris: Gallimard, 1973), 8.

57 This is the greyness of *Thomas* sitting and looking at the sea, the greyness of abstraction, the night in which all cats are grey, indeterminate, and in which the glow of the indeterminate seems to be the only real thing.

the "essayai" of the next sentence, there is the "si j'étais là." These tense relations will maintain their tension and keep coming back throughout the book. We will try to keep to commenting them, duratively, punctually, and frequentatively. "This time," however, presents other problems. Is this time different from any other time? If so, how so? Will we get an account of what happened this time? I think so. – But, given the vagaries already described in terms of the way other elements of the sentence are capable of absolving themselves of relation to the or a story – in terms of whether they will be, in any way, progressively determined – we should not be too quick to assume that we'll get anywhere this time, or be in any way further illumined.[58]

In truth, no one has spoken yet. We do not know the gender of the narrating voice; but are willing enough to assume a kind of ubiquitous, grammatically masculine proto-neutrality. If we take the title as referring to the (as yet enthymimetically unannounced) counterpart-companion, then we can assume that "he" is masculine: celui *qui ne m'accompagnait pas*. The first words are given to *him*: " 'Mais vous ne l'êtes pas,' remarquait-il." In between the first sentence and the first remark there is the "à mon tour," which is not to be taken lightly in this story, which has so many *voltes*, on a page where it occurs along with "cette fois" and with "ma part." My turn was a blowout: I had exhausted my resources.

Given the (non)dialectics we have already sketched out above, though, we can take this as the most sincere kind of gambit. These two are playing chess with words, taking turns, as usually happens. But the *tour* comes back further along: "je cherchai à tourner la chose autrement." – These turns, turn and turn about, turn around the calm and the silence of the vortex of a Maelström. When you have exhausted your resources, reached your limit, you try another gambit, another strategy – even if the attempt to make it seem that one's taking another tack is part of a grander, more masterful plan belonging to some more original strategy. But we may not yet be at the limits of this room in this house outside the city: I tried, after all, to make him or leave him to understand that I couldn't go any further. But that doesn't mean I can't, a fact which

[58] The difference between this and the opening absolutions of *L'Entretien infini* is that here, this time, in *Celui qui ne m'accompagnait pas*, the book does what it does, in its *attack*, in its *abord*, in words, and not in any kind of pseudo- or quasi-mathematical machinery.

he remarks in recognizing my gambit as a kind of petulant, spoiled child's complaint: "I can't go on! I'm tired." That didn't work. He wouldn't, didn't let me get away with it, and said, you are not at the end, you have to play on some more.[59]

Let us remark (for we have already remade) here the notorious difficulty of description. What voice, what grammatical person am I to use to talk about what happens between "I" and "he?" Do I have to go through and make decisions and quotation marks each time I try to comment a passage, sentence, or word of this book?

I will not do so. I will stick to the pragmatic device of trying to put it all into basic English in order to get at the ruses and turns of this complex piece of language made up of everyday words. And furthermore, actually I find it useful that my I, my authorial persona, will have to stand in jeopardy, on its own merits, as a kind of placeholder in this possible-world semantics scheme. Let us remember: a possible world is specified and stipulated in sentences, not projected on a wall or seen through a telescope. You cannot see it, but you can read it and write it: it has no phenomenal existence.[60] My words remain my words, and I am not going to put my paraphrases into quotation marks, which would run the risk of allowing them to be confused with Blanchot's words. Then we would really be lost. I will consider my I to be rigorously impersonal and you will not know anything more of me after you have finished this than you did at the beginning. Presume nothing: you have no rights. My I has thoroughly absolved itself of you – but not of him. Now it is possible to understand why I had to go through all that business about sacrifice.

Let us begin to think again about the relations between "cette fois," "à mon tour," and "ma part." That this time might not be this time, that my turn might never arrive, because I myself didn't know what or when it would or could or might be, that likewise my part in this is unclear. My part would be my turn, my twist on these things – but there are so few things: "L'obstacle, c'est que justement – alors – les événements paraissait avoir reculé prodi-

---

[59] On the subject of *this time*, we should note that, in addition to the notes about it scattered upon the waves of "Pas," there *zerstreut*, Derrida has written an entire book about what only takes place once, or this time. It is a book to which my mind recurs as I write these pages, and it is called *Schibboleth pour Paul Celan* (Paris: Galilée, 1985).

[60] I am turning around the examples given by Saul Kripke in his *Naming and Necessity* (Oxford: Blackwell, 1980).

gieusement." (And of the prodigious we will see more soon.)

Che cosà? What's up? What is "the thing" here? It is very hard to tell. This constant shuttling back and forth between the positive and the negative, the active and the passive ('je ne luttais pas, je ne cédais pas non plus, céder aurait demander plus de forces que je n'en avais" – this is not the passive voice here, properly speaking, but a manifestation of a kind of will to passivity by saying that that's all that's possible or available) is not the anxiety or "pathos of uncertain agency,"[61] but the anxiety over what voice or pole or form something like an *action* or an *event* might take – when, and if, it does take place. For all there is, here and now, seems to be a kind of letting, a *lassen*, which seems to be more a manifestation of anxiety than an attitude of purportedly more dignified philosophical indifference.

Do not think for a second that simply because these descriptive sentences seem to be moving along so placidly I am not, at every instant, rent with my anxiety about the potential *arbitrariness* of every single one of these purportedly critical thrusts – or are they feints? What is criticism? What is it, if it is neither the machine-like application of grammar to texts on the one hand, nor the willful arbitrariness of aestheticizing caprice on the other? – It is the activity that shuttles back and forth, in its anxiety, between specters of these alternatives (and neither is viable), and thus is never sure. To leave philosophy, the discourse of the concept, for criticism, is something like leaving behind the paranoia latent in every system-building impulse for obsessional neurotic and autophagic self-doubt. Criticism is an autoimmune "activity," but the agent of its autoimmune disorder is not a foreign agent, something that arrived, one day, from the outside. This Penelope-like activity is both anabolic and catabolic, thus metabolic. Criticism is the anxiety of making choices, or just making choices, with all the anxiety attendant thereto – including the anxiety as to whether one is making choices or one's hand is being forced.

– Whence this anxiety? Well, if you said to someone, "It seems to me that I have everything, except . . .," and they responded, "Except?," wouldn't you be a bit anxious, too? This puts the

---

[61] Hertz has argued strongly for the use of this expression to get at what is going on in several places in the work of Paul de Man and the expression sticks in the mind because it is so well used. Rather than disagreeing with Hertz, what I am doing here is simply using the idea as a foil. See his "Lurid Figures," in *RMR*.

burden on "I" to gloss: "He gave me the impression now of being more attentive, even though this attention was not directed upon me, it was rather a silent direction, a hope for himself, a sort of daybreak that, finally, revealed nothing but the word 'except.' A little bit more, however, for I was compelled to add: 'Except that I want to be rid of it.'"

"I thought I was at the end;" "'You aren't,'" "'I would like to be,'" we remember from the first and preceding page, where "I" was left to reflect on this "'I wanted.'" The "'I would like...'" has *already* been absorbed into the imperfect, thus durational, lasting, "'I wanted'" ("'je voulais'"). The conditional of the "I would like" has already been converted into the continuous past of the "I wanted," which is itself embedded within quotation marks, quotation marks that in fact surround words that weren't uttered: "je voudrais" has become "'je voulais.'" As the reader turns this over in his mind, it turns him over, over and over again. We are left to reflect on it. We are not I: the situation is ever harder for me, for us, because we don't have only "his" words to deal with, we have to deal with the web between "his" words and "my" words, that is to say, with Blanchot's words.

We are not in a space within which a *phenomenology* of the reading experience, modeled upon the Reader's identification with the Narrator's voice, would help. When Poulet writes that this is in fact what takes place when we pick up a book, that we relate the predicates of the narrator's experience to ourselves, he assumes that the language is some kind of medium transparent to consciousness. No wonder this is called *thematic* criticism. Blanchot's book, which consists of nothing but the words of these two "voices," and the voice-off narration of the first person's *for intérieur*, denudes the possibility of such criticism, which would be condemned to repeat everything, word for word, but *without a difference*.

Such criticism is the most egotistical and the most idealist criticism imaginable, for it would level any and all distinctions having to do with time and context. The time of reading would be the time in which the reader was to cancel the difference with the time of writing – where writing, it is assumed, was the vehicle for the author's speaking. Perhaps such a criticism could imagine this book staged as a play, with two characters on stage, and most of the speaking coming from the first character's taped voice, offstage. This would be amusing and interesting and perhaps very beautiful and not altogether out of keeping with the spirit of this book. But is there a spirit of this book that would permit such a phenomenal manifestation? Or is this book not rather an exercise in what writing can do, an exercise in the "possible-world semantics" of the narrative form? Or the no-longer-possible world of no-longer-possible semantics? Perhaps, in a move which would be more ambitious, much more violent, and certainly more true, the voice-off narration, instead of being spoken by the taped voice of the narrator, "offstage," could be spoken by a kind of choros of one, a choragos, who would thus intervene as a third, "between" the two other "persons." This choros, in its reduction to its singular speaker, would speak the "interior monologue" of the narrator as a kind of permanently interposed parabasis, the very parabasis of narration itself. He (or it) would, by a violent catachresis, personify (or perhaps better yet: emblematize) not only the splitting that takes place in the narrative voice, in this book, which "watches" itself(?) go upstairs to the garret, go to the kitchen to get a glass of water, etc., but at the same time would give presence or face, even more violently, to the insubstantial third person (a reflection?), who is always threatening to make something other than a non-entrance, that is to say, to enter this narrative: "Isn't there someone outside the window?" – "No, there is no one."[62]

Let's go on:

Je crois que j'attendais de lui, malgré tout, une invitation à aller de l'avant et peut-être un risque, un obstacle. Je ne luttais pas, mais je ne cédais pas non plus, céder aurait demandé plus de forces que je n'en avais. Je ne puis nier que la nécessité de lui parler et de parler le plus souvent le premier, comme si l'initiative eût été de mon côté et du sien, la discrétion, le souci de me laisser libre – mais cela même n'était peut-être de sa part qu'impuissance et, par conséquent, impuissance aussi de ma part –, cette nécessité me paraissait si épuisante, si harassante que, souvent, il ne me restait pas même assez de forces vraies pour user de cette nécessité. Je n'avais pas le sentiment que parler fût pour lui le moins du monde nécessaire, ni agréable, ni, non plus, désagréable. Il faisait toujours preuve d'une extrême loyauté, il me ramenait avec la fermeté la plus grande d'un

[62] In writing these remarks, I have been animadverting to Georges Poulet, "Conscience de soi et conscience d'autrui," and "Phénoménologie de la conscience critique," both in his *La Conscience critique* (Paris: Corti, 1971).

mot moins vrai à un mot plus vrai. Parfois, je me demandais s'il ne cherchait pas à me retenir à tout prix. J'en venais à croire qu'il m'avait toujours barré la route, bien que, s'il manifestait une intention, ce fût plutôt celle de m'aider à en finir. D'après lui – mais je dois ajouter que jamais il ne me l'avait affirmé avec autant de précision que je le fais –, de son aide, je m'approchais le plus quand je me décidais à écrire. Il avait pris un bizarre ascendant sur moi pour toutes ces choses, si bien que je m'étais laissé persuader qu'écrire était le meilleur moyen [as I type this, I realize: "écrire" contains "rire"] de rendre nos relations supportables. Je reconnais que pendant quelque temps ce moyen fut assez bon. Mais un jour je m'aperçus que ce que j'écrivais le concernait toujours davantage et, quoique d'une manière indirecte, semblait n'avoir d'autre but que de le refléter.

(In spite of everything, I think I awaited from him an invitation to go on ahead and perhaps a risk, an obstacle. I didn't fight, but I didn't cede either, ceding would have demanded more strength than I had. I cannot deny that the necessity of speaking to him and most often of speaking first, as if the initiative had come from my side and from his, the discretion, the care to leave me free – but this itself was perhaps only impotence from his side and, consequently, impotence also from my side – this necessity seemed to me so exhausting, so harrassing that, often, there did not remain to me even enough strength to make use of this necessity, to exhaust it. I did not have the feeling that speaking was the least thing necessary in the world for him, neither agreeable, nor disagreeable either. He always gave proof of an extreme loyalty, he brought me back with the greatest assurance from a word less true to one more true. Sometimes, I asked myself if he didn't seek to hold me back at any cost. I came to believe that he had always blocked the road for me, even though, if he manifested an intention, it was rather that of helping me to be done with it. According to him – but I must add that he had never affirmed it to me with as much precision as I am doing – I approached his help the most when I decided to write. He had assumed a bizarre ascendancy over me in all these things, so much so that I had allowed myself to be persuaded that to write was the best means of making our relations bearable. I recognize that these means were pretty good for some time. But one day I realized that what I was writing concerned him always more and more and, even though in an indirect way, seemed to have no other goal than to reflect him.

[C, 8–10; my translation])

What does "I" want to be dispensed with? Is it the everything that I has? Or is it my except, my lack, the thing I lacks? Or is it his interrogative and interruptive "except?"

We can do nothing in this reading except try to lay out the alternatives. There will not be any foreclosures; or rather, *we* will not make any foreclosures. If the book makes them, fine. For us there is only the trying, the rest is not our business – and this business is trying, indeed.

There is a kind of exhausting passivity in this mutually assured standoff. There is, above all, or at any rate first, the necessity that I speak first. But this first speaking is dictated by an imperative ("necessity") that comes from both of us, from the situation – a rather bare version of a total speech-act situation (and more total because more bare) – from his side and from mine. (From his part and from mine?) This is glossed, this passivity, as perhaps his impotence, perhaps mine as well, in a chiasmus that holds the strange tension of this mutuality: the initiative comes from my side and from his, the impotence is perhaps his and perhaps mine (I cannot tell what is his part and what is mine). Altogether, this tension is exhausting – I don't have the force even to do what I can, to partake of, to take advantage of the necessity. I am left with the fact that *I speak first and it exhausts me.* His passivity, his indifference exhaust me: I have the impression that speaking is not at all necessary for him. In his silence, though, and perhaps in the impotence of his waiting, thus he leads me from less true to more true words. He is not a subject who is supposed to know, even though I know he does know – what? – because he leaves me to sort it out; but thus he is in fact the very function of the subject who is supposed to know. This then *is* the story of someone who has survived, if not lived through, the events recounted; through this intolerable situation which lasted, for a time, in the imperfect, but ended – when? In writing? – Clearly not, for I began to write already in the midst of these things. But at any rate, now that I is writing this, it is over. And how did he get on? We will have to keep reading for any hope at all of finding out. "Are you writing? Are you writing *at this moment?*" (C, 126) These are the only words given emphasis in this book, this *at this moment* in *his* voice (repeated twice, in the narrator's voice, four pages later). The emphasis of this question, and its decided answer with a "Yes" (C, 130), are the subject of this book.

In any case, regardless of whether he is trying to keep me on or back (from what?) at any cost (as his patient, and in his very patience) he was extremely loyal to me – I paid him, in my presence, for his patience. I think of Winnicott's scandalously true dedication to *Playing and Reality*: "To my patients, who have paid to teach me."[63] The first chapter of this book is a reprinted version of the famous "Transitional Objects and Transitional Phenomena," about which, in respect of these Blanchot's voices, many *analogies* could be made. I think these analogies would be relatively unconventional or *catastrophic*, though, in that they would tend to disfigure Winnicott's narrative more than Blanchot's. This is (and should always be) the risk run by any analogous reading, which operates on the base of a chiastic exchange between some text put into the position of a theoretical model and a text to be read in terms of the model text. Properly read, the text, as text, will always render the model unintelligible, or even the analogizing itself impossible. Theorize at your peril, always.

And now it is more explicit: I came to believe that he had always blocked the road for me, even if, if he manifested an intention, it was to help me to come to the end of it.

Next, I will have to start to make some choices.

I have an idea, a modest proposal: I should conceive that I might begin by writing *badly*. Let me allow myself to be bad. Let us see if, in starting out badly, we might end up somewhere a little bit better. If we start out worried about being good from the start, we will never get anywhere, because we will be paralyzed – not by fear, but by terror. It is the terror of not getting all the moves right from the very beginning. It is the terror of the writer to be confronting his reader – before the writer has written anything, before the reader has anything to read. It is the fear of the writer's thinking: the moment someone gets to this moment, in my writing, he will see that I have made an error, and he will tune out. In order to keep his attention, I have to be perfect, and perfection means, being perfect from the very beginning.

But was this ever a choice?

[63] London: Tavistock, 1971.

5

❖❖❖

Afterword: er, or, borrowing from Peter to pay Paul: further notes on Celan's translation of Shakespeare's sonnet 105

❖❖❖

The fact is that an external object has no being for you or me except in so far as you or I hallucinate it, but being sane we take care not to hallucinate except where we know what to see. Of course when we are tired or it is twilight we may make a few mistakes . . .[1]

Why now choose to discuss the poetry of Paul Celan? To bring Celan into a discussion of the limits of the thematic today? One might, after all, choose Kafka or Blanchot, or Pseudo-Dionysios the Areopagite, or Nicholas of Cusa, or any one of a number of others. Perhaps because in reading Celan's work one does not know so easily what he is talking about, and this thematic disorientation comforts itself by determining the power of this negativity in a particular thematic, in a concern with a very particular historical fact, the extermination of the Jews. I do not at all want to suggest that Celan's poetry is not marked by this event. It can (also) be read as an extended name for that event, as an epithet or an epitaph. While my primary concern here has to do with some of the intrinsic, linguistic factors of Celan's poems themselves, I hope to suggest not only some ways in which these poems may well, in their very resistance to reading, contribute to

---

[1] D. W. Winnicott, "The Fate of the Transitional Object," in his *Psycho-Analytic Explorations*, ed. Clare Winnicott, Ray Sheperd, and Madeleine Davis (Cambridge, MA: Harvard University Press, 1989), 54.

the frantic search for extrinsic, extra-textual, causes or occasions, but also how these poems – as well as this recourse to the historical they somehow seem to encourage – may have something to tell us about their own historical positing and about the occurrence of texts in general.

Peter Szondi, whose last book, still incomplete at the time of his death, is a study of Celan, attempts in this monograph an examination of Celan's poetry based largely on lexical considerations.[2] It is not that Szondi sees his work in terms of a rarefied, hyper-formalized, textual aestheticism, as an attempt to remove the serious study of Celan's poetry, which at the time of Szondi's writing was still in its infancy, from historical considerations. On the contrary, Szondi wants to suggest that the approach to Celan's texts provided by closer reading might bring critical awareness towards an understanding of Celan's historical importance through the consideration of his treatment of signification in his poetic practice. But certainly these readings by Szondi, like those of his earlier *Hölderlin-Studien*,[3] have a strong polemical moment that is bound up with the attempt to bring German literary studies away from the weight of the primitive accumulation of empirico-biographical data (though not at all to dispense with these) and into a productive encounter with American New Critical and also with more recent French structuralist and post-structuralist analyses of poetry.

In the case of each of Szondi's three written essays on Celan, the occasion for the choice of the particular poem to be read is thematically centered. The extended reading of "Engführung," commissioned by *Critique* and written in French,[4] attempts to show a kind of parallelism between two deportations. The one leads to the death camps, and the other carries the reader – from the first line or even from the very title on – from the outside to the inside of a poem. It is no accident that Szondi chooses "Engführung" for this purpose, since it is itself Celan's major attempt to write himself out of the more thematically accessible language of

---

[2] *Celan-Studien* (Frankfurt-on-Main: Suhrkamp, 1972); now in Peter Szondi, *Schriften* vol. II, *et al.* ed. Jean Bollack (Frankfurt-on-Main: Suhrkamp, 1978). The essay on Celan's Shakespeare translation, "Poetry of Constancy – Poetik der Beständigkeit," occupies pages 321–44 of this volume; the "Eden" essay, to which I will also refer, pages 390–98.   [3] Now in his *Schriften*, vol. I.

[4] "Lecture de *Strette*: essai sur la poésie de Paul Celan," in *Critique* 288 (May 1971); reprinted as "Durch die Enge geführt," in Szondi, *Schriften*, vol. II, 345–89.

his earlier "Todesfuge," the publication of which canonized its author immediately, but also largely vitiated the reading of his work by placing it under the rubric "poetry of the Holocaust," thus treating it simply as a form of historical documentation to be cited in a pious manner on state occasions. It takes only the most cursory inspection of Celan's work to imagine his contempt for such a use of his – or anyone else's – poetry, and his equal or greater contempt for poetry written for such a purpose. "Engführung" was a provocative declaration: *harter Stil, nicht glatt.*

"Eden," the last and incomplete essay in Szondi's book (the editor's apparatus also contains notes for two unwritten texts), is a reading of a late Celan poem, itself written during one of the poet's rare visits to Berlin. In this final essay, the critic-witness makes explicit many of the recondite references in the poem by referring to the celebration of the Christmas holiday and to the police reports of the murders of Karl Liebknecht and Rosa Luxemburg. While Szondi was with Celan during much of his stay in Berlin and reports on many of the events which took place there during that time, he warns at once that a narrative containing all the *facts* of which he speaks, while apparently helpful, does not amount to a reading of the poem. Still, the body of the discursively written-out part of the essay is devoted to the presentation of these facts, while the lexical considerations with which a closer reading of the poem would have to begin remain only in note form, and have been reproduced for us by the editors as such.

Szondi reports that a manuscript version of the poem that is the subject of his incomplete essay bears the title "Wintergedicht," which has been effaced, along with the date of composition, from the version published in the posthumous volume *Schneepart*.[5] What remains to be done in order to complete Szondi's essay on this poem, which he was writing at the time of his death, is to pick up where he leaves off, that is at his assertion that to relate as much as possible of the context or of the occasion of the poem's composition is not to do a reading of the poem.

At the very moment where the written-out part of the book breaks off, in the "Eden" essay on Celan's Berlin winter poem, at the moment where Szondi relates and must relate – must relate

---

[5] Frankfurt-on-Main: Suhrkamp, 1971. Apparently this kind of effacement of dates and titles between the fair copy of the single poem and the book manuscript was not an uncommon practice for Celan.

because he has related them – the facts that he and only he knows about the circumstances surrounding Celan's composition, his testimony is written in the decorous third person. He refers to himself as "someone," "a friend," etc. Szondi's modesty, as well as his sense of embarrassment at not being able to complete the task, may account for the fact that he has given us an eyewitness account written in the curious impersonality of this third person. We will come back to this strange third person, the apparent decorum of which may call attention to a different necessity. But the fact remains that while his essay ends – curiously enough in a manner similar to the poem's (non)ending in "Nichts / stockt." – with this injunction to the necessity of intrinsic criticism, the matter of the essay which leads up to that (non)ending relates for the most part a piece of biography, an episode in the poet's life to which the critic was a witness. Thus, what is called for – an internal analysis of the poem that would concentrate on morphology and not on semantics – is preceded by an account of phenomenal, and not of textual events.

An intrinsic reading of this poem might want to take account of the way in which the "nichts / stockt" at its end not only stops the poem (among Szondi's notes for the Celan essays occur the following two fragmentary lines: "Darüber, das nichts stockt, stockt das Gedicht," and "Das nichts stockt, macht das Gedicht stocken").[6] But by forcing the poem to spill over onto the fourteenth line of type on the page, Celan makes this poem, which begins with an unnamed *du*, into a kind of degenerate sonnet that stops/does not stop. A poem originally entitled "Wintergedicht," by the poet Paul Celan, cannot have been written without that other twentieth-century lyric in mind, that is Trakl's "Ein Winterabend," the sacramental final line of which, "Auf dem Tische Brot und Wein," has been transposed into the "Du LIEGST im großen Gelausche" of Celan's first line, as well as into the center of the later poem, in the verses "Es kommt der Tisch mit den Gaben / Es biegt um ein Eden." The Trakl poem is one of the ostensible subjects of a Heidegger essay that both Celan and Szondi knew well.[7]

But the only necessity that can be attributed in literary history

---

6 See Szondi, *Schriften* vol. II, 429.
7 See Martin Heidegger, "Die Sprache," in his *Unterwegs zur Sprache* (Pfullingen: Neske, 1959).

has to do first with the occurrences of texts, and only secondarily with the narrative–temporal order within which such events are incorporated into a history after the fact. There is no prediction in literary history because there is no principle of sufficient reason for the occurrence of texts. The necessity of any relation construed between any given texts is a necessity constructed after the fact, even if such explanation often occults this by telling a story of genesis, or of decline, or of regression, or whatever as though it were a relation between texts themselves – as though such entities were imaginable. In this respect, much literary history is more formalist than supposedly hyper-formalist readings, which insist on the positing, occurrence, eventhood, or singularity of texts.[8]

The other complete essay in Szondi's book, and perhaps the most successful one, is devoted to a historical inscription of another kind. Here the friend-critic turns his attention to one of Celan's translations from Shakespeare's sonnets, to sonnet 105, "Let not my love be called idolatry, nor my beloved an idol show . . ." And in his reading it is a matter of making explicit, of thematizing the way in which Celan's *version* acts out lexically, or performs a linguistic constancy, where Shakespeare's poem *describes* the constancy of his poetic attention to his beloved as the theme of the verse. Thus the relation between Shakespeare's poem and Celan's own illustrates what I have called in my introduction the thematic scar, that (non)site or opening/closing that takes place between Shakespeare's melodic model of epideictic verse and, as I will argue in the following pages, Celan's potentially de-thematizing, lexically disarticulating (Szondi would say performative) reading of it.

In each of these three essays, then, there is this constant grappling with what I have called the thematic scar, that is with the seal (Celan's poetry contains both the figure of the scar as well as that of the seal in prominent places, see, for example, the end of "Engführung" and the opening of "Mit Brief und Uhr," respectively) that provides the occasion for the thematic choice of the particular poem for reading and which has some kind of relation, even if it is that of a non-relation, to the lexical or morphological analysis which ensues thereupon.

[8] On the crucial question of how and why what is called deconstruction is *not* a formalism, see de Man, "Kant and Schiller," in his *AI.*

It would not be uninteresting to describe this relation – between Szondi's essays and Celan's poems – in terms borrowed from the description of psychic structures, as emblematic of the paradoxes of mourning considered as a narcissistic wound, of the necessity of a subject's divestment of whatever value it has – not necessarily previously – put into an object. In a preliminary fashion, it would not be wrong to characterize Szondi's little monograph as his own kind of textual mourning poem to and for Celan. And it would be neither wrong nor monstrous to try to write an account of this relation that would tell the story of two suicides, and to read Szondi's interrupted text as enacting the paradox of mourning as being always on the one hand necessary and inevitable, and on the other impossible and "in error." "Dem gleich fehlet die Trauer" is the last line of "Mnemosyne," a poem which looms large over the work of Paul Celan, and which has been translated powerfully as "For him, mourning is in error."[9] Lest these comments provoke a knee-jerk accusation of the worst form of psychologizing, I add that the kind of situation within which such a *Trauerarbeit* would take place would be one in which any psychoanalytic terminology employed would have to be thought through in terms of the linguistic structures which have proven so useful in being taken up by analytic theory and practice. It is neither a question of assimilating psychoanalysis to linguistics nor vice versa, and the kind of work to which I am alluding has progressed a great deal since Lacan's seminar on the psychoses, and his reflections there on pronominal fade-outs in relation to subjective fade-outs.[10]

Szondi's analysis of Celan's Shakespeare translation is meticulously morphological – to a point. And here our revisionary, if you will – but not in Harold Bloom's sense of the word – reading of Szondi reading Celan properly begins again. Shakespeare and Celan's texts read thus:

[9] See Friedrich Hölderlin, *Hymns, Elegies, Fragments*, trans. Richard Sieburth (Princeton: Princeton University Press, 1984), 119.

[10] See Jacques Lacan, *Le Séminaire* vol. III: *Les Psychoses* (Paris: Seuil, 1981); as well as Derrida's work with Abraham and Torok ("Fors," preface to Nicholas Abraham and Maria Torok, *Le Verbier de l'homme aux loups* [Paris: Aubier, 1976]). This progress is due largely to the efforts of Cathy Caruth, Cynthia Chase, Shoshana Felman, Neil Hertz, and Avital Ronell.

Let not my love be call'd idolatry,
nor my belovèd as an idol show,
Since all alike my songs and praises be
To one, of one, still such, and ever so.

Kind is my love today, tomorrow kind,
Still constant in a wondrous excellence;
Therefore my verse, to constancy confin'd,
One thing expressing, leaves out difference.

"Fair, kind and true" is all my argument –
"Fair, kind and true" varying to other words;
And in this change is my invention spent –
Three themes in one, which wondrous scope affords.

"Fair, kind and true" have often liv'd alone,
Which three till now never kept seat in one.

Ihr sollt, den ich da lieb, nicht Abgott heißen,
nicht Götzendienst, was ich da treib und trieb.
All dieses Singen hier, all dieses Preisen:
von ihm, an ihn und immer ihm zulieb.

Gut ist mein Freund, ists heute und ists morgen,
und keiner ist beständiger als er.
In der Beständigkeit, da bleibt mein Vers geborgen,
spricht von dem Einen, schweift mir nicht umher.

"Schön, gut und treu," das singe ich und singe.
"Schön, gut und treu" – stets anders und stets das.
Ich find, erfind – um sie in eins zu bringen,
sie einzubringen ohne Unterlaß.

"Schön, gut und treu" so oft getrennt, geschieden.
In Einem will ich drei zusammenschmieden.[11]

Borrowing a celebrated expression from Benjamin, Szondi characterizes the difference between the Shakespeare poem and Celan's
translation as a difference in intention towards language, *Intention
auf die Sprache*.[12] In trying to isolate what he wants to call the

[11] The texts of both poems are to be found in Paul Celan, *GW* vol. v, 344–45.
[12] See Walter Benjamin, "Die Aufgabe des Übersetzers," in *Gesammelte Schriften*
vol. IV, ed. Rolf Tiedemann, Gretel Adorno, *et al.* (Frankfurt-on-Main: Suhrkamp,
1972, 1980), translated by Harry Zohn as "The Task of the Translator," in Walter
Benjamin, *Illuminations*, ed. Hannah Arendt (New York: Schocken, 1969).

enacting, as opposed to the descriptive elements of Celan's version of the sonnet, Szondi speaks a great deal about minimally varied repetition, the *Dauer im Wechsel* that has become the staple food of the Jakobsonian version of poetics in this century: *treib/trieb* in line 2; *ihm/ihn/ihm* in line 4; *singe/singe* in line 9; *stets . . . stets* in line 10 and so on. But what he himself identifies as the most risky move in his reading, as well as the emblem of Celan's success, has to do with line 11. With the *ich find, erfind*, the "I find, invent," the critic insists that the reader of the poem must draw an artificial hiatus, and read not *ich find, erfind*, but *ich find, er[ ]find*, "I find, he finds." Beginning with Celan's boldness, Szondi proceeds with his own assertion that these lines show the most violent break with a traditional notion of translation which would depend on the presupposition of interlinguistic allosemes:

Designation is replaced by speaking: *Ich find, erfind*. In linguistic terms, this is one of the boldest passages in Celan's version, surpassed perhaps only by the immediately following one. For here the repetition of the verb, that is, of the word for the activity, does more than simply convey the activity's constancy . . . [T]o understand the phrase *Ich find, erfind*, it is not sufficient to read the expansion of "find" in the repetition (*erfind*) as a delayed translation of "invention"; nor should it be viewed as a substitute for the dimension of "change" that Celan refuses to mention explicitly or even to accept a possible means of expressing variation . . . [W]ith the phrase *Ich find, erfind* Celan pierces the facade of linguistic performance, that is, of *parole* (speech), making it possible to glimpse the inner workings of the linguistic system, of *langue* (language). . . . What is thereby revealed are parts of the conjugation paradigm, once with respect to tense (*was ich da treib und trieb*) and once with respect to person: *ich find, erfind* (*=er find*). Admittedly, this reading is not compelling in the first case . . . it becomes so only when the first case is considered together with the second (*Ich find, erfind*). Our interpretation of the second case presupposes that, in this position, the prefix *er* carries the connotation of the personal pronoun *er* ("he").[13]

For Szondi, the departure from a view of translation as paraphrase into one of translation as performance is yet another way in which

---

[13] See "The Poetry of Constancy: Paul Celan's Translation of Shakespeare's Sonnet 105," in Peter Szondi, *On Textual Understanding and Other Essays*, trans. Harvey Mendelson (Minneapolis: University of Minnesota Press, 1986), 170–71. The original title of Szondi's essay, the point of which seems to be lost on the translator, is "Poetry of Constancy – Poetik der Beständigkeit: Celans Übertragung von Shakespeares Sonett 105," now in Peter Szondi, *Schriften*, vol. II (Frankfurt-on-Main: Suhrkamp, 1978).

Celan's poem exhibits linguistic constancy in the lyrical chanting, or the dead repetition, of a linguistic paradigm. But, having done this, what the critic fails to do, most importantly, I think, is to see that once he has separated this small piece of *Er-Sprache* from the poem in order to bolster a notion of linguistic constancy, the automatisms that pervade the entire linguistic structure are made manifest. *Er* is one of the most common diphones to be found in German, perhaps the most common, and seeing it draw attention to itself here (I think Szondi's move should hardly be considered a risky one) in this line must lead us to perform a recursive scanning of the poem, which Szondi does not do.

His discovery of *er* does not, to take an example which is not merely one among others, take him back to line 6, "Und kein-er ist beständig-er als er," which demands now to be read as "und kein-er ist beständig-er als er." Not: "And no one is more constant than he." But: "and no he is more constant than he," or even: "and no he is he-constant[er] than he." But as translation is precisely the problem here, and having already admitted that it is not a question of an allosemic plugging-in of equivalent, translinguistic values, and hence that there are no equivalent translations of *faits bruts de langue*, we must write, finally: "And no er is constant-er than er": Er, er, er.[14] In answer to the question "*Wer* ist er?," we cannot even say "*Der* ist er!," maybe only "Er ist er," or better yet "Das ist er," for even the pronominal function itself has dissolved in its specificity, leaving only the stuttering automatism of the marks on the page.

While this translation thus makes it difficult to see any particular face on the portrait of Mr. W. H., we should not rush to say that this pronominal profusion empties the poem of meaning. Such a move has perhaps become a shibboleth of contemporary criticism, and a point could also be made by the opposite formulation, that this er-proliferation over- or hyper-means, has one meaning, making explicit a kind of verbal-apophantic boy-craziness on Shakespeare–Celan's part. All one meaning, no meaning – neither one of these is my point, which I choose to express in the tension of a question: What can be said to be the referent of such massive

---

[14] I cease to underline "er" at this point, since, according to my argument, while belonging to language, it does not belong to any particular language, hence not to the impure German language. Being further than foreign, it is not simply a foreign word, or even a word at all. It is a piece of pure language in Benjamin's sense. See Benjamin, "Die Aufgabe des Übersetzers."

overinsistence of such a general, deictic, almost syncategorematic word – *if it be one or a word?*

Lest these er-findings seem arbitrary or trivial, I now point out that while there is not a single occurrence in Shakespeare's poem of a first-, second- or third-person pronoun, in any grammatical case – no I, no me, no you, not a single he or even a him, only "my" – all three "persons" are present in Celan's version, which is so bold as to open with the lyrically speaking egregious second-person plural, *ihr*, which we can read in one way as an almost-er. But to the extent that this *ihr*, which, of all the German personal pronouns most resembles er, does *not* enter into a rhyme with another er, and thus is not being phonetically pushed into a near er-identity, we can say that this *ihr* points out the complete absence of the second person throughout the rest of the poem, thus calling attention to the fragility of its own second personhood, even in this abstract world of pronouns.

Metrically, Celan could have written *du* here without any problem, as he does, for example, in his translation of the first line of the first sonnet. The *ihr*, in addition to being phonemically closer to er, is also capable, thematically speaking, of encompassing the company of an entire future history of readers, in a move that would not have been too bold for Shakespeare himself. – Despite the fact that while er may be the most common of German syllables, the second-person plural is the least common grammatical person to be found in the written language. Perhaps we can say something more about *ihr*.

As Szondi duly notes, the quotation marks around the three epithets "Fair, kind, and true" may have been deliberately chosen by Celan, who was the most meticulous of poets when it came to the mechanical.[15] But at the level of our argumentation, this is an irrelevant point. Why does it matter whether Celan chose an edition which used the quotation marks, or if he just happened to be working from the English text opposite some handy copy of Schlegel–Tieck translations, or from some dime-store copy? The point here is that the consideration of what is going on in Celan's poem does not depend on his intention, in the same way that the frequency of the occurrence of er (or of re) does not depend on his

---

[15] The story of his withdrawing his own first volume of poems from circulation because it contained too many printer's errors is well known.

intention. In attributing an intention toward language to Celan which is different than that of Shakespeare, Szondi makes Celan into an allegorical name for something like language or language power. Intention toward language here must rather be taken in a thoroughly non-intentional, non-consciousness-oriented sense, as the *poem's* slant on language. Speaking psychologistically, Szondi has lost a friend and been left with a poem, and what he has done – as reader – in his essay is to transfer the constancy of the friend into a property which he can save by attributing it to the poem. This forces him to misread Benjamin's notion and to give an all too intentional account of intention. While the quotation marks are included in numerous editions of Shakespeare, and thus are not Celan's invention, they do not appear in the Quarto text of 1609 and have been dropped from contemporary critical editions. They too can be read as intentional *stricto sensu* or as without intention, forcing a question similar to the one posed above about the instance of er. Szondi points to what I would call the ontological transformation of the three epithets accomplished by the quotation marks, which call attention to the merely verbal existence of these allegorical names.

Stephen Booth, whose annotated critical edition of the sonnets is as good a standard as any, speaks of this sonnet as being playfully and mockingly engaged in a parody of Trinitarian language. He opens his commentary on the poem with the following paragraph, before proceeding to gloss it line by line:

The wit of this playful experiment in perversity derives from the false logic resulting from the speaker's studiously inadequate understanding of idolatry. Idolatry has traditionally been almost synonymous with polytheism: in Shakespeare's England its commonest occurrence was in self-righteously puritan attacks on Roman Catholics; it referred not so much to *substituting* worship of idols or other false gods (such as the golden calf in Exodus) for worship of the Christian god as to real or apparent worship of other gods (e.g. the saints – Mary in particular – and relics), *in addition to* the Christian god . . . However, although all polytheism is idolatrous, it does not therefore follow that any and all monotheisms are orthodox as the speaker here pretends. In the narrow and misleading sense of *idolatry*, the poem makes its case, but the diction of the poem is ostentatiously reminiscent of Christian doctrine (lines 12–14 cap the litany-like repetition of the suggestively triple *Fair, kind and true* with a specific echo of the doctrine of the Trinity), and of the forms of

Christian devotion (line 4 echoes the *Gloria Patri*: "Glory be to the father, and to the sonne, and to the holy ghost. As it was in the beginning, is now, and ever shal be: worlde wythout ende"). Thus the same rhetoric that strengthens the argument for innocence of idolatrous polytheistic beliefs not only testifies to the idolatrous nature of the speaker's allegiance to the beloved but sharpens the evidence with overtones of active sacrilege.[16]

My own recourse here will not be precisely to the Trinity, but to a motif which is ever-present in Renaissance literature, which prefigures the Trinity in a conventionally historical sense and which has been compendiously documented by Edgar Wind in his *Pagan Mysteries in the Renaissance*.[17] That is to say, we are here involved with the personification of the dynamic triad of the Three Graces, an illusion to which opens Szondi's own essay.

That to which Wind's iconography returns, in its patient tracing of the depiction, both verbal and pictorial, of the Three Graces, is the ambiguity of the position of the third Grace. The debates centering around the use of the allegory always seem to center on the role of this third figure. There is giving and there is receiving, but how does one best represent returning so as to keep the tableau *vivant*, so as to keep the economy in circulation? I do not know if there is an answer to this question, except to say that the story Wind tells is an objective historico-textual account of the recurrent difficulties in reading a figure, and is thus a second- or third-level narrative, or allegory.

When de Man writes of allegory as a second- or third-level narrative (*AR*, 205), the ambiguity in the ordination must be accounted for, which I propose to do in the following way, following de Man's discussion. If the figure in the text is level one, then the text being read is assigned to level two, and the critical reading thereof level three. But a naked figure as such is not something which is given to be read, so alternately the figure could be conceived of as a zero-level after-the-fact construction to which the reader has abduced from the text (level one) in the course of the reading (level two). This may be a heuristic device for the understanding of one sentence in the paragraph in question; but it is important to remember that de Man's greater point is that the levels are always contaminating each other and that an *unambigu-*

---

[16] See *Shakespeare's Sonnets*, edited with an analytic commentary by Stephen Booth (New Haven: Yale University Press, 1977), 336–37.

[17] New York: Norton, 1958, 1968.

ous scheme such as the one just proposed would pertain only to a model or ideal, that is to say to a non-existent language. Another way of saying this is that in the case of a text for which an un-double account could be given, reading would not be necessary, or to put it in de Man's own words, rhetorical readings are "consistently defective models of language's impossibility to be a model language" (*RT*, 19).

In our account of Celan's poem, however, the *sprachontologische* shadiness does not relate to the grammatical *third* person, which is, in this poem, omnipresent, but to the strangeness of the second, which flickers into whatever existence it may have in and as the opening of the poem and just as quickly disappears.[18] The ambiguity that centers on the figure of the third Grace (who is, however, also the second, in the sense that she often stands between giving and receiving as the figure of their relation, that is as returning) also centers on the second person of Celan's poem.

To whom is this sonnet addressed? When Paul Celan wants to speak to a reader, he most often writes *du*, although the ontological status of the *du* in many of Celan's poems could not possibly be interpretatively foreclosed in such a manner. *Ihr* is perhaps an address to these three verbal non-entities, these three words *schön, gut, und treu* – "you [three] should not call the one whom I loved there an idol, nor idolatry what I do and did" – but its secondness is also a kind of thirdness.

While I have just foregrounded the *ihr*, I would like to conclude my remarks on this sonnet with some more remarks in the field of the automatism of the impersonal or grammatical opened up above. As I have noted, Szondi comments Celan's repetitions as performing linguistic constancy. Continuing in our recursive reading of the poem, and moving one line further up to "Gut ist mein Freund, ists heute und ists morgen," we may now have to take seriously the (in German rather conventional) fading out of *er* into the contracted *es* as a shading off into the neutrality of the third person, which is not really a person at all. A noun may (pretend to) be the name of a person, place or thing, but what, I ask, is a pronoun?

We can say of pronouns what we can say of other shifters as well

---

[18] I have discussed the difficulties of tracking pronominal persons in my chapter on Blanchot above.

as of deictic marks in general, such as "this," "here," "now," and so forth, precisely what Benveniste, who translates the most traditionally Hegelian philosophemes into something like a linguistics,[19] says: namely, their abstract generality phagocytes the particularity of each speech event in which they are spoken. The linguistic necessity of allegory – the necessity to speak the other, because that is all that can be spoken – exists, if anywhere, most clearly in the occurrence of deictic language, for it is in deictic language that apparently referential statements can be seen most clearly to lose their referential moment in the very act of being uttered. The reading of the predications consequent to the utterance of any pseudo-deictic act of the form "this is x," where x is any predicate whatever, narrates the fall of positional language into abstraction, which is hence an inextricable part of any referential statement or description, no matter how "definite" it may hope to be. Thus the fall into the thematic is a necessary linguistic moment that accompanies every positional speech act, and that embeds thematization as a structural moment in predicative utterance. Thematization is the name for this fall, for this fated process which befalls the (non)moment of positing of any utterance, which utterance can be spliced in as a moment of some account – such as is the case in Szondi's as well as in the present essay – and thus be made into the matter or theme of that account. Such is the disjunction at the core (or on the surface – it is the same) of all speech acts considered in the linguistic truth of and as allegory. What occurs here is prior to any consideration of a conflict between codes, or between natural languages. It is this rupture, attendant to syntactic structure, which constitutes and inhabits the code as such.

An exemplary analysis of such disruption at the grammatical level occurs in Lacan's analysis of the difference between the sentences "tu es celui qui me suivras" and "tu es celui qui me suivra."[20] This moment of Lacan's text, which concerns a node of

---

[19] The section of Benveniste's *Problèmes de linguistique générale*, vol. I (Paris: Gallimard, 1966), entitled "L'Homme dans la langue," is largely a recounting of Hegelian commonplaces. This does not, however, invalidate it as a set of observations about language or about linguistics, given that it is not at all assured that any linguistics could ever emancipate itself from any such ideological translation, even and especially in its founding gestures, such as those which would try to define its object.

[20] See his *Le Séminaire*, vol. III: *Les Psychoses* (Paris: Seuil, 1981).

contiguity between the registers of the imaginary and the symbolic, is an expansion of Benveniste's cliché concerning the way in which the personhood of the second grammatical person is just as "imaginary," as it were – that is, symbolic – as the purported specificity, the haeccity of the first or third. All poems or letters written in the intimate second person might as well, in this sense and according to this line of thinking, be addressed "dear occupant." But the rhetorical irreplaceability of the *you* has to do with the very *attempt at* address, even if, in technical–linguistic terms, the pronominal function effaces the specificity of any given addressee. Anyone knows that he or she cannot address a lover as a "second-person function," but it is precisely this nexus of (ir)replaceability which makes the transference, and hence psychoanalysis, possible. – And, *a fortiori*, according to Freud and Lacan, all interpersonal relations, inasmuch as all of our relations are based on what Freud calls *Anlehnung*, or anaclitic object choice. The theory and practice of psychoanalysis could be said to exist in the space between the need to have an address for any given second person and the actual, linguistic, leveling impersonality of the structure of that – and of all other – "persons."

Back to our poem: speaking of *ich*, *ihr*, and er, we are principally concerned with the first and third, inasmuch as the second, according to our analysis, reveals itself as an address to the constituent figures of an allegorical tableau that already has something of the third person about it. Its secondness, considered as a plurality of phenomenal addressees, of singular yous, drops out, as it were. *Ich* and er, he and I: the *and* unites and divides. But to keep up in our pursuit of the automatisms at the heart of this poem, of the ers, *unds* and *ists*, we should now draw the logical conclusion of our argument thus far, namely, that *ich*, I, in its abstract, (non)positional generality, is no more personal than the so-called third person. In his *Meridian* speech in acceptance of the Georg-Büchner Prize of 1960,[21] speaking of that day upon which Büchner's Lenz went into the mountains, Celan writes of that Lenz who thus goes, "er als ein ich." This was first translated into French as "Lui en tant que moi,"[22] then corrected as "Lui en tant

[21] In *GW* vol. III.
[22] "Le méridien," trans. André du Bouchet, in Paul Celan, *Strette* (Paris: Mercure de France, 1971), 188.

qu'un moi."[23] But it should perhaps be even "Lui en tant que je," "He as an I." Having gone through the required analysis of the asymmetrical symmetry of the relation between the first and third persons, we can now say, inverting Celan's maxim: *ich als ein* er, I as a he.

While Szondi reads Celan's couplet as the expression of a hope, the hope the fulfillment of which would be the performance of the constation of line 7, "In der Beständigkeit, da bleibt mein Vers geborgen," "In constancy, there remains my verse sheltered," it would be more accurate to say that the expression of the wish "In Einem will ich drei zusammenschmieden" ('I want to forge these three in One") is precisely the correlate of a kind of failure, although the failure here is a necessary and linguistic one, and not one which should be interpreted in the register of the pathetic. It is a failure in the sense that it is the disjunction of Celan's translation – of the disjunction which is his translation, that is to say, the very achievement of this poem, of the translation of Shakespeare's song without a singer into his – Celan's – prose poem[24] which overflows with impersonal personalities – it is this success/failure (I would not try to subordinate one of these terms to the other), this *Fehlleistung*, which results in the impossible wish of the last line, which speaks a hope of something which cannot be, rather than the satisfaction of a desire already gratified. The first line of Shakespeare's poem, with its exhortation, speaks of a present love, whereas Celan's speaks not only in the simple past of a perfected action, but also of another place, "den ich *da* lieb," of a *da* which is *fort*. This *da* occurs three times in Celan's poem. Where or what is this place?

It is the place (1) of the one whom I loved; (2) of the activity which I do and did; and (3) where my verse remains sheltered. Critics perhaps too numerous to count have interpreted the first and greater portion of Shakespeare's sonnets as consisting, for the most part, of the narrative of the singer's love for a young man. In this reading, the narrative is often taken referentially, as the story of a chain of events, beginning with the so-called procreation sonnets and ending with a sequence of poems in which the

---

[23] "Le méridien. Discours prononcé à l'occasion de la remise du prix Georg Büchner," trans. Jean Launay, in *Po&sie*, 9 (1979), 75.

[24] It is a prose poem, in this account, because it highlights, or backlights, the craftwork of grammar, and not the artwork conceived of in symbolic terms.

speaker's idealization of his love into an abstract object, as opposed to a love object, leads to the waning of the relationship. In keeping with this fabular reading, we could say that the place of this *da* is the place of the preceding poems in which the poet spoke of his beloved, and not so much of his love. But this would be to miss the point of (our analysis of) Celan's poem, as well as to efface the one occurrence of the *da* in a line where it relates both to present as well as to past activity: "was ich da treib und trieb."

Once we have said that this is a poem about er, if not about him or about my or his love, we will no sooner realize that we cannot say this. For this level of analysis is not "about" anything. The question of the "about," which we posed at the beginning in our remarks on the thematic scar, is the question from which we departed when we left behind the considerations of the theme of the theme. Instead of saying that this is a poem about er, we might, in a move which appears to be at first glance a pathetic attempt at the recuperation of the *melos* purported to exist at the root of the lyric – we might want to adopt the more musical expression and say that this is a poem in er. This would be no melocentrism in the traditional sense, but rather some kind of asymmetrical inversion on the order of "the birth of music from the dead letter of poetry," or from the illusion of the existence of poetry. Thus here, in the kingdom of *ich, ihr,* er in which there is no *du* – as there is no you in Shakespeare's poem either, the poet at this point being fully engaged in his activity of writing, which activity is not being addressed, as in many of the earlier sonnets, to a singularly beloved you – in this kingdom from which all "persons" have been deported, the poet's activity is always already accomplished in the preterite of *den ich da lieb*. There are more reasons than one why one always fails to speak of whom – or of what – one loves.

Index

Index